The End of Children?

Edited by Nathanael Lauster
and Graham Allan

The End of Children?
Changing Trends in Childbearing and Childhood

UBCPress · Vancouver · Toronto

20 19 18 17 16 15 14 13 12   5 4 3 2 1

Printed in Canada on FSC-certified ancient-forest-free paper
(100% post-consumer recycled) that is processed chlorine- and acid-free.

Library and Archives Canada Cataloguing in Publication

The end of children? : changing trends in childbearing and childhood / edited by Nathanael Lauster and Graham Allan.

Includes bibliographical references and index.
ISBN 978-0-7748-2192-6 (bound) ISBN 978-0-7748-2193-3 (pbk.)

1. Children – History – 20th century. 2. Child development – History – 20th century. 3. Human reproduction – History – 20th century. 4. Children. 5. Child development. 6. Human reproduction. I. Lauster, Nathanael II. Allan, Graham

HQ767.87.E53 2012   305.2309'04   C2011-903983-4

Canadä

UBC Press gratefully acknowledges the financial support for our publishing program of the Government of Canada (through the Canada Book Fund), the Canada Council for the Arts, and the British Columbia Arts Council.

This book has been published with the help of a grant from the Canadian Federation for the Humanities and Social Sciences, through the Aid to Scholarly Publications Program, using funds provided by the Social Sciences and Humanities Research Council of Canada.

Printed and bound in Canada by Friesens
Set in Stone by Artegraphica Design Co. Ltd.
Copy editor: Stacy Belden
Proofreader: Kate Spezowka

UBC Press
The University of British Columbia
2029 West Mall
Vancouver, BC V6T 1Z2
www.ubcpress.ca

For Amy, Ezra, and Sheila, with love

Contents

Figures and Tables

Tables

Acknowledgments

We first met each other in the fall of 2005 when we both joined the Family Studies group at the University of British Columbia (UBC), · Nathanael Lauster as a newly appointed assistant professor and Graham Allan as a visiting professor from Keele University in the United Kingdom. The idea for this volume arose as a result of the numerous research discussions we had with each other and with our colleagues at UBC. Without the warm support of the Family Studies group, then part of the School of Social Work and Family Studies, now located within the Department of Sociology, this book would not have been written. We are very grateful to all of our colleagues in Family Studies, and in the School of Social Work and Family Studies more widely, for the encouragement they gave us.

There is one person in particular, though, from this group whom we would like to single out for thanks – Dan Perlman, now chair of the Department of Human Development and Family Studies at the University of North Carolina in Greensboro, but then the recognized leader of the Family Studies group at UBC. As everyone in Family Studies at UBC at that time would have recognized, Dan was the heart and soul of the group. He was also an extremely good colleague who always had time to listen to others' ideas, whether about research, teaching, or new academic initiatives. He made us both very welcome when we arrived at UBC, and we benefited greatly from his knowledge, enthusiasm, and commitment to interdisciplinary family studies. We are very grateful to him for the support he gave us, both with this project and more generally.

There are other people we would also like to thank. First we owe a great deal to our current colleagues, in the Department of Sociology at UBC and in the School of Sociology and Criminology at Keele University, respectively. They have provided us with highly supportive academic environments in which to pursue our interests. We are also very grateful to Darcy Cullen, acquisitions editor at UBC Press. She has been an enthusiastic supporter of this project since our first tentative discussions with her. She has provided us with sound and helpful advice throughout the various stages of bringing the book to fruition. We are highly appreciative of her professional guidance and knowledge. We would also like to thank Megan Brand who has been extremely helpful and efficient throughout the process of preparing the typescript for publication. We are also very grateful to the two anonymous reviewers who commented extensively on earlier drafts of this volume. Their comments have helped make it a better book than it would otherwise have been.

Finally, we would like to thank Amy Hanser and Sheila Hawker for their continuing support and Ezra for reintroducing us to childhood at close quarters. It is to them we dedicate this book.

The End of Children?

Introduction

Nathanael Lauster and Graham Allan

In 1900, Ellen Key (1900), the Swedish educationalist and writer, pro-claimed the coming twentieth century as "The Century of the Child." In many ways, this contention can be seen as highly prescient. Throughout the twentieth century, there was a far greater concern for the physical, moral, and economic welfare of children than there had been in earlier eras. Particularly, but not only, in Western societies, the rise of educational provision clearly reflected changed understandings of children's social and economic location. However, changes in the social organization of motherhood, the creation of new legal protections for children, and later the extension of "childhood" into a new phase of "adolescence" all served equally to highlight the greater attention and prominence bestowed on "pre-adult" life phases across the twentieth century. By the time the UN's *Convention on the Rights of the Child* was published by the United Nations in 1989, the special significance of childhood in twentieth-century thought and practice had become firmly established (United Nations 1989).

These changes in understandings of children's place – or, better still, places – within society reveal the analytical importance of viewing child-hood as a social, rather than as a natural, construction. The value placed on children, what is expected of them, how they are treated, what pro-tections they are granted, and the like vary significantly depending at least in part on the economic contributions required of the young within the family to sustain normative lifestyles. Moreover, the social pos-itioning of children and the social construction of childhood continue to alter. In the period that Anthony Giddens (1991) characterizes as late modernity – broadly speaking the period since 1975 – widespread demo-graphic shifts have occurred, especially, though not only, within indus-trialized societies. For example, divorce rates have grown, marriage rates have fallen, and the incidence of cohabitation and lone parenthood have increased. In addition, birth rates and the age at which people first become parents have also changed, representing altered pathways into adulthood and greater diversity in the structure of the life course.

The origins of the current volume can be traced back to the numerous and wide-ranging discussions that the editors had with their colleagues in the Family Studies group at the University of British Columbia about these demographic and social changes, especially as they affect children and childhood. As a result of these discussions, we decided to solicit papers for a collected volume from scholars with different backgrounds – including sociology, demography, history, anthropology, family studies, social work, and education – with the goal of encouraging an interdisciplinary debate about the implications and significance of children in contemporary life. Borrowing from the title of Arthur C. Clarke's science fiction novel *Childhood's End* (1953), in which the children of Earth are taken and transformed by aliens, leaving their forlorn parents behind, and P.D. James's similarly futuristic *The Children of Men* (1992), in which children simply stop being born, we asked our contributors to focus their essays broadly on the theme of "The End of Children?: Changing Trends in Childbearing and Childhood." Our intention was to look critically – hence, the question mark in the title – at what is happening to children and childhood, given declining birth rates and public concerns over perceived dangers to children's well-being and "natural" innocence. In the main, the chapters that follow concentrate on children and childhood in a North American context, but cases from outside Canada and the United States are also considered in a number of the chapters. Along the way to producing the book, we were able to gain the support of the University of British Columbia to organize a two-day symposium to bring contributors and others together to discuss the various issues raised in their chapters. Prior to this symposium, we had some concern that the different disciplinary discourses around issues of fertility and childhood might lead to disparate papers from which little discussion would emerge. However, throughout the symposium the debate was extremely lively, with specialists from the different areas engaging fully in the range of subjects being presented.

Notwithstanding their different theoretical and methodological approaches, it was apparent that individuals schooled in different disciplinary traditions "connected" with one another in stimulating and productive ways. Despite their differences, there was a resonance in the knowledge and understanding brought to the various themes and topics being addressed. As many of the authors have told us, the development of their chapters undoubtedly benefited from the debates that were generated during the symposium.

Of course, each discipline and field provides unique insights into the issues surrounding childbearing and childrearing. The questions they ask and the mode of analysis they develop are rooted in the intellectual concerns that define their subject and discipline. This makes it all the more striking that a number of common themes emerge from the works contained here. Scholars seeking to understand changes in childbearing trends speak to many of the same concerns as those working to understand changes in the construction and experience of childhood. We hope the chapters we have included in this volume capture for the reader the "connectivities" apparent in the symposium and the value of considering the issues we address from different disciplinary perspectives. For this reason, we also hope readers will delve into the different chapters rather than just those that are most directly relevant to their own disciplinary base. To be clear, the volume is "multidisciplinary" rather than "interdisciplinary." Each chapter addresses its concerns from its own disciplinary perspective, but, collectively, we think the book illustrates the advantages that can be gained from a willingness to engage in interdisciplinary dialogue.

Before outlining some of the integrative themes of the book and the contents of the chapters included, we want to clarify our use of the terms "children" and "childhood." In talking of children, we are referring both to children as embodied individuals and to their generational position. Normally, when we use the term "child," we are implicitly referencing someone who is considered "pre-adult," according to whatever social and cultural criteria are conventionally used in the relevant society to define adulthood. However, at times, "child" may be used solely to convey a generational status, irrespective of the age of the individual concerned. That is, a daughter or son remains her or his parents' child no matter what age the child happens to be.

In contrast, "childhood" is not directly about embodied individuals or generational connections. Instead, it refers to the general social position assigned to those who are considered pre-adult in a given society. It concerns the social construction of a particular age category – the rights, responsibilities, protections, and understandings that define what it means to be pre-adult. The construction of childhood is not uniform; it varies across societies and across time. It varies in the length of time a child is considered dependent; it varies in the constitution of that dependence; and it varies in the social arrangements devised to protect the child while he or she is seen as dependent. For example, in contemporary

Western society, part of being pre-adult is that you go to school for a given period. This practice has not always been the case, but now education is a major business. Similarly, the legal system now understands children and their capabilities quite differently from the ways they were understood a century or so ago. In a simple sense, the child has not altered, but what has changed is his or her childhood – the set of experiences seen as normative for those who are pre-adult.

The End of Children?

Until quite recently, the bearing of many children was an expected part of life for most people. People could expect to replace themselves and more through their children. "Replacement fertility" is a concept invented by demographers to describe the replenishment of populations through childbearing. The total fertility rate (TFR) represents an estimate of the number of children a woman is likely to have over the course of her lifetime. Approximately 2.1 children are needed for a couple to replace themselves under conditions of low mortality (the extra 0.1 being needed to make up for child mortality). At the extreme, women among the early French-Canadian colonists (born before 1660) tended to bear between eleven and twelve children during their lifetimes, one of the highest completed fertility rates ever recorded (Livi-Bacci 2007). TFRs of six to seven children per woman have been far more common historically, and they continue through the present in some countries such as Yemen, Afghanistan, Niger, and Mali. However, for most of the world's population, children are no longer quite so inevitable. Indeed, according to the Population Reference Bureau (2008), populations are no longer successfully replacing themselves (TFR < 2.1) in some seventy-one countries, which contain approximately 2.5 billion of the world's 6.7 billion people.

Indeed, across the course of the twentieth century, most countries around the world have experienced dramatic declines in childbearing. While widespread baby booms in the post–Second World War decades garnered significant attention, in reality they were deviations from the long-term trends. Declines in fertility that began in Europe and North America well before 1900 reached new lows by the last quarter of the twentieth century. In both Canada and the United States, the TFR first dropped below the rate at which couples replace themselves by 1972. The United States recently rebounded to replacement level again for the first time in 2006. By contrast, Canada's childbearing rates have remained quite low, with a TFR of approximately 1.6.

Despite fertility declines, we are clearly not experiencing the end of children, at least not in the sense that they have all disappeared, as in the novel *The Children of Men* (James 1992). While fertility rates have decreased nearly everywhere quite dramatically, most people alive today, even in North America and Europe, have had, or will have, one or more children at some point in their lives. However, the decline of childbearing to the point where generations are no longer replacing themselves through their children remains a cause of concern for many. Declining fertility rates mean that there are fewer workers to replenish workforces, to provide tax bases for governments, and to support aging populations. Fewer children also mean fewer consumers in the long run, challenging a variety of industries and institutions – including universities! Overall, some forty-five countries estimate their fertility rates are too low and are adopting policies aimed at boosting childbearing (Population Reference Bureau 2006). Many countries, such as Canada and the United States, are also turning to immigration as a possible solution to concerns over declining labour forces.

For others, declining fertility rates are a cause for celebration. The publications entitled *The Population Bomb* (Ehrlich 1968) and *The Limits of Growth* (Meadows and Meadows 1972) have contributed to widespread concern about the negative impacts of overpopulation toward the latter third of the twentieth century. Too many children were thought to constitute a barrier to development, a position prominently adopted by China (see the Conclusion in this volume). Similarly, high birth rates have been seen by many as an environmental problem, following concerns that the Earth may be exceeding its human "carrying capacity." More nuanced analyses have emphasized that consumption patterns matter at least as much as family size as determinants of environmental impact (Curran and de Sherbinin 2004). In this sense, the low fertility rates of high-income countries, where most of the world's consumption takes place, may be particularly encouraging for environmentalists. The authors in this volume speak to questions of fertility decline – a concept that has implications beyond demography and the replenishment of populations. They attempt to forward explanations, interpretations, and implications of this decline. At the same time, they often address related questions about changes in the social construction of childhood.

The End of Childhood?
A host of authors bemoan the state of childhood today, ranging from popular accounts, such as Neil Postman's *The Disappearance of Childhood*

(1994) to more academic accounts, such as Anne-Marie Ambert's Vanier Institute report *The Rise in the Number of Children and Adolescents Who Exhibit Problematic Behaviours: Multiple Causes* (2007). As documented by Scott Coltrane and Michele Adams (2003), a specialized cottage industry has sprung up inside and outside academia detailing the challenges faced by children from so-called "broken" homes (for examples, see Popenoe 1996; Wallerstein, Lewis, and Blakeslee 2000; and Marquardt 2005). Other proposed threats to childhood include advertisers intent on turning children into mindless consumers (Schor 2004) or forcing girls to grow up and embrace their sexuality too soon (Ward 2003), schools that fail to allow boys to be boys or adequately prepare them to become adults (Tyre 2008), the decline of religion (Zhai et al. 2007), the rise of new drugs (Degrandpre 2000), and the omnipresent dangers of predatory adults (Kincaid 1998).

Contrary to many reports, by most measures, children do not seem to be doing worse and worse. In a basic sense, children in most places are far more likely to survive childhood today than ever before (Bongaarts 2006). According to time-use studies in the United States, parents seem to be spending as much or more time with their children today as in the heyday of the stay-at-home housewife (Bianchi, Robinson, and Milkie 2007; though also see Edward Kruk's arguments in Chapter 7 of this volume). In their longitudinal study of generational change, Vern Bengtson, Timothy Biblarz, and Robert Roberts (2002) note that youth today have greater aspirations than their parents and often have better relationships with family members. Youth crime rates do not seem to be rising, and they have dropped considerably since the 1990s (Snyder 2005; Gannon 2006). As revealed in Allison Pugh's *Longing and Belonging* (2009), children's consumption is more complicated than most analysts have considered, driven by the very old desire to belong rather than by new forms of advertising. Trends in sexual debut appear to be changing in North America such that young adults are postponing sex more often now than ten or twenty years ago (Biddlecom 2004; Rotermann 2008). Yet despite much evidence to the contrary, the idea that a normative childhood is under threat remains powerful. As argued by Coltrane and Adams (2003), the moral panic generated by declaring childhood under threat can be used to rally popular action and influence policy. As Mona Gleason and Anita Garey suggest in Chapters 8 and 9 in this volume, ideas of the normative childhood being under threat can also be used to discipline real children in disturbing ways.

Common Themes

Overall, this collection of essays is premised on the idea that researchers concerned with declines in fertility and with changes in the ways in which childhood is experienced and understood have much to say to each other. A number of common themes are worth drawing out here.

Heterogeneity

One of the most striking themes sounded by the contributors to this volume, and a prominent critique of discourses promoting the idea of an end to children or childhood, is the fact that circumstances differ for different people. Speaking to the disappearance of children, fertility has tended to be in a decline across the globe. Yet global trends, and even national trends, mask substantial variation in fertility rates. Many populations are continuing to replace themselves and even grow in size through the addition of their offspring, even as other populations have begun to decline. Historical patterns also differ. Many nations seem to be on a steady downward trajectory, but some, such as the United States, Sweden, and France, have seen fertility rates decline since the 1970s only to rise once again, if modestly, in more recent years.

Heterogeneity in fertility trends is mirrored by heterogeneity in ideas about what childhood should entail. Few people would honestly suggest that a singular notion of childhood could capture all of the diverse ways childhood is imagined or experienced. Yet positing an end to childhood entails imagining such a singular experience. This sort of imagining ignores the diversity of childhood experiences. It further ignores the diversity of opinion concerning what childhood should be like. One notion of childhood may fall into decline without dooming all notions of childhood – indeed, the decline of one notion of childhood is usually accompanied by and/or caused by the rise of another. Similarly, one set of experiences thought to characterize childhood may change for one population (say Midwestern, middle-class, suburban White children) without changing similarly for another (East coast, urban, minority children).

The Idea of the Child

Children exist as ideas in their parents' minds before they are born and often (but not always) before they are even conceived (see Chapter 3 by Rebecca Upton in this volume). The idea of the child, then, informs whether or not prospective parents act in such a way as to bring a child into the world. In short, the idea of the child matters for fertility. Conversely, of course, concerns about the end of children are as often as not really concerns about the end of a particular idea of the child. Moreover, echoing the theme of heterogeneity, the idea of the child differs for different people at different times. Context matters. At one point in time, the idea of a child might frighten a person away from any sort of behaviour that even remotely carries a risk of pregnancy. At another point in time, the idea of a child might be so compelling to the same person that he or she would spend enormous amounts of energy, time, and money to see that idea made flesh.

The changing meaning of the child as an idea is a central preoccupation of all the chapters that follow as well as being key to understanding the ongoing and massive changes in fertility around the world. In this way, the child is a symbol that may be adopted or avoided, depending on the meaning attached. Childbearing breathes life into the symbol, providing children with an agency of their own. Yet the agency of children is carefully circumscribed by their relationships with those more powerful others around them. As such, to be a child is to occupy a particular social role. Children actively navigate their ways through this role, transitioning in the process from childhood into adulthood (see, as an example of this idea, Chapter 6 by Adena Miller in this volume). Childhood and adulthood exist in opposition to one another, yet everyone is expected to cross the boundary between the two at some point or another. In this sense, the changing meaning of the child is also key to understanding the changing world of adults.

Any tour of the idea of the child must begin by wrestling with how children once seemed inevitable and unavoidable. Thomas Malthus (1826), for instance, saw children as the by-products of deeply ingrained human desires. Only by taking control of human desires, by subjecting them to rational consideration of costs and benefits, and by planning accordingly could humanity avoid creating too many mouths to feed. Malthus advocated abstinence. These days, other more erotically enabling options are available for most people to avoiding childbearing.

If children are not inevitable, then a child becomes a decision. As such, having a child may entail costs and benefits. The rational choice framework has become particularly powerful in demographic research as a means of thinking about changes in childbearing. Various authors have forwarded the notion that the costs of children have risen over time, while the benefits have declined. In particular, it costs more to educate children, to house them (see Chapter 4 by Nathanael Lauster in this volume), and to look after them than in the past. Yet they provide less labour, less remuneration, and less financial protection as an old age security system (in comparison to pension systems) than ever before. Mira Whyman, Megan Lemmon, and Jay Teachman discuss many of the relevant demographic theories in Chapter 1 of this volume.

While demographers tend to discuss the benefits of children in terms of their economic costs and benefits, it seems obvious that the symbolic value of children cannot be entirely translated into monetary terms. This notion has a variety of implications. First, if children have symbolic value, then this value has to be understood within the context of culture – a point that is developed strongly in Chapters 2, 3, 4, and 5 of this volume. Culture is that which provides symbols with meaning. Second, the value of children is attached to the value of parents. A child imbues its maker and/or caretaker with the status of parent, and parents, like children, can be good or bad. In this way, children can make their parents better or worse people through their own performance. Finally, this moral element to the meaning of the child is accompanied by an emotional element. Children are usually seen as providing a source of much happiness for parents, although a recent study by Hans-Peter Kohler, Jere Behrman, and Axel Skytthe (2005) has indicated that this effect may be limited, and they are, of course, equally capable of generating a good deal of sadness.

The Child We Live By and the Child We Live With

The idea of the child becomes manifest in the creation of children. As many authors suggest, the contrast between the child as imagined and the child as manifest may be stark. Evoking John Gillis's (1997) distinction between the mythical families we live by and the very real families we live with, the ideas of the child that we profess may be quite distinct from the way children actually intrude on our realities. This notion can have important implications for fertility. As parents take on a first child, they may feel unready for any more (see Upton's analysis in Chapter 3 in this volume), but the implications for the lives of children already born may be even more important.

What happens when parents find discrepancies between the idea of the child motivating their childbearing decisions and the reality of the child they bear? Only parents with a high tolerance for cognitive dissonance might be able to ignore these discrepancies. Otherwise, such dissonance tends to push parents in one of two directions. They can adjust their ideas of children so they better fit parental experiences of interacting with children, or they can attempt to adjust their children to better fit with their ideas of what a child should be like. The latter solution speaks to the profound differences in power between parent and child. The agency of the child to shape his or her own circumstances is reduced as the potency of the idea of the child increases in the parental imagination.

Ideas about the child, or the children we live by, do not just affect the relationship between parents and children. Ideas about the child also become manifest in a variety of institutional relationships. These ideas may be detached from the reality of children's circumstances, resulting in a sort of social dissonance. Policy makers may ignore resulting discrepancies, as Kruk discusses in Chapter 7 in this volume. Various agents may also act to bring children in line with social expectations or ideas about what a child should be like. The courts and medical professionals are particularly key actors in this regard, as Gleason and Garey illustrate in Chapters 8 and 9 respectively in this volume.

Chapters Ahead

While there are connections made throughout the book, the next five chapters tend to concern questions about the end of children, while Chapters 6 to 9 focus more on questions about the end of childhood. In this way, the book begins by thinking about how the child as an idea relates to whether or not people have children and ends by thinking about how the child as an idea takes on (or fails to take on) institutional forms, contrasting with and informing the lives of real children. In Chapter 1, Whyman, Lemmon, and Teachman provide an introduction to common demographic perspectives that inform discussions of the end of children. They discuss the demographics of fertility decline, with special focus on recent trends in North America. They also detail basic changes in fertility patterns by age and discuss the impact of abortion, contraception, and marriage patterns. In examining the links between childbearing and marriage for self-identified Black and White populations in the United States, they raise the issue of heterogeneity within nations. This chapter sets the stage for further attempts to understand childbearing trends and helps inform the chapters that follow.

In Chapter 2, Nathanael Lauster, Todd Martin, and James White consider the intersection of immigration and fertility, both expanding and dissecting in the process the discussion of heterogeneity in demographic patterns opened by Whyman, Lemmon, and Teachman in the previous chapter. Their focus is on the extent to which immigration can help reverse fertility declines, which is a matter of major consequence for population policies in Canada and other receiving countries. Drawing on data from the Canadian Ethnic Diversity Survey, Lauster, Martin, and

White demonstrate how the different conceptualizations of culture embedded in Canadian multiculturalism – specifically with regard to language, ethnicity, racialized grouping, and religion – have led to different
conclusions about fertility trends among immigrant populations.
Ironically, given population policy objectives, they find that it may be
only where immigrant children are less accepted as belonging that immigrants are likely to maintain higher fertility rates.

The decisions people make about childbearing clearly involve agency.
However, in line with the underlying premises of Chapter 2, this agency
is structured by cultural understandings, not least of which, as we have
argued earlier, are those informing people's ideas of the child at different
life-course phases. This is a theme developed further in Chapter 3 where
Upton highlights the centrality of discourses of actively planning fertility
and the informal pressures that operate in this context. Drawing on her
ethnographic research in the United States, she analyzes how childbearing norms can become burdensome for some people, especially in the
face of competing work demands and the high financial costs of childbearing. A revealing facet of her study is how some respondents drew
– misleadingly – on the discourses of physiological infertility to resist
informal pressure to meet American norms of the two-child family.

Like Upton, Lauster in Chapter 4 also addresses questions of why and
when people choose to have – or not to have – children, questions that
are core to the themes of this book. However, he adopts a quite different
theoretical and methodological approach from Upton, although like
her he is concerned with the social pressures encouraging people to
conform to prevailing cultural standards. He focuses particularly on the
idea of performance, theorizing that privileged parents set the performance standards for everyone else. Using US census data from 1900 to
2005, he explores how over time parents in materially advantaged positions have progressively raised the bar on what is taken to constitute
good parenting to a point where many others with fewer resources have
difficulty attaining it. He argues that increased expectations governing
good parenting represent an important, though so far under-examined,
explanation for contemporary fertility declines. If young adults do not
feel adequately equipped to perform parenthood properly, they may
well be choosing not to perform it at all.

In exploring when and why people choose to have children, Upton
and Lauster both address, albeit from quite different perspectives, the
interplay of moral and economic considerations in these decisions. In
Chapter 5, Nicholas Townsend, an anthropologist, draws on a generational framework to assess further the symbolic benefit of children for

parents. In making this assessment, he focuses on childhood not as a phase of personal and social development but, instead, as one of a set of positions, or roles, within a social structure. In this sense, the category "childhood" needs to be understood in the context of the notion "parenthood." Thus, the disappearance of childhood also implies the disappearance of parenthood, with all of the implications that this carries for our conceptions of "adulthood." Drawing on his fieldwork in South Africa, Townsend expands our understanding of the idea of the child, in part by focusing on children as signifiers of our inevitable death while also offering the possibility of immortality through their celebration of our lives.

In the volume's final four chapters, we turn to consider the end of childhood, both as a distinct stage in any individual life course (how do we know when someone becomes an adult?) and as a singular notion of what youth experience. In Chapter 6, Miller addresses a core element within contemporary notions of childhood's ending – leaving the parental home. Children can leave home relatively early, on time, or relatively late – hence, beginning the entry into adulthood and the ending of childhood at different ages. The categories of early, on time, and late reveal both the heterogeneity of childhood experiences (and transitions to adulthood) and the normative elements that can bind people to certain common expectations. Using a Canadian data set, Miller focuses in detail on the relationship between the timing of leaving home and the experience of parental divorce. In doing so, she illustrates how different childhoods can structure different pathways into adulthood and thereby signify different endings to childhood.

As we argued earlier, childhood altered dramatically during the twentieth century, with many of the changes becoming established through legislative action. The state, in other words, played a significant part in creating modern childhood, with both education and child welfare programs being key components. In Chapter 7, Kruk examines what contemporary Canadian child welfare policies reveal about the state's support for parental involvement in childhood. He analyzes three different sets of child welfare policies – those concerning child care, child custody, and child protection – and argues that in each sphere the state has implicitly endorsed the disappearance of at least some children from parental involvement. Kruk is not arguing that such parental disengagement from the lives of children represents an explicit and clearly formulated idea of the child constructed by those involved in Canadian policy formation. Rather, he points to the surprising absence of an explicit idea of the child in these different policies.

In Chapter 8, Gleason is also concerned with how the idea of the child is represented and utilized in social welfare, this time from a historical perspective. She focuses specifically on early to mid-twentieth-century responses to childhood disabilities in Canada, examining the manner in which discourses drawn on by health and educational professionals at the time pathologized disabled children as "defective." Notwithstanding the good intentions of the professionals involved, the children were defined as "abnormal" and thus in need of "normalizing." Frequently, these actions involved their removal for different lengths of time and in different ways from other children and thus, somewhat paradoxically, from the ordinary experiences and modes of participation of "normal" childhood. In this regard, disability represented a particular end of childhood, one in which the child was separated from the institutionalized social arrangements that had become central for signifying childhood as a special phase of life.

In the final substantive chapter, Chapter 9, Garey continues with the exploration of how specific state policies impact on the experiences of children. She draws on ethnographic fieldwork on truancy courts in the United States to explore how the boundaries of childhood are constructed and policed in the routine procedures of the official agencies involved. Her research connects in interesting ways with Gleason's analysis in the previous chapter, in that both are explicitly concerned with the processes of pathologizing children. However, the understanding of childhood's end that she draws on in her chapter is distinct from those that are used in the previous chapters. Garey focuses on childhood's end in the sense of childhood's purpose and benefits. The argument she develops is that while childhood is no longer productive in terms of familial economic contribution, the therapeutic perspective that has come to dominate official responses to children who are seen as experiencing problematic childhoods benefits adult actors within the therapeutic professions. In this regard, her analysis explores the mobilization of resources when the actions of particular children cross the boundaries of acceptable childhood and compromise normatively constructed ideas of the child.

Conclusion

As we hope can be seen from the chapters included in this volume, there are numerous ways in which ideas about "the end of children" can be interpreted and understood. Our starting point comprised demographic questions of fertility decline and population replacement levels. As various commentators have recognized, the social and economic consequences of such decline are both intriguing and imperative. As an example, in the week that we were first drafting this introduction, David Brooks (2009), the *New York Times* columnist, wrote a speculative piece on the potential impact of a declining birth rate on the social fabric. Interestingly, while he recognized the long-term dangers to people's material and religious well-being of such a decline, he emphasized most heavily the consequences of losing generational connection. In this observation, he is surely right. Any population decline would inevitably alter the structure of relationships between the generations, and in the process modify our ideas of the child.

There is, of course, nothing new in this idea. In all eras, our ideas of the child are emergent, shaped by a variety of complex factors. Across the twentieth century, the increasing institutionalization of childhood in Canada, the United States, and other Western countries has been particularly significant. There are two key elements at play in this development, which both reflect a sense of the appropriate separateness of childhood. First, there has been the growth of social institutions – some private, some public – that are concerned specifically with catering to the perceived (and changing) needs of the child. The school remains the primary example, but the growth of specialist health care, judicial provision, leisure activities, and the like all attest to a social recognition that the needs of adults and children are distinct. Second, the social institutions that have been developed to cater to these emergent needs of children help to constitute prevailing ideas of the child that, in iterative fashion, inform public policies. Thus, as the later chapters of the book argue, the practices of these social institutions themselves signify the end of childhood, in the sense of constituting the boundaries between understandings of normal and pathological childhoods.

We are well aware that the topic of "the end of children" offers numerous research avenues, only some of which have been addressed in this volume. Many interesting and important questions about the constitution of social relationships come to the fore through an analysis of potential changes in the ways that children and childhood are situated in contemporary societies. We are also aware that many of these research avenues can be approached from different directions. One of the exciting aspects of the symposium that accompanied this volume was the interdisciplinary debates that flourished in it. While the individual chapters in this volume are written from particular disciplinary perspectives, we hope that the potential of interdisciplinary research is apparent from the different ways our contributors have addressed their research concerns. As editors, we are certainly aware of the benefits that an interdisciplinary focus can bestow on the research issues addressed in the chapters that follow and hope that this volume serves to encourage further collaborations in these areas.

References

Ambert, A-M. 2007. *The Rise in the Number of Children and Adolescents Who Exhibit Problematic Behaviours: Multiple Causes.* Ottawa: Vanier Institute of the Family, http://www.vifamily.ca/library/cft/behavior.pdf.

Bengtson, V., T. Biblarz, and R. Roberts. 2002. *How Families Still Matter: A Longitudinal Study of Youth in Two Generations.* Cambridge: Cambridge University Press.

Bianchi, S., J. Robinson, and M. Milkie. 2007. *Changing Rhythms of American Family Life.* New York: Russell Sage Foundation.

Biddlecom, A. 2004. "Trends in Sexual Behaviours and Infections among Young People in the United States." *Sexually Transmitted Infections* 80 (Supplement II): 74-79.

Bongaarts, J. 2006. "How Long Will We Live?" *Population and Development Review* 32: 605-28.

Brooks, D. 2009. "The Power of Posterity." *New York Times,* 27 July 2009, http://www.nytimes.com/.

Clarke, A.C. 1953. *Childhood's End.* New York: Harcourt Brace Jovanovich.

Coltrane, S., and M. Adams. 2003. "The Social Construction of the Divorce 'Problem': Morality, Child Victims, and the Politics of Gender." *Family Relations* 52: 363-72.

Curran, S., and A. de Sherbinin. 2004. "Completing the Picture: The Challenges of Bringing 'Consumption' into the Population-Environment Equation." *Population and Environment* 26(2): 107-31.

Degrandpre, R. 2000. *Ritalin Nation: Rapid-Fire Culture and the Transformation of Human Consciousness.* New York: W.W. Norton.

Ehrlich, P. 1968. *The Population Bomb.* New York: Ballantine Books.

Gannon, M. 2006. *Crime Statistics in Canada, 2005.* Ottawa: Canadian Centre for Justice Statistics, Statistics Canada.

Giddens, A. 1991. *Modernity and Self-Identity: Self and Society in the Late Modern Age.* Cambridge: Polity Press.

Gillis, J. 1997. *A World of Their Own Making: A History of Myth and Ritual in Family Life.* Oxford: Oxford University Press.

James, P.D. 1992. *The Children of Men.* London: Faber and Faber.

Key, E. 1900. *The Century of the Child.* New York: Putnam, 1900.

Kincaid, J. 1998. *Erotic Innocence: The Culture of Child Molesting.* Durham, NC: Duke University Press.

Kohler, H., J. Behrman, and A. Skytthe. 2005. "Partner + Children=Happiness? The Effects of Partnerships and Fertility on Well-Being." *Population and Development Review* 31: 407-45.

Livi-Bacci, M. 2007. *A Concise History of World Population.* Oxford: Blackwell.

Malthus, T.R. 1826. *An Essay on the Principle of Population.* London: Murray.

Marquardt, E. 2005. *Between Two Worlds: The Inner Lives of Children of Divorce.* New York: Three Rivers Press.

Meadows, D., and D.L. Meadows. 1972. *The Limits of Growth*. New York: New American Library.

Popenoe, D. 1996. *Life without Father: Compelling New Evidence That Fatherhood and Marriage Are Indispensible for the Good of Children and Society*. New York: Martin Kessler/Free Press.

Population Reference Bureau. 2006. *2006 World Population Data Sheet*. Washington, DC: Population Reference Bureau.

–. 2008. *2008 World Population Data Sheet*. Washington, DC: Population Reference Bureau.

Postman, N. 1994. *The Disappearance of Childhood*. New York: Vintage.

Pugh, A. 2009. *Longing and Belonging: Parents, Children, and Consumer Culture*. Berkeley, CA: University of California Press.

Rotermann, M. 2008. "Trends in Teen Sexual Behaviour and Condom Use." *Statistics Canada Health Reports* 19: 1-6.

Schor, J. 2004. *Born to Buy: The Commercialized Child and the New Consumer Culture*. New York: Scribner.

Snyder, H. 2005. *Juvenile Arrests 2003*. Washington, DC: US Department of Justice, Office of Juvenile Justice and Delinquency Prevention.

Tyre, P. 2008. *The Trouble with Boys: A Surprising Report Card on Our Sons, Their Problems at School, and What Parents and Educators Must Do*. New York: Crown.

United Nations. 1989. *Convention on the Rights of the Child*. New York: United Nations, http://treaties.un.org/.

Wallerstein, J., J. Lewis, and S. Blakeslee. 2000. *The Unexpected Legacy of Divorce: A Twenty-Five-Year Landmark Study*. New York: Hyperion.

Ward, L.M. 2003. "Understanding the Role of Entertainment Media in the Sexual Socialization of American Youth: A Review of Empirical Research." *Developmental Review* 23: 347-88.

Zhai, J., C. Ellison, N. Glenn, and E. Marquardt. 2007. "Parental Divorce and Religious Involvement among Young Adults." *Sociology of Religion* 68: 125-44.

1

Fertility Change in North America, 1950-2000

Mira Whyman, Megan Lemmon, and Jay Teachman

There have been many changes in the structure of fertility in Canada and the United States over the past fifty years, and the current demographic profile of fertility suggests a future that is much different from that previously predicted. In our analysis of changing fertility, we focus on aggregate trends rather than subgroup differentials, although such differentials are present and are sometimes substantial. Two shifts characterize the change in fertility. The first change is the considerable decline in overall fertility experienced over the last half of the twentieth century. The second shift is a weakening of the formerly strong link between marriage and childbearing. Fifty years ago, a birth in North America almost certainly occurred within a marriage. This is not the case today, as non-marital fertility has increased substantially. As a consequence, the United States and Canada are now experiencing low birth rates, with a substantial fraction of those births occurring outside of marriage.

The United States and Canada are far from being alone in the world as nations with fertility near or below replacement level, generally a total fertility rate (TFR) of less than 2.1. Indeed, about one-half of the world's population now lives in a country with fertility that is sufficiently low to imply an absolute population decline (see Table 1.1), at least in terms of natural processes. In low-fertility nations, international immigration has therefore assumed a more important role in demographic change than in nations with high fertility. It is important to note that low fertility does not come without consequences, and we list several of the most important societal-wide implications of sub-replacement fertility. We also discuss the implications of a shift in the births outside of marriage and the growing importance of international migration for countries with low birth rates.

Table 1.1

Low-fertility countries in the world

Country	Total fertility rate 2000-5	Implied growth rate (%)	Implied years to halve	Years with sub-replacement fertility
Europe				
Germany	1.32	-1.5	46	30
France	1.87	-0.4	196	25
Russia	1.33	-1.6	43	35
Spain	1.27	-1.6	42	20
Italy	1.28	-1.6	42	25
Greece	1.25	-1.7	41	20
Sweden	1.64	-0.8	88	30
Asia				
China	1.7	-0.9	75	10
Japan	1.33	-1.5	46	45
Australia	1.75	-0.1	119	25
United States	2.04	-0.4	196	25
Canada	1.61	-0.8	88	35

Source: Morgan and Taylor (2006).

Theories of Fertility Decline

Many theories of fertility decline emphasize that with economic development children become economically disadvantageous to families (Kirk
1996). The most commonly cited theory that follows this perspective is
the demographic transition argument, which is largely built on the assumption that economic changes associated with industrialization have
rendered previous family functions incompatible with new economic
institutions (Davis 1997). For example, the specialization of labour that
occurred during the industrial revolution triggered a change in women's
roles, within and outside of the home, contributing to incompatibility
with traditional childbearing patterns and reducing the number of children that women bore. Opportunity cost theory is complementary to
demographic transition theory. It states that as changes in women's roles
enable them to acquire income by working outside the home, the opportunity costs of having children increase. In contrast, women who
are secluded in the home and do not have the opportunity to be gain-
fully employed lose little by having children (Mason 1987). These opportunity costs increase as women's wage levels increase because they

are sacrificing a higher potential income to bear and raise children, leading to further fertility decline. Consequently, as a country develops economically and gives women the potential to acquire income outside of the home, fertility rates decrease. As a result of changing economic conditions, the direct costs of having children also increase, providing another potential deterrent to having children. One notable example is the dramatic increases in the length and cost of education that children must receive to enter the labour force successfully.

Another, more distinct, theoretical perspective emphasizes the role that is played by ideological change in the form of shifts in dominant cultural schema that interpret contemporary contexts in ways that produce low fertility (Morgan and Taylor 2006). The primary ideological shift responsible for lower fertility involves a greater emphasis on individualism, replacing an altruistic theme in which children were the centre of family life. As these individualistic norms become more common, men and women are allowed to pursue a life that they find fulfilling, which need not include children and the necessary sacrifices they entail. The diffusion of fertility trends that occur along language and cultural lines is often cited as evidence of ideological influences on fertility. Diffusion occurs when individuals within certain linguistic and cultural groups adhere to the dominant fertility norms of their group, regardless of dissimilar economic conditions and the dominant fertility norms of the country in which they reside (Kirk 1996).

Another perspective focuses on how changes in institutions, such as the family and the state, contribute to decreasing fertility. Within the family, gender equity, and the changing roles that it entails, is often cited as a reason for lower fertility, which occurs because shared family tasks and increasing incompatibility between home and work tasks generate less motivation to have children. Changes that affect the fertility rate within the family are slow to occur because the family system is strongly linked to conservative institutions such as religion (McDonald 2000). At the state level, factors such as the availability and cost of child care also influence decisions to have children (Blau and Robins 1989). In addition, national laws concerning family leave policies impact the costs and benefits of having children (Caldwell and Schindlmayr 2003).

A final perspective on declining fertility is associated with technological change, which argues that technological innovations are important to consider when explaining declining fertility. Although technologies include those operating in the workplace or in the home that have altered the costs and benefits of having children, major consideration is also given to contraceptive technologies that sever the link between sex and reproduction. In turn, the ability to easily limit reproduction has allowed women to devote more time to intensive and extensive investments in their human capital, such as their own education or career, which further increase the cost of childbearing (Mason 1987). Furthermore, if a woman were to experience an unwanted or unplanned pregnancy, the availability and safety of abortion procedures has increased greatly since *Roe v. Wade* legalized the procedure in 1973.[1] In fact, the ratio of legal abortions to live births increased from 0.24 abortions per live birth in 1973 to 0.43 abortions per live birth in 1981 in the United States (Preston 1986). Although the legalization of abortion does not drastically affect fertility rates, it is an important component of the cultural schema surrounding fertility to consider when examining fertility in the United States, Canada, and other countries that have legalized the procedure.

Although these theoretical mechanisms are sometimes presented as having unique influences on fertility rates, it is more likely that they exert influence interdependently. Indeed, it would be difficult to understand any large-scale decline in fertility as the result of anything less than a combination of each of these theories. What might differ from case to case is the importance of the given factors and the order in which they interact and unfold.

Describing the Fertility Decline in the United States

The focus of this chapter is fertility decline in North America, but Table 1.1 (p. 18) is included for international comparison.[2] Table 1.1 shows the TFR values for a selected set of countries with sub-replacement fertility. The TFR represents the average number of children that would be born to a woman over her lifetime if she were to experience current age-specific fertility rates throughout her lifetime. Since China is included, about one-half of the world's population now lives in a country with fertility low enough to imply population decline in the absence of international migration (Morgan and Taylor 2006). Most of Europe is experiencing a period of sub-replacement fertility, and, in some countries such as Germany, Russia, Spain, Italy, and Greece, the fertility rate is so low that it would take less than fifty years for the population to halve without in-migration (ibid.). It is also interesting to note that below-replacement fertility is not just a recent phenomenon. For many countries, low fertility has been in place for at least a generation.

Since the late 1970s, Canada's fertility has dropped below that of the United States. Nevertheless, the long-range trend in fertility has been broadly similar between the two countries (see Bélanger and Ouellet 2001, for a more in-depth treatment). Focusing on the United States for

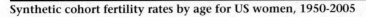

Figure 1.1

Synthetic cohort fertility rates by age for US women, 1950-2005

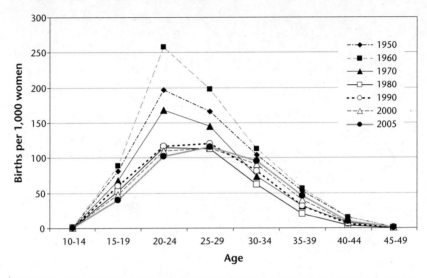

illustration, the timing and number of children that women chose to have greatly affected the fertility decline experienced from 1950 to 2005. We recognize that beginning with 1950 provides a somewhat artificial image of US history, given the magnitude of the baby boom that followed the Second World War. Yet the pattern still reflects the fact that fertility in the United States has generally fallen since the nation was formed. Figure 1.1, which plots fertility rates for women by age from 1950 to 2005, illustrates two important points about recent change in US fertility. First, overall fertility has fallen considerably, from a TFR of approximately 3.5 in 1960 to a TFR of approximately 2.04 in 2005. This is most clearly indicated by the sharp decline in peak fertility rates experienced by women aged twenty to twenty-nine. Second, the distinctive age gradient associated with baby boom fertility has altered. There has been a dramatic decrease in fertility among women aged twenty to twenty-nine and a more modest, but still pronounced, increase in fertility among women aged thirty to thirty-nine. Thus, women are having fewer children and having them later in life. Changes in both number and timing of having children affect the TFR. For example, 1980 stands out as a period of very low fertility with a synthetic cohort TFR of 1.8. In part, however, the 1980 fertility rate was artificially low, representing

Figure 1.2

Median age for all births and median age at first birth

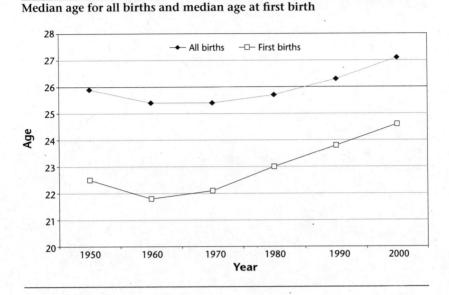

a shift in the timing of births from younger to older ages as well as a decrease in the number of births. After 1980, following the substantial change in the timing of fertility, fertility rates have rebounded slightly but still remain slightly below replacement levels.

Figure 1.2 provides another view of the striking delay in fertility experienced by US women over the past half-century. Two lines are shown: the median age of women at any birth and the median age of women at first birth. Both lines have shifted sharply upward since 1960, with the changes in age at first birth being particularly noticeable. The median age at first birth is now more than two years older than it was in 1960. The median age at any birth has increased by approximately one-and-a-half years. These trends are important because throughout history delayed fertility is a strong indicator of lower fertility.

The Weakening Link between Fertility and Marriage in the United States

Fertility and marriage are no longer as strongly linked as they used to be. It used to be the case that marriage came first, followed soon after by children. Consequently, almost all children were born within marriage. Out-of-wedlock childbearing was not unknown, but it was relatively

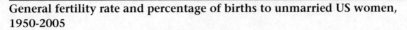

Figure 1.3

General fertility rate and percentage of births to unmarried US women, 1950-2005

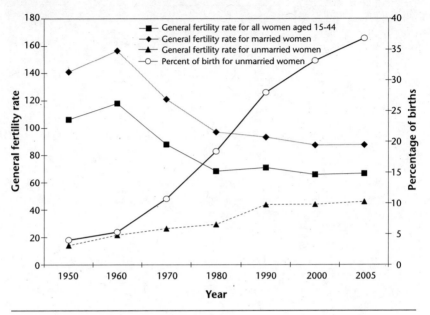

uncommon. If a single woman became pregnant, the event usually spurred a marriage.

Using the general fertility rate (GFR) rather than the TFR, Figure 1.3 demonstrates that the link between marriage and fertility is weakening. Although the two measures of fertility are closely related, we use the GFR, which measures the rate of births to women between the ages of fifteen and forty-four, because it most easily relates changes in fertility to changes in marriage. In particular, the fertility of both married and unmarried women can be easily shown using the GFR. Figure 1.3 plots the GFR for married and unmarried women from 1950 to 2005. The figure demonstrates the rise in the percentage of births occurring to unmarried women in the United States over the past fifty years. It demonstrates that the GFR for married women has fallen dramatically, whereas the GFR for unmarried women has escalated rapidly (but not enough to offset the decline in marital fertility). As a consequence, by 2005, over one-third of all births in the United States occurred to unmarried women. Clearly, marriage and childbearing have become

Figure 1.4

Percentage of births to unmarried women

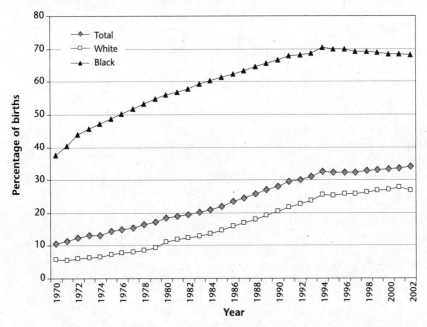

decoupled over time. Of course, because cohabitation rates have increased dramatically since 1950, some of these births have occurred to women in stable cohabiting unions, but we do not have the data to take the effect of this cultural shift into account (Smock 2000).

Overall, marriage rates have declined, with this trend being particularly pronounced for the Black population in the United States. Consequently, the disassociation between marriage and childbearing has been strongest in the Black population (Bumpass and McLanahan 1989). Figure 1.4 illustrates the weakened link between marriage and fertility in the United States, especially for Black women. Almost 70 percent of the births to Black women in 2000 occurred outside of marriage compared to approximately 27 percent of births to White women.

Consequences of Changes in Fertility, and Why Mortality Is Important

We are just now beginning to understand the social impact of pronounced and widespread changes in demographic processes. There have been many well-documented societal-wide implications of changes in fertility. However, in order to better understand the demographic impact of changing fertility, we must also consider the effect of changes in mortality. Historically, mortality and fertility have both declined, albeit at different rates and starting at different points in time. A shift in the way mortality declines, however, has important implications for the social consequences of demographic change. In the past, mortality generally declined more rapidly at the youngest ages and has resisted change at the oldest ages. Thus, until recently, increases in life expectancy have largely resulted from declines in infant mortality. This pattern has changed over recent decades, starting in 1950 when declines in mortality slowly shifted from younger to older ages. Since then, mortality has continued to decline at all ages, but it is now declining most rapidly at older ages. In the United States, during the decade from 1950 to 1960, about 40 percent of the decline in mortality occurred at older ages. During the decade from 1990 to 2000, this figure was 80 percent, indicating the growing importance of mortality decline at older ages (US Census Bureau 2008).

Lower fertility, in conjunction with the shift in the nature of mortality decline, has led to populations that are rapidly aging. Declining and low fertility ages a population because fewer people are born each year, decreasing the number of young persons in a population. Declining mortality at older ages increases the number of older persons in a population, further enhancing aging. What is occurring in Canada is instructive in this instance. Since 1950, the median age of Canadians has risen from 27.2 to 38.8 years, and the percentage of persons aged sixty-five and older has increased from 7.7 to 13.2 (Foot 2008). By mid-century, these percentages are expected to increase to 46.8 and 26.4 respectively.

In turn, an aging population, particularly in the policy context of entitlement programs indexed by age, places a considerable burden on younger cohorts. The provision of health and social benefits to a growing elderly population can severely tax the ability of a nation to invest in required infrastructure needed for subsequent growth. In Canada, for the year 2001-2, 43 percent of the $95 billion spent on health care went to the 13.2 percent of Canadians aged sixty-five and older (Health Canada 2002). As the proportion of Canadians who are older than sixty-five years of age continues to grow, health expenditures will also grow, stressing other programs that will compete for limited resources. A similar scenario appears with respect to old age pension plans, which are on the point of being stressed by the bulge of retiring baby boomers (Foot 2008).

Thus, declining fertility and mortality are likely to redefine the implicit bargain that has long existed between generations. Parents are increasingly likely to live most of their adult years without childrearing responsibilities and are more likely to need their accumulated resources to live a relatively long period of time following retirement (King 1999; Schrier 2010). Consequently, younger cohorts of men and women will be forced to pay higher levels of tax to support an aging population, reducing their ability to invest in their own future (Grant et al. 2004).

An aging population also means that labour shortages are possible, if not inevitable. When populations fail to reproduce themselves, yet still need a viable work force to support an elderly population, the pressure and need for immigration increases. Already, Europe, the United States, and Canada have attracted vast numbers of immigrants from Asia, Africa, and Latin America. In part, the flow of immigration is spurred by poor living conditions and the lack of opportunities in countries of origin. At the same time, declining populations in more developed countries often count on a cheap source of unskilled labour drawn from these migration streams. Many European nations such as France and Germany have long relied on immigrants to fill needs in their labour force (Martin and Zurcher 2008). As a result, there is likely to be continued tension between pro- and anti-immigration groups in many nations with declining populations. The situation in France has been particularly illustrative of this issue, as clashes between immigrants and native inhabitants spiked as the French economy stagnated. In part, this tension led to the rise of Jean-Marie Le Pen's party, the Front National, in the 2002 presidential election. Running on a platform advocating strict limits on immigration, Le Pen's campaign made it to the second round of the presidential election, displacing the socialist party, which was much more progressive and better established.

Another implication of declining fertility and mortality is the fact that the family has become a less central component of everyday life. In part, this situation is a function of the declining role played by children in adults' lives. As noted earlier, nearly two-thirds of an adult's lifespan in North America is spent without childrearing responsibilities (Morgan and Taylor 2006). Without the demands and structure that having children entails, adults are freer to pursue their own interests. In addition, without the added constraints of having to care for children, most nations with declining populations have also experienced rapid rises in rates of divorce and cohabitation (Preston 1986; Kiernan 2000). In the United States, nearly one out of every two marriages will end in divorce, and more than half of all marriages will be preceded by a period of cohabitation, with an even higher fraction of second marriages preceded by cohabitation (Smock 2000). On the global stage, the United States has the highest divorce rate among more developed countries, although Canada and many countries in Europe have higher cohabitation rates (Furstenberg 1994; Kiernan 2000; Le Bourdais and Lapierre-Adamcyk 2004).

Another consequence of these shifts in fertility and mortality is that children are increasingly likely to experience some form of disruption in their family life. Despite declines in the risk of becoming an orphan, greater numbers of children witness a parental divorce, parental marriage, and non-marital cohabitation. Greater instability in the adult life course has meant that children are more likely to have multiple parental figures throughout their childhood. And because poverty is closely linked to marital status, particularly statuses other than marriage, children are increasingly likely to experience economic instability (Iceland 2003; Amato and Maynard 2007). Such instability in childhood living arrangements, along with poverty, are in turn linked to poorer socio-economic outcomes for children such as dropping out of school, engaging in sex at an earlier age, and having children out of wedlock (Furstenberg 1994; Amato and Maynard 2007).

Hence, a very delicate relationship exists between fertility and mortality, and once the balance has been disturbed the resulting demographic changes inevitably spur changes in social relationships. At the most basic level, these changes are the result of norms and roles linked to our most basic demographic characteristics such as age, sex, race, and marital status. Several authors have noted that demographic shifts in sex ratios affect social functioning and can affect patterns of marriage and divorce (Guttentag and Secord 1983; Blau and Schwartz 1984). Shifts in age structure have also been linked to change in social relationships, largely because organizations and individuals interact based on age (Ryder 1965; Gordon and Longino 2000). For example, shifts in age structure affect the number of workers available to an economy or the number of students heading to college. And, as noted earlier, the growth of the elderly population substantially impacts costs for health care and social insurance programs.

Of course, social institutions are not immutable, and policy shifts can alter the linkages between population structure and social organizations. As David Foot (2008) notes, various proposals have been suggested to keep workers in the workforce longer in Canada. In the United States, the aging of the baby boom cohorts has led to many proposed changes in social security. For example, in his 2005 State of the Union address, President George W. Bush proposed a partial privatization of social security as one means of addressing the looming shortfall in social security revenues associated with the impending retirement of baby boomers. The same projected shortfall has led to recent increases in the age at which full retirement benefits can be received (from age sixty-five to age sixty-seven). Projected deficits associated with Medicare are one of the stated reasons for President Obama's call for health care reform.

Conclusion

Fertility rates have drastically changed in North America over the last half-century, decreasing almost to the point of causing overall natural population decline. The United States and Canada are not alone in experiencing this phenomenon. Countries such as Germany, France, Spain, Russia, Italy, Greece, and Australia would all be experiencing rapid population declines due to sub-replacement fertility rates without in-migration. In an attempt to explain these changes, many competing theories exist, but they are complementary at best because no one theory is able to entirely account for declining fertility. In both Canada and the United States, as well as in many European countries, the declining fertility rate can be largely attributed to changes in the timing and number of children that women are choosing to have. It is obvious that such drastic changes in fertility and related changes in mortality unavoidably spur additional demographic changes. Across North America, the population must adapt to accommodate an aging population, placing considerable strain on younger cohorts. Such changes will inevitably have a widespread effect, which will influence many aspects of daily life ranging from marital behaviours to immigration policies.

Notes

1 *Roe v. Wade,* 410 U.S. 113 (1973).
2 Unless otherwise noted, all data presented in this chapter are taken from various issues of the National Vital Statistics reports available from the Centers for Disease Control and Prevention, http://www.cdc.gov/nchs/products/nvsr.htm.

References

Amato, P., and R. Maynard. 2007. "Decreasing Non-Marital Births and Strengthening Marriage to Reduce Poverty." *Future of Children* 17: 117-41.
Bélanger, A., and G. Ouellet. 2001. "A Comparative Study of Recent Trends in Canadian and American Fertility, 1980-1999." In *Report on the Demographic Situation in Canada,* 107-36. Ottawa: Statistics Canada.
Blau, D.M., and P.K. Robins. 1989. "Fertility, Employment, and Child-Care Costs." *Demography* 26: 287-99.

Blau, D.M., and J. Schwartz. 1984. *Crosscutting Social Circles: Testing a Macro-sociological Theory of Social Structure*. Orlando, FL: Academic Press.

Bumpass, L., and S. McLanahan. 1989. "Unmarried Motherhood: Recent Trends, Composition, and Black-White Differences." *Demography* 26: 279-86.

Caldwell, J., and T. Schindlmayr. 2003. "Explanations of the Fertility Crisis in Modern Societies: A Search for Commonalities." *Population Studies* 57: 241-63.

Davis, K. 1997. "Kingsley Davis on Reproductive Institutions and the Pressure for Population." *Population and Development Review* 23: 611-24.

Foot, D. 2008. "Some Economic and Social Consequences of Population Aging." In *Canadian Priorities Agenda,* Brief no. 7, http://www.irpp.org/cpa/briefs/foot.pdf.

Furstenberg, F. 1994. "History and Current Status of Divorce in the United States." *Future of Children* 4: 29-43.

Gordon, C., and C. Longino. 2000. "Age Structure and Social Structure." *Contemporary Sociology* 29: 699-709.

Grant, J., S. Hoorens, S. Sivadasan, M. van het Loo, J. DaVanzo, L. Hale, S. Gibson, and W. Butz. 2004. *Low Fertility and Population Aging: Causes, Consequences, and Policy Options*. Santa Monica, CA: RAND Corporation.

Guttentag, M., and P. Secord. 1983. *Too Many Women? The Sex Ratio Question*. Beverly Hills, CA: Sage.

Health Canada. 2002. *Canada's Aging Population,* http://www._dsp-psd.pwgsc.gc.ca/Collection/H39-608-2002E.pdf.

Iceland, J. 2003. "Why Poverty Remains High: The Role of Income Growth, Economic Inequality, and Changes in Family Structure, 1949-1999." *Demography* 40: 499-519.

Kiernan, K. 2000. "European Perspectives on Union Formation. In L. Waite et al., eds., *Ties That Bind: Perspectives on Marriage and Cohabitation,* 40-58. Hawthorne, NY: Aldine de Gruyter.

King, R. 1999. "Time Spent in Parenthood Status among Adults in the United States." *Demography* 36: 377-85.

Kirk, D. 1996. "Demographic Transition Theory." *Population Studies* 50: 361-87.

Le Bourdais, C., and E. Lapierre-Adamcyk. 2004. "Changes in Conjugal Life in Canada: Is Cohabitation Progressively Replacing Marriage?" *Journal of Marriage and the Family* 66: 929-42.

Martin, P., and G. Zurcher. 2008. *Managing Migration: The Global Challenge*. Population Reference Bureau, *Population Bulletin* 63(1): 1-24.

Mason, K.O. 1987. "The Impact of Women's Social Position on Fertility in Developing Countries." *Sociological Forum* 2: 718-45.

McDonald, P. 2000. "Gender Equity in Theories of Fertility Transition." *Population and Development Review* 26: 427-39.

Morgan, P., and M. Taylor. 2006. "Low Fertility at the Turn of the Twenty-First Century." *Annual Review of Sociology* 32: 375-99.

Preston, H.S. 1986. "The Decline of Fertility in Non-European Industrialized Countries." *Population and Development Review* 12: 26-47.

Ryder, N. 1965. "The Cohort as a Concept in the Study of Social Change." *American Sociological Review* 30: 841-61.

Schrier, D. 2010. "Consequences of an Aging Population: Can Existing Levels of Social Services be Sustained?" http://www.bcstats.gov.bc.ca/DATA/pop/pop/agingpop.pdf.

Smock, P. 2000. "Cohabitation in the United States: An Appraisal of Research Themes, Findings, and Implications." *Annual Review of Sociology* 26: 1-20.

US Census Bureau. 2008. *Statistical Abstract of the United States,* 127th edition, Washington, DC: US Census Bureau.

2

Changing Children and Changing Cultures: Immigration as a Source of Fertility and the Assumptions of Assimilation

Nathanael Lauster, Todd F. Martin, and James M. White

In visions of the future, including both the books *Childhood's End* (Clarke 1953) and *The Children of Men* (James 1992), the disappearance of children precipitates larger crises of meaning. These crises of meaning quickly become extended and interwoven with the icons of international immigration – the alien and the refugee. Similarly, as fertility continues to fall around the world, particularly in more developed countries, questions about the meaning of children have increasingly become conflated with questions about the meaning of immigration (see also Chapter 1 by Mira Whyman, Megan Lemmon, and Jay Teachman in this volume). Concerns over where the labour force of tomorrow will come from become joined with concerns over what the societies of tomorrow will look like. Sometimes these concerns result in explicitly anti-immigrant analyses. Mark Steyn (2006) provides a somewhat hyperbolic claim that the higher birth rates of non-Western immigrants will lead their children to out-number more "Westernized" groups, resulting in a "cultural decline" for immigrant-receiving countries with low fertility rates. Others argue that higher fertility rates for immigrants from less developed regions might have positive implications such as changing dependency rates for countries where fertility is currently below the replacement level (for example, Lutz and Scherbov 2008). Many of these arguments assume that immigrants are more likely to have children and that they (and possibly their descendants) will retain higher fertility rates long after arriving in more developed countries. In this chapter, we explore the intersection of immigration, ethnicity, and fertility in Canada.

Fertility decline is a recognized trend across most of the developed world. Of those countries that tend to be considered more developed, only the United States and Iceland retain near-replacement fertility (each approaching a total fertility rate (TFR) of 2.1 as of 2006). Other countries have attempted to respond to fertility declines by developing pro-natalist policies, but only recently have any of these countries made substantial gains in raising fertility, and, even then, the outcome has still been below replacement level. For example, France moved from a TFR of about 1.71 in 1995 to about 1.98 in 2006 (Population Reference Bureau 2007). While much of France's increase in fertility has been attributed to pro-natalist policies, including free nurseries and family-friendly work policies, immigration has also played a large role in the rise in its fertility. Depending on the method of estimation, immigrant TFRs appear to be between 0.46 and 0.85 higher than native-born TFRs (Toulemon 2006). The case of France, then, gives increased credibility to the idea that immigration and fertility are linked, with immigrants providing a boost in birth rates to offset the lower fertility of native-born populations.

However, there are several assumptions regarding the positive effects of immigration on fertility that call for closer scrutiny. First, the assumption that immigrants will always come from places with higher fertility rates should be questioned. Indeed, as Laurent Toulemon (2006) notes, immigrants to France from Italy and Spain are coming from places with lower fertility rates. Second, even immigrants coming from higher-fertility regions are often both institutionally screened and self-selected in ways that make them different from the people they are leaving behind. As a result, immigrant cohorts are not typically representative of others from their countries of origin, and they may be quite likely to demonstrate different fertility patterns. Third, we argue in this chapter that the assumption that immigrants will in some way carry the culture of their sending country into their receiving country should also be called into question. We address all three of these assumptions in the following pages, though we focus mostly on the third claim, investigating the relationship between culture and fertility in multicultural countries.

Immigration and Theories of Fertility Decline

Contemporary theoretical arguments have largely emphasized that fertility decline is tied to development, but exactly how this connection is made remains vague (Bryant 2007). Most often, development has been assumed to make children less useful and more expensive, leading rational adults to weigh the costs and benefits and reduce the number of children they bear (Goode 1963, 1993). For some analysts, the usefulness of children as labourers changes with the movement away from agriculture and toward industrialization (despite the widespread use of child labour in many factories) (Caldwell 1976). For many analysts, development also involves a change in institutional responsibility, allowing elderly people to avoid relying on their children for care in later life. There is a corresponding drop in fertility as the usefulness of children changes, altering intergenerational wealth flows (Caldwell 1976, 1982; Boldrin, DeNardi, and Jones 2005). The costs of childbearing are typically assumed to rise as education becomes required (Caldwell 1982).

Demographic theories of fertility decline that are based on developmental explanations largely ignore or downplay the importance of culture (Easterlin and Crimmins 1985; Bryant 2007). Applying these theories to understanding the relationship between immigration and fertility, one would expect that immigrants would quickly become subject to all of the same pressures and incentives that others face in their receiving country. Cultural differences should not matter, at least not for long. As a result, immigrants and the descendants of immigrants should not display markedly higher (or lower) fertility rates than those who are native born.

Other scholars, however, have argued that culture remains important in understanding fertility change. Ron Lesthaeghe (1995) and Johan Surykin (1988) have made the case that widespread cultural change favouring a new post-material individualism has accompanied economic development. Children, and family living in general, are no longer as bound up with identity as in the past, and, as a result, fewer people are having children. This cultural change, they argue, amounts to a second demographic transition and explains the low fertility rates of Europe, Canada, and other more developed nations (Lesthaeghe 1995), arguably even the United States (Lesthaeghe and Neidert 2006). According to many researchers, the role of culture should also be accorded more respect in analyses of the first demographic transition (Kirk 1996; Bryant 2007). In particular, historical researchers note that the spread of fertility limitation has been contained by cultural boundaries, especially linguistic and religious boundaries, far more than would be expected if development were the sole or even primary force promoting fertility change.

If culture, rather than development, is the key force promoting fertility decline, then immigrant groups might maintain substantially higher fertility rates in receiving countries. To the extent that immigrant parents pass on their culture to their children, higher fertility might become "ethnicized," leading to differences between cultural groups within the same country. In this vein, Samuel Huntington (1996) raises the issue that certain groups might change their "materialistic culture," adopting the same orientation toward developmental factors assumed to influence fertility in the developmentalist analysis, while maintaining their "symbolic culture," an orientation toward children and family life that is quite possibly at odds with Lesthaeghe's individualism. Similarly, Goran Therborn (2004) argues that certain groups seem relatively stable in the maintenance of their family cultures regardless of diverse economic and social influences. This sort of cultural indelibility, or resistance to assimilation, may allow fertility differences to persist between immigrant groups and their descendants and the population of receiving countries.

The introduction of culture into questions of immigration and fertility raises fundamental questions about how culture should be defined and how it might work to influence fertility. The notion of cultural indelibility posits a unitary, coherent system of symbolic understandings – or a worldview – that might be passed on between generations. Among different worldviews, the value and meaning of children and family life might differ, leading to very different fertility outcomes. This model of culture would seem to provide a possible explanation for fertility differences between groups. Yet two problems arise with this vision. First, there is little guidance as to what should define the boundaries of a given cultural group. Is cultural categorization a matter of the strictures imposed on a worldview by language, self-defined ethnic history, socially defined and racialized marginalization, or religious ideology and belief? It is not coincidental that these four bases for identifying cultural boundaries – language, ethnicity, race, and religion – also form the basis for Will Kymlicka's (2001, 2008) defence of Canadian multiculturalism. Political philosophers have given thought to how culture might be meaningfully defined and assigned, but demographers have mostly ignored this most critical issue.

Second, the notion of cultural indelibility provides a unitary and homogeneous view of culture that leaves little room for contestation and change, complex culture-to-culture interactions, and ultimately even little room for traditional views of assimilation. Individuals are assumed not to negotiate identities or to contest and construct worldviews outside of the cultural systems passed on to them.[1] Instead, a categorical view of individuals is promoted by this vision – one in which individuals can be tagged and labelled by culture. Culture is ultimately (and problematically) conceived of as a property of individuals rather than as the interaction between individuals (Emirbayer 1997). This problem may be especially intractable for demographers since making group comparisons requires assigning people into groups in a categorical fashion (Hammel 1990). At this point, we will discuss more relative ways of thinking about culture that might be important for understanding how it influences fertility.

Culture, Multiculturalism, and Fertility

The first task in breaking down fertility trends by cultural groups is to decide who belongs to what group. Assortment is typically performed on the basis of dividing the population into mutually exclusive, but exhaustive, categories. Through surveys, individuals are usually given the chance to assign themselves to one of various groups based on racial or ethnic or other cultural categories. In practice, researchers often take these self-assignments as indicative of meaningful group membership, assuming that everyone fits himself or herself into one, and only one, grouping. Where individuals fit themselves into multiple racial groupings, as in the most recent US census, they are still considered to belong to only one group by many researchers.

What type of grouping is appropriate for defining an explicitly cultural group? This depends on how one envisions culture as working. First, culture could be conceived of as linguistic. Language assigns the symbols and signifiers by which most people relate to the world, hence serving as the architecture of one's worldview. Dividing people up by first language would be one approach to practically and meaningfully defining cultural groups. Since there are different words for child in different languages, so the meanings swirling around children and fertility can be expected to differ across languages. In the Canadian context, Kymlicka (2001, 2008) describes the support for a multiculturalism policy as relating first to the linguistic distinction between Francophones and Anglophones – two distinct cultural groups within Canada. These two languages together define the official heritage of Canada. According to this approach, immigrants, and the children and grandchildren of immigrants, who speak a non-Anglophone or non-Francophone first language would be considered to be culturally distinct groups within Canada. However, the children of immigrants to Canada who grow up speaking English or French as a first language would quickly blend in with other Francophone or Anglophone Canadians, breaking down any notion of cultural indelibility.

Many would argue that culture transcends language and can be passed on from parents to children even when their first language differs. This ethnic view of culture involves some notion of belonging to a historical group that is distinct from other groups. This belonging can be expressed in the maintenance of deep traditions and rituals that distinguish one group from another even when they speak the same tongue. Alternatively, this belonging can be expressed in no more than surnames or genealogical records. Hence, an ethnic notion of belonging can be genealogically passed on from parent to child to create a sense of cultural continuity, which can be further reinforced by the maintenance of shared rituals and traditions. These shared rituals and traditions can result in different orientations toward children and childbearing, resulting in different fertility patterns. Kymlicka (2008) argues that multiculturalism in Canada quickly spread from support for linguistic differences to a broader, more expansive inclusiveness based on support for ethnic differences. As a result, the maintenance of distinct ethnic rituals and traditions within Canada is supported by multicultural policy (Bloemraad 2002).[2]

Ethnicity is primarily a matter of how individuals and families define themselves and record their own heritage in rituals and observances. As such, ethnicity is usually defined by those belonging to the group recognizing their affiliation with a given group designation. By contrast, individuals can also be placed into marginalized groups by others. Cultural groupings can be produced by the ideologies of race and racism, producing various histories of discrimination and marginalization. A history of marginalization and oppression, in conjunction with ongoing discrimination, can produce different orientations toward children and childbearing for different groups. Kymlicka (2008) finds that the framework of multiculturalism in Canada quickly came to be enlisted in the fight against racism, placing racialization at the centre of definitions of culture. This framework has produced the "visible minority" categorization within Canada, so that individuals can be categorized according to how they are perceived by others and within the context of their historical marginalization within racist ideologies.

Finally, aside from locating cultural affiliation in linguistic, ethnic, and racialized terms, individuals can also be categorized by religion. As such, religion can also be considered culture. Religions can provide moral and ideological guidance regarding childbearing behaviours, laying out prescriptive and proscriptive norms that should be followed by adherents. Many scholars suggest that religion has an influence on fertility (McQuillan 2004; Derosas and van Poppel 2006; Goldscheider 2006). Kymlicka (2008) includes religious difference as the latest incarnation of multiculturalism in Canada, with many groups making claims to specific religious rights.

Another, perhaps more intractable, problem with linking culture to fertility in most demographic accounts builds on these difficulties in determining how to categorize people. It is difficult to determine how to group people into cultural categories because these categories are only contextually defined. Cultural identities are evoked (or elided) in

the process of social interaction. As a result, the salience of social difference can vary a great deal depending on the context. For immigrants,
the salience of language, ethnicity, race, and religion as determinants
of fertility may depend on how often these factors are evoked in daily
life or how these factors are internalized as important parts of constructed
identities. To the extent that one speaks a different language at home
from the surrounding society, then language becomes more tangible. To
the extent that ethnicity determines with whom one interacts socially
or how one views conceptions of self, then ethnic difference becomes
more tangible. To the extent that religion is considered important, then
religious difference becomes more tangible. To the extent that discrimination prevents one from getting a job, then racial difference becomes
more tangible. As cultural differences become more tangible in everyday life, they serve as more plausible barriers to assimilation within the
cultural mainstream. Unless cultural affiliations are tangible in daily
life, they are unlikely to have much effect on fertility. However, to the
degree that symbolic cultural differences become embedded in regular
interactions, they can translate into barriers to the diffusion of fertility-
related behaviour.

We explore different ways of measuring culture and estimate the resulting fertility differentials between cultural groups in the sections that
follow. Canada is in many ways an ideal country in which to explore
the relationships between culture and fertility that are likely to develop
given immigration trends around the world. Canada is broadly representative of more developed countries, with high education levels and
relatively expansive social supports in evidence. At the same time,
Canada has an explicit and legally enshrined multicultural policy that
encourages immigrant groups to maintain their cultures.[3]

Methods

Data

The sample for this study was derived from the Ethnic Diversity Survey
(EDS), which was conducted jointly by Statistics Canada and the
Department of Canadian Heritage. The EDS was a post-censal survey,
and its participants were selected from the 2001 census based on answers
to specific questions from the long-form questionnaire. The EDS's target
population consisted of persons aged fifteen years and older living in
private dwellings in all ten Canadian provinces, but excluding First
Nations reserves and territorial populations. The response rate of the

survey (75.6 percent) was relatively high, producing a sample size of 42,476 respondents. For analysis of fertility patterns, we further constrained this sample to focus on the 16,036 women in the age range fifteen to fifty-four, which corresponded roughly to those women at risk of having children. This sample size seems quite large, but it still served to limit the analyses possible for smaller cultural groupings, as discussed further later in this chapter.

The EDS data was collected between April and August 2002. Interviews were conducted in English and French as well as in several other non-official languages. In order to represent the target population, a probabilistic survey was used to gather a random sample. The survey was specifically designed to ensure sufficient numbers of persons belonging to non-British or non-French ethnic groups. Specific steps, including a detailed stratification structure, were taken in order to collect data on certain sub-populations. The sample selection was designed to have an over-representation of peoples who were first- and second-generation non-Canadian, non-British, non-French, and non-American, Australian, and/or New Zealander origins (CBFA+). The EDS sample's distribution was established with two-thirds of the sample representing Canadians from non-CBFA+ origins in an attempt to remain relevant to all people in Canada. As a result of the complex sampling design, the data required weighting. In our analyses, we follow the weighting guidelines suggested by Statistics Canada (2002, 10-11). Although the use of normalized weights do not correct for design effects such as stratification and clustering, they do take into account the unequal probabilities of selection.

Measures
The dependent variable that we used in our fertility analysis was the presence of children under age three. This most closely approximates childbearing given the limited information available in the EDS, and a similar, though more precise, variable has been used to study fertility in other Statistics Canada reports (Malenfant and Bélanger 2006). This variable tends to be downwardly biased with respect to capturing all childbearing and is particularly influenced by the timing of childbearing (children born close together only count once) as well as infant mortality effects (children dying before age three are likely to be missed). Furthermore, for any given age range, relatively few women will have toddlers or infants at any given time, limiting the power of the measurement. Like measures of TFR, this measurement provides only a cross-sectional measure of fertility rather than a total summation of fertility across the

life course of survey respondents. We configure the fertility variable this way primarily because of data limitations. However, using the presence of children under age three also has some advantages for this analysis. In particular, we focus only on recent fertility, which means that this fertility was likely to have occurred in Canada. We also avoid missing many children of older ages who might have moved away from their mothers. Overall, we argue that biases resulting from using this variable are likely to be distributed more or less evenly across the population and that the resulting variable serves as a reasonable proxy to capture between-group differences in fertility within the constraints of this particular data set.

Culture is our primary independent variable of interest. We consider and compare a variety of cultural categorizations, including linguistic, ethnic, racial, and religious. We discuss these different categorizations in the following sections.

Linguistic

Language, as the basis for a symbolic understanding of the world, could prevent people from assimilating in terms of fertility behaviour. We begin by considering linguistic categorization based on first language spoken. This specification of culture speaks to the culture of origin and possibly to socialization, but it does not speak to current context. We compare this specification of culture to a linguistic categorization based on language currently spoken at home. We argue that this second specification more adequately captures a contextual understanding of cultural barriers to assimilation that might lead to differences in fertility.

Ethnic

We also consider a categorization based on ethnicity. Ethnic understandings and practices could work to prevent people from assimilating in terms of childbearing behaviour. We begin by using the first ethnic ancestry listed in the survey (out of many possible ethnicities) as a means of dividing up the population into mutually exclusive cultural groups and comparing the fertility for these groups to the base group of Canadians who simply listed Canadian as their first ethnic ancestry. Limiting individuals to one ethnicity is problematic since many individuals (over 40 percent in the sample) list multiple ethnicities, but this approach is commonly taken in studies of culture. We next construct a measure of ethnic affiliation to account for the multiplicity of ethnicities that an individual could claim. In this case, individuals are not limited to one ethnicity. Instead, each ethnic affiliation is estimated to provide an additive effect on overall fertility. We continue to use ethnic ancestry as the basis for understanding ethnicity in this measure. While individuals may recognize their ethnic ancestries, they may or may not be important to them. So we also measure whether or not an individual feels a given ancestry is important (ranking at least a four on a scale of one to five). For this measure, we continue to treat cultural categories as potentially additive rather than as mutually exclusive. Finally, an ancestry may or may not be considered part of a person's current identity. This factor is also measured in the EDS, and we use an additive measure of cultural identity to explore this understanding of culture.

Racial

In Canada, racialization is understood in terms of the visibility of one's minority status. Patterns of social exclusion could also prevent individuals from assimilating in terms of fertility behaviour. Canadians are divided into visible minorities, defined by the Employment Equity Act as "persons other than Aboriginal peoples, who are non-Caucasian in race or non-white in colour."[4] The assumption is that individuals can be grouped into visible categories that resemble contemporary understandings of race in such countries as Canada, the United States, and many other contexts. To capture this grouping of individuals into racialized groups, we first use their listed visible minority status. However, individuals may recognize themselves as being in a visible minority group without feeling as though they have faced discrimination as a result of their status. We create a second measure of visible minority that includes as visible minorities only those who have felt discriminated against in the past five years based on ethnicity, race, skin colour, language, accent, or religion. This is an attempt to measure how racialization might actually work to influence individuals' sense of social exclusion (recognizing that actual categories of exclusion might be more difficult to assess). Finally, we create a measure of visible minority status based on identity, which only includes as visible minorities those people who have listed visible minority status and who have also incorporated something besides "Canadian" or "French Canadian" into their own ethnic identity.

Religious

We consider the role of religion as it creates cultural difference and barriers to assimilation in terms of childbearing behaviour. First, we simply consider religious affiliation, assigning individuals to groups by their sense of belonging to a specific group. Next, we consider whether or not religion is important to people and assign individuals to religious groups only if they feel that religion is important in their lives (at least four on a scale of one to five).

Controls

Controls are also important to our analysis since immigrant groups differ in composition by a number of variables known to influence fertility. We control for age group in our analysis (fifteen to seventeen, eighteen to twenty-four, twenty-five to twenty-nine, thirty to thirty-four, thirty-five to forty-four, and forty-five to fifty-four), using the categories available in the EDS. We also control for partnership status, dividing individuals into single, married, common-law, and formerly partnered categories. We control for current schooling to separate out students from non-students. We also control for the level of completed education (advanced degree, bachelor's degree, college/technical diploma, some university, some college, high school diploma, and less than high school). Finally, and importantly, we control for generation, separating the population into first generation (immigrants), second generation (children of immigrants), and third or later generations. This division provides some control for the selection effects of immigration itself.

Results

In the various figures illustrated in this chapter, we demonstrate the odds ratios for the likelihood of having one's own child under the age of three in the household by different conceptualizations and measures of culture. These odds ratios are obtained from logistic regression models including the relevant measure of culture along with age, partnership status, schooling, education, and generation. In all models, age shows the expected curvilinear relationship with fertility, predicting an increasing likelihood of having a child under age three in the household up until age twenty-five and a decreasing likelihood after age thirty-four. Not surprisingly, being married or in a common-law relationship dramatically increases the odds of being a mother to a young child. Having been in a relationship has a much lower, but still significantly, positive effect. Being in school significantly lowers the likelihood of being a mother to a young child. Level of education has a limited impact, although those attaining an education level beyond high school tend to be somewhat more likely to be mothers of young children.

In nearly all models, generation has an important influence on fertility, but only for first-generation immigrants. First-generation immigrants are generally more likely to be mothers of young children than third- or

Figure 2.1

Odds ratios for the likelihood of having a child under the age of three, by language (relative to English) for women aged fifteen to fifty-four

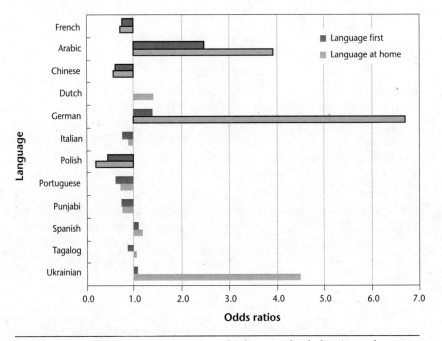

Note: Model controls for age, partnership status, schooling, completed education, and generation. Outlined bars indicate significance at p < 0.10.

higher-generation individuals. By contrast, the likelihood of motherhood for second-generation immigrants never differs significantly from the likelihood of motherhood for third and higher generations. This result provides further support for the selection effects of immigration itself, but it offers little evidence that the children of immigrants "carry on" the childbearing patterns of their parents in the absence of compelling cultural reasons.

To explore the influence of culture on fertility, we consider a variety of different categorizations and conceptualizations of culture. For the purposes of modelling, we run each of these categorical conceptualizations separately but include all of the earlier-mentioned controls for each model. Although we recognize and ultimately suggest that the various categories and conceptualizations ought to be combined in a more theoretical fashion, even with a moderately sized survey devoted to ethnic diversity, we encounter severe problems with inferential power when exploring distinct groups. We suggest that this is likely to be a persistent problem with many attempts to measure fertility differentials by culture. As a result, in Figure 2.1, we begin with a comparison of the odds ratios for different groups using two conceptualizations of a linguistic categorization. The odds ratios that differ in at least a marginally statistically significant fashion (alpha = 0.10 level) are outlined in this bar chart.

The first thing noticeable in the results is that language does seem to have significant effects on fertility in whichever conceptualization is used. Growing up speaking French, Arabic, Chinese, or Polish results in significantly different fertility outcomes than growing up speaking English. However, strikingly, the type of difference depends on which language was spoken. While growing up speaking Arabic increases the likelihood of being a mother to a young child, growing up speaking French, Chinese, or Polish decreases the likelihood. In this way, linguistic barriers to assimilation can result in both lower and higher fertility, depending on the language learned while growing up. Perhaps even more strikingly, the results differ in comparing whether or not individuals grew up speaking a different language at home and whether or not they currently do so. In this second conceptualization of language, speaking French, Arabic, Chinese, or Polish at home still matters to fertility and produces similar results to a conceptualization of language incorporating first language. However, speaking German at home also matters a great deal. In fact, speaking German at home is the strongest linguistic predictor of being a mother of a young child. In this way, changing the conceptualization of linguistic categories changes the interpretation of where one is likely to find group differences. Depending on how culture is defined, different linguistic groups emerge as distinctly important for tracking cultural resistance to assimilation.[5]

In Figure 2.2, we focus on ethnic categorizations. A relatively small proportion of ethnic categorizations results in significant differences from being Canadian, which likely reflects the small sample size for many groups. However, some significant differences by group do emerge. According to the first, most simplified, and mutually exclusive version of categorizing people by the first ethnic ancestry they choose (the top bars), people listing themselves as Ukrainian, African, West Asian, or Caribbean/Latin American demonstrate significant differences in fertility behaviour from ethnic Canadians. In all cases, these individuals have a significantly higher likelihood of having children than ethnic Canadians.

Figure 2.2

Odds ratios for the likelihood of having a child under the age of three, by ethnic ancestry or identity (relative to Canadian) for women aged fifteen to fifty-four

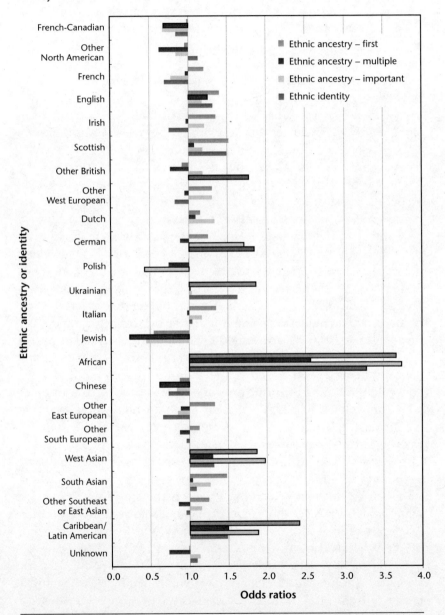

Note: Model controls for age, partnership status, schooling, completed education, and generation. Outlined bars indicate significance at p < 0.10.

However, this result does not recognize the contextual and complex nature of ethnic ancestry, where a single person might share multiple ancestries. Recognizing people's multiple ancestries produces the results in the second set of bars. Interestingly, the effect of having Ukrainian ancestry disappears in this analysis, and the effect of having West Asian ancestry loses its significance. Having African or Caribbean/Latin American ancestry remains significant, but the estimate of the amount of positive influence these ancestries have on fertility diminishes. Moreover, other groups take on new significance in this conceptualization of culture. Having English ancestry increases fertility, while having French-Canadian, Jewish, or Chinese ancestry reduces it.

In the third conceptualization of ethnicity as culture, ethnicity is only recorded as being different from Canadian if an individual considers it important. Here, again, the change in conceptualization of culture has important implications for which groups emerge as significantly different from the Canadian category. Looking at the third set of bars, having German, African, West Asian, or Caribbean/Latin American ancestry and valuing this ancestry as important significantly boosts fertility relative to having Canadian ancestry or ancestry that is self-defined as unimportant. Having Polish ancestry and considering it important decreases fertility. Here again, a different conceptualization of culture, which takes account of the self-rated importance, reveals different groups of interest.

Finally, we shift from ethnic ancestry to ethnic identity with the last set of bars in Figures 2.2 and 2.3. An entirely new group, the "Other British" group (including Welsh), suddenly becomes important, with individuals who strongly identify as being part of this group more likely to have children than those who do not identify strongly as anything but Canadian. Germans and Africans also retain their importance in this analysis, but all other groups fall away. Changing the conceptualization of ethnicity clearly has a substantial effect on the groups that are likely to be considered important in fertility analyses. Notably, only those with an African ethnicity retained a significant difference from Canadian ethnicity through all shifts in conceptualization.

In our next categorization of culture, we focus on race. Being racialized could represent an obstacle preventing assimilation in terms of fertility behaviour. In our first conceptualization, we look at self-identified visible minority status as it reflects racialized categories. In this analysis, being racialized as Black, Latin American,[6] or Arab has a significantly positive effect on fertility relative to those remaining unracialized. A Statistics Canada report focusing on the fertility of self-identified visible minority

Figure 2.3

Odds ratios for the likelihood of having a child under the age of three, by visible minority status (relative to non-visible minority) for women aged fifteen to fifty-four

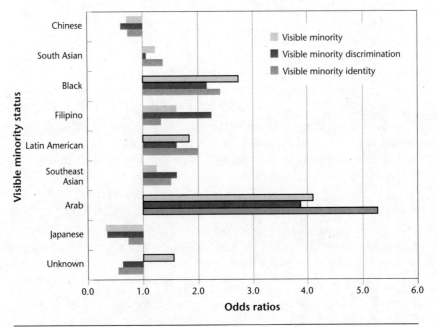

Note: Model controls for age, partnership status, schooling, completed education, and generation. Outlined bars indicate significance at p < 0.10.

women in Canada with a larger sample size finds similar differences in the likelihood of having a child under the age of one in the household, providing some confidence in these results (Malenfant and Bélanger 2006). Racial categorizations are often linked to discrimination, and this connection may pose a real barrier to cultural assimilation. We next conceptualize race in terms of discrimination and include racial categories for only those individuals who have experienced discrimination. In this analysis (indicated in the middle bars), only Arabs demonstrate a significant fertility difference from non-racialized Canadians. Finally, we consider racialization in terms of how it may operate on identity, using the same indicator of ethnic identity explored earlier. For those people both racialized and accepting of a non-Canadian ethnic identity, only Arabs, again, demonstrate a significant difference in fertility from non-racialized Canadians.

Figure 2.4

Odds ratios for the likelihood of having a child under the age of three, by religion (relative to non-religious) for women aged fifteen to fifty-four

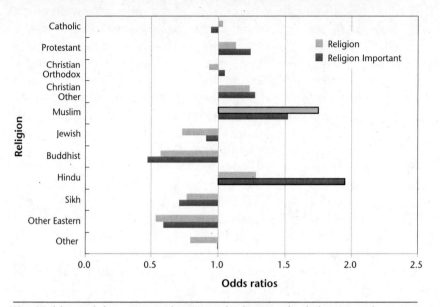

Note: Model controls for age, partnership status, schooling, completed education, and generation. Outlined bars indicate significance at p < 0.10.

Lastly, we explore cultural categorization by religion (see Figure 2.4). First, we model religion by self-identification (in the top bars), and then we model religion by whether or not it is important to the respondent (in the bottom bars). In the first case, which simply looks at religious affiliation, being Muslim is the only category that has any significant relationship to fertility. Being Muslim raises fertility relative to not being religious. In the second case, focusing more specifically on those who actually consider their religion to be important, the group demonstrating a significant difference from the mainstream changes (in this case, the mainstream incorporates those who are non-religious and those who consider religion not to be especially important). Being Muslim is no longer significantly different from the mainstream, which seems to represent a change both in effect size and in the sample size after discarding those Muslims who do not consider their religion to be very important. However, being Hindu and considering one's religion as Hindu important has a significant and positive effect on fertility relative to the mainstream.

Discussion

The preceding results leave us with a number of preliminary findings on how culture works as a determinant of fertility. First and foremost, in the multicultural context of Canada, culture appears to be important in understanding fertility. No matter how we specify culture, some groups stand out from the Canadian mainstream as having different fertility patterns. Such results occur even with analyses using a moderate sample size. With a larger sample size, it is likely that even more groups would stand out from the mainstream. However, as discussed in the beginning of this chapter, cultural differences in fertility patterns can lead to both higher fertility and lower fertility outcomes. This result follows from the fact that immigrant groups to more developed countries may come from places with higher fertility (such as Africa and Western Asia) or lower fertility (such as China and Eastern Europe). Furthermore, the effects of culture are distinct from the selection forces of immigration itself. Immigration consistently boosts the fertility of the first generation but has no effect on the subsequent generations apart from culture.

Second, while culture is important, the varying categorizations used to describe culture matter in how cultural differences in fertility are interpreted. Theoretically, there are a variety of ways that culture could work to influence fertility across different groups. Cultural barriers to assimilation could come in the form of linguistic differences, ethnic differences, racialized differences, and religious differences. In this study, we have separated these categories out to explore each separately. In each category of cultural difference, some groups stand out as being significantly different from the mainstream. However, ultimately, categories of cultural difference are unlikely to work alone. It is probable that the accumulation of differences across each cultural category works to create barriers to assimilation and distinct ways of understanding the world.

Figuring out how to join categories together is not a trivial task, especially if one wishes to avoid being left with very small respondent numbers in each resulting subcategory. For instance, for those listing themselves as Arab visible minorities, only 61 percent speak Arabic at home, and only 53 percent list themselves as Muslim. Just over three-quarters of those listing African ethnic ancestry declare themselves to be Black, while 57 percent of Blacks list no African ancestry. Only 63 percent of those with Jewish ancestry report being Jewish as a religion, while 58 percent of those reporting their religion as Jewish do not report Jewish for their ethnic ancestry. If, using independent effects, we were to look across the categories to construct the group with the highest fertility, we would identify ethnically African practising Hindus who are racialized as Arabic and who speak German at home – a very small population indeed. For this reason, further research should be devoted to understanding how to combine different categorizations of culture together.

Third, we can conceive of a variety of ways in which cultural differences within a category might matter. How we conceive of cultural differences as mattering should influence how measurements of culture operate. If we assume that cultural differences matter because it is important to people to carry on their various traditions, then we should include people as culturally different only if they feel their culture is important to them. Crucially, the results in this study show that within the same sample, and even the same category of culture, different conceptualizations of how culture matters provide different estimations of which groups are different from the mainstream. The results of dividing people by first language differ from the results of dividing people by language spoken at home. The results of using only first ethnicity as a categorization method differ from allowing multiple ethnicities, allowing only important ethnicities, or allowing only ethnicities that correspond to people's notions of their own identities. Similar issues arise in using visible minority status to divide people into groups. If we assume that visible minority status matters because of discrimination, then discrimination ought to be part of the measurement, and the results are different when we use this categorization from when we simply categorize people into visible minority groups regardless of their experiences. Finally, the results of religion differ by whether or not religion is important to those involved. Since conceptualization matters for each category, we argue that researchers interested in understanding cultural difference should have a clear idea of how they think culture works to produce differences in behaviour.

Attempts to measure fertility differentials by culture will always necessitate grouping people by culture. However, as discussed earlier, these groupings do not have to be mutually exclusive, and it may best reflect the complexity of real life to allow people to assume multiple identities. This is one step toward a more relational model of culture. We would like to suggest that further steps could also be useful. Cultural closure should not be assumed but, rather, should be explored as a process in its own right.

As mentioned earlier, cultural analyses should be embedded within an understanding of how culture operates in daily life. The greater the tangibility of cultural differences, and the more that various aspects of cultural difference overlap, the more they might be likely to influence fertility in ways that are opposed to a cultural mainstream. These factors could create conditions for the production of social closure, resulting in exclusive social interaction. This sort of exclusive social interaction creates the context for symbolic differences – in language, ethnic background, race, or religion – to translate into behavioural differences. Behavioural differences, in turn, can translate into fertility differentials. In effect, processes of social closure create subcultures that allow different worldviews to maintain themselves as distinct from the mainstream and to maintain correspondingly distinct fertility patterns.

Developing a better grasp of the processes of social closure relevant to the creation of subcultures is not just important for understanding how different cultural worldviews might operate within the same multicultural nation. Processes of social closure might also have an independent influence on fertility. Those individuals located within subcultural enclosures, whether the barriers are erected or encountered, necessarily find stronger limits placed around their social interactions. This situation could result in a severe limitation of the overall volume and quality of their social interactions. In other words, those individuals located within subcultural enclosures experience more limited opportunities for developing social capital (Bourdieu 1984; Coleman 1990; Portes 1998). Raymond Breton (2003, 1-2) suggests that this scenario might be linked to the utility of ethnic social capital. He states:

> Members of ethnic minorities expect to find the social capital they need primarily in social relations and organizations of the larger society. But it will also be found that this is not the experience of all groups. First, for immigrants, social capital appears to be more easily available within their community than in the larger society. Second, for many non-whites, Arabs or non-Christians, there are barriers to integration in the larger society and this creates an impetus to search for social capital in the minority community. That is to say, exclusion from mainstream social networks and especially from institutional opportunities is among the most important factor[s] that [lead] to the search [for] social capital within the minority community.

Childbearing offers a solution to this problem in that it would be one major way of increasing the density of ethnic social capital (Schoen et al. 1997).

Children represent both a direct and indirect expansion of social capital for their parents (Astone et al. 1999). In a direct sense, children provide new sets of relationships with people of similar culture. Having children is an act of cultural reproduction for parents. In an indirect sense, having children may also be seen as an act of cultural reproduction for a wider group of people involved in a subculture. As such, there may be significant support for parents to have children, and subcultural networks may provide more advantages to those who reproduce, expanding the group's social capital.

Fundamentally, we suggest that the meaning of children is important for understanding fertility trends and differentials. The meaning of children is also inextricably bound to culture. Yet children often carry on aspects of their parents' cultural worldviews. In this way, culture produces children, leading to biological reproduction, and children produce culture, leading to cultural reproduction. However, in neither case is reproduction really the right word. Children extend beyond the sum of their parents, and culture constantly changes. The processes by which children come to experience cultural identification are embedded within their daily lives beyond the control of their parents, shifting with language, recognition of various ethnic ancestries, experiences of discrimination, and religious awakenings (or increasing religious drowsiness). In the end, all children are at least a little bit alien.

Notes

1 This is actually a level-of-analysis problem since the cultural or ethnic group is at an aggregate level and the culture carried by the individual captured in constructs such as "identity" is clearly at an individual level of analysis. The notion that culture emerges from individuals' interactions would supply the theoretical linkage between these levels.
2 While the Canadian Multiculturalism Act, R.S.C. 1985, c. 24 (4th Supp.), of 1988 clearly advocates separate groupings such as: "(d) recognize the existence of communities whose members share a common origin and their historic contribution to Canadian society, and enhance their development; ... (h) foster the recognition and appreciation of the diverse cultures of Canadian society and promote the reflection and the evolving expressions of those cultures." The act also provides for equality: "(e) ensure that all individuals receive equal treatment and equal protection under the law, while respecting and valuing their diversity." And it includes inequality: "(i) preserve and enhance the use of languages other than English and French, while strengthening the status and use of the official languages of Canada; and (j) advance multiculturalism throughout Canada in harmony with the national commitment to the official languages of Canada."
3 Canadian Multiculturalism Act, R.S.C. 1985, c. 24 (4th Supp.), of 1988.
4 Employment Equity Act, S.C. 1995, c. 44.
5 Note that speaking Ukrainian at home might also be important, but the sample is too small to get a significant estimate.

6 Note that Latin American descent is considered distinct from Caribbean for the purposes of visible minority designation, though they are considered jointly for ethnic designation.

References

Astone, N.M., C.A. Nathanson, R. Schoen, and Y.J. Kim. 1999. "Family Demography, Social Theory, and Investment in Social Capital." *Population and Development Review* 25: 1-31.

Bloemraad, I. 2002. "The North American Naturalization Gap: An Institutional Approach to Citizenship Acquisition in the United States and Canada." *International Migration Review* 36: 193-228.

Boldrin, M.B., M. DeNardi, and L.E. Jones. 2005. *Fertility and Social Security*. National Bureau of Economic Research Working Paper no. 11146, http://www.nber.org/papers/w11146.

Bourdieu, P. 1984. *Distinction: A Social Critique of the Judgement of Taste*. Translated by R. Nice. Cambridge, MA: Harvard University Press.

Breton, R. 2003. "Social Capital and the Civic Participation of Immigrants and Members of Ethno-Cultural Groups." Paper presented at the Conference on the Opportunities and Challenges of Diversity: A Role for Social Capital? Montreal, November, http://www.horizons.gc.ca/doclib/OECD_RaymondBreton_E.pdf

Bryant, J. 2007. "Theories of Fertility Decline and the Evidence from Development Indicators." *Population and Development Review* 33: 101-27.

Caldwell, J.C. 1976. "Toward a Restatement of Demographic Transition Theory." *Population and Development Review* 2: 321-66.

–. 1982. *Theory of Fertility Decline*. New York: Academic Press.

Clarke, A.C. 1953. *Childhood's End*. New York: Harcourt Brace Jovanovich.

Coleman, J. 1990. *Foundations of Social Theory*. Cambridge, MA: Harvard University Press.

Derosas, R., and F. van Poppel. 2006. "Introduction." In R. Derosas and F. van Poppel, eds., *Religion and the Decline of Fertility in the Western World*, 1-21. Dordrecht: Springer.

Easterlin, R.A., and E.M. Crimmins. 1985. *The Fertility Revolution: A Supply-Demand Analysis*. Chicago: University of Chicago Press.

Emirbayer, M. 1997. "Manifesto for a Relational Sociology." *American Journal of Sociology* 103: 281-317.

Goldscheider, C. 2006. "Religion, Family and Fertility: What Do We Know Historically and Comparatively?" In R. Derosas and F. van Poppel, eds., *Religion and the Decline of Fertility in the Western World*, 41-57. Dordrecht: Springer.

Goode, W. 1963. *World Revolution and Family Patterns*. New York: Free Press.

–. 1993. *World Divorce Patterns*. New Haven, CT: Yale University Press.

Hammel, E. 1990. "A Theory of Culture for Demography." *Population and Development Review* 16: 455-85.

Huntington, S. 1996. *The Clash of Civilizations and the Remaking of World Order*. New York: Simon and Schuster.

James, P.D. 1992. *The Children of Men*. London: Faber and Faber.

Kirk, D. 1996. "Demographic Transition Theory." *Population Studies* 50: 361-87.

Kymlicka, W. 2001. *Politics in the Vernacular: Nationalism, Multiculturalism, and Citizenship*. Oxford: Oxford University Press.

–. 2008. "The Three Lives of Multiculturalism." UBC-Laurier Institution Multiculturalism Lecture Series, Vancouver, BC, 15 April.

Lesthaeghe, R. 1995. "The Second Demographic Transition in Western Countries: An Interpretation." In K. Mason and A. Jensen, eds., *Gender and Family Change in Industrialized Countries*, 17-61. New York: Oxford University Press.

Lesthaeghe, R. and L. Neidert. 2006. "The Second Demographic Transition in the United States: Exception or Textbook Example? *Population and Development Review* 32: 669-98.

Lesthaeghe, R. and J. Surkyn. 1988. "Cultural Dynamics and Economic Theories of Fertility Change." *Population and Development Review* 14: 1-45.

Lutz, W., and S. Scherbov. 2008. "Can Immigration Compensate for Europe's Low Fertility?" *European Demographic Research Papers*, http://www.oeaw.ac.at/vid/download/edrp_no1.pdf.

Malenfant, E.C., and A. Bélanger. 2006. "The Fertility of Visible Minority Women in Canada." In A. Bélanger, ed., *Report on the Demographic Situation in Canada, 2003 and 2004*, 79-96. Ottawa: Statistics Canada.

McQuillan, K. 2004. "When Does Religion Influence Fertility?" *Population and Development Review* 30: 25-56.

Population Reference Bureau. 2007. "Fertility Rates for Low-Birth Rate Countries: 1995 to Most Recent Year," http://www.prb.org/pdf07/TFRTable.pdf.

Portes, A. 1998. "Social Capital: Its Origins and Applications in Modern Sociology." *Annual Review of Sociology* 24: 1-24.

Schoen, R., Y.J. Kim, C.A. Nathanson, J. Fields, and N.M. Astone. 1997. "Why Do Americans Want Children?" *Population and Development Review* 23: 333-58.

Statistics Canada, 2002. *Ethnic Diversity Survey: User's Guide to the Public Microdata File*, Catalogue no. 89M0019GPE. Ottawa: Government of Canada.

Steyn, M. 2006. *American Alone: The End of the World As We Know It*. Washington, DC: Regnery Publishing.

Therborn, G. 2004. *Between Sex and Power: Family in the World 1900-2000*. London: Routledge.

Toulemon, L. 2006. "Fertility among Immigrant Women in France: New Data, a New Approach." Presentation at the Population Association of America Meetings, Los Angeles, CA, 31 March 2006.

3

Using Infertility, Useful Fertility: Cultural Imperatives on the Value of Children in the United States

Rebecca L. Upton

This chapter explores the perceived necessity of having children and the subsequent strategies that individuals use to facilitate and fashion identities as reproductive or non-reproductive bodies at different life cycle stages. Drawing on research from the United States, I demonstrate how families, and women in particular, have increasingly delayed childbearing in the pursuit of demanding career responsibilities and yet still find themselves confronted with the equally demanding cultural imperatives to have, perform for, and maintain a family. This chapter draws on ethnographic research among US middle-class and dual-earner families. It examines how reproductive identities and subsequent strategies of reproduction factor into cultural narratives about the value and timing of children and how these narratives vary cross-culturally. Ideally, this chapter provides some insight into people's daily lives and how individuals use fertility, both as a concept and as a real and tangible aspect of everyday life. I attempt to provide insight into the perceived "rationality" of childbearing and the timing of having children and suggest that only through careful analysis of why and how individuals fashion reproductive identities at particular points in time can we begin to understand why they do not at other times. Through examination of the stories of several American families, these identities come into clearer focus and understanding.

The Problem of Pregnancy

In my fieldwork as a cultural and medical anthropologist in southern Africa, I have found some interesting and important comparisons to my work among couples in the United States when it comes to discussions about childbearing and pregnancy. For example, in northern Botswana, it is typical, non-problematic, and even *expected* that one would "prove" one's fertility by having a child while still a teenager and regardless of marital status. Such a situation, while perceived as problematic in the US context, is both normative and beneficial to the social status of Tswana men and women, boys and girls. In marked contrast, in the United States, teen pregnancy rates are always a topic of concern, and recent events such as reported high school "pregnancy pacts" draw attention to how very different these constructions of timing and appropriate ages to bear children can be. There is, one is to assume, a "right" time and even place in one's career and life to have a child/children. Yet, childbearing in the United States, which has recently been lauded in pop culture through a focus on "baby bumps" and a cultural glorification of pregnancy and the chic that goes with it, has become "problematic" in a culture of increasing instances of paid labour force participation by women and delayed first marriage and childbirth. Working women and families receive multiple and conflicting messages: have children but do it on your own time; have a career but just make sure you have children.

For working women and families in the United States, then, timing becomes everything and fertility becomes less of a natural fact and more of a cultural liability and asset. In the Western context, culturally determined time periods for childbearing are both rigidly understood and enforced, while, at the same time these same time periods and rates of fertility are paradoxically challenged by the active manipulation of the young and old(er) alike. However, this chapter is not about the perceived "problems" of pregnancy pacts and teen pregnancies – planned or unplanned – in the United States. Rather, it is about the careful and methodical attention paid culturally to the construction of the "ideal" family and what this perception means in terms of actual children and their presence, absences, and numbers in contemporary society. Pregnancy is a "cultural" problem in some ways, but in others its very absence can be seen as both problematic and beneficial, manipulated and yet naturalized. The cultural value of children for middle-class working families and women in the contemporary United States becomes a matter of planning – of planned and unplanned fertility and, as I argue here, even a matter of unplanned and planned infertility.

Planned Fertility

In this chapter, I do not deal directly with the cultural phenomenon of unplanned pregnancy or teen pregnancies in the United States but, rather, focus more on the planning and assumption of fertility among Americans. I mention pregnancy "pacts" earlier in contrast to the cultural assumption in southern Africa that I have encountered where proving fecundity is important in order to attract a stable partner. While this tradition is seemingly at odds with the cultural norm in the United States, however, this study highlights how important "proving" fertility can be to contemporary American couples and women. As one woman I met early in my research commented: "Everyone just expects to have kids, I mean, everyone expects you to have them, and to have a certain number of them, so I guess you don't think about it much."[1] In ways that are similar to other forms of crafting identity and of "imagining community," bearing children is both understood as normative and simultaneously tacit and unspoken in ways that contradict increasingly challenging obligations to career and other goals (Anderson 1983).

The cultural expectation to have children has increasingly come into conflict in the past several decades with the rising numbers of women in the paid labour force. Women have delayed not just their age at first marriage but also their age of childbearing, and greater numbers of women and couples are experiencing problems becoming pregnant. The rise of reproductive technologies in the West has come hand in hand with these cultural shifts and serves to illustrate just how the importance of childbearing comes into direct and ironic conflict with the importance of wage labour and career trajectories for women. In the remainder of this chapter, I focus on the interesting ethnographic tensions between planned and unplanned (in)fertility as grounded in a larger cultural assumption that one can and should actually have, plan, and manipulate something called one's "fertility." Fertility has become reified and a cultural fact that, similar to other cultural aspects in our lives, is assumed to be manageable.

Central to this manageability, however, is the notion of time. Time and timing of children are key to the American cultural narrative about how to "balance" work and family (Hochschild and Machung 1989; Schor 1992; Hochschild 1997) and, at the same time, to be sure to do it all – to achieve the entire package and be successful in the timely pursuit of a family alongside a successful career (Townsend 2002). In this study, for example, a familiar refrain became: "We are just doing our best to balance everything!" Couples reiterated over and over again just how important "managing" work and family life are in everyday life and how having a daily schedule was one step toward achieving that goal. Fertility is managed and planned in the long term – most couples talk about the cultural expectation to have two children as I note elsewhere (compare with Axinn, Clarkberg, and Thornton 1994; Upton, forthcoming) – but it becomes expressed in everyday language, narrative stories, and in schedules posted on kitchen walls.

Keenan and Linda Cooper: A Matter of Timing

For some couples, the spacing and timing game is central. When I was researching the necessity of having two children in cultural lore in the United States, it was common for people to talk about and ask the question as to what the "perfect" spacing and timing are for having children. The latter tends to be a question about when is a good time to have children in one's life course, tempered by career choices and age at marriage, which was not the specific focus of my study but did allow an ethnographic glimpse into just how individuals set about negotiating a perceived and even latent fertility. However, the question of spacing has more to do directly with what I have called in the title of this chapter the negotiation and literal "usefulness" of fertility.

For Keenan and Linda Cooper, their decision to have a family was very much a planned and placed decision. Their strategies in family planning revealed just how "managed" the notion of the constructed family really is. Throughout their narratives, the Coopers relied on a powerful notion of "fertility" as being readily available and something to be manipulated. Clearly, they were the actors in the various situations, and they themselves were not seen as the ones being manipulated. When I asked about their decisions to have a family, and when, Linda answered:

> We were pretty clear in our heads about when we would start a family. There was a lot we wanted to do, like job-wise and career-wise and luckily we were both on the same page with this because otherwise I think it would have been really hard, like we were both going for the same things and we didn't talk about it all the time, but we both sorta *knew*, you know? We didn't push each other or challenge each other about it. We knew that we would have a family but we also knew that it wouldn't be right away. There was a time for it all.

Linda described a sense of absolute certainty that fertility was something attainable, achievable, "out there" – to be chosen when the time was right. As she repeated several times, she and Keenan were sure they would "know" when the time was right to start a family and have children. She was clear in her narrative that while she and Keenan were married and working for common goals they were not yet a "family" in the sense of having children to complete that picture. Keenan also talked about a "plan" and a linear sense of when things were supposed to happen in their lives. He said:

> Linda was working to finish her nursing degree. We've always thought that that had good flexible hours and Linda is the kind of person who is really good taking care of people, so she wanted to do that as a job and it made sense. So, we planned on that, planned out when she would be done. And meanwhile I was working my way through training at Citibank who were paying for classes I could take while I was working that would go for my MBA. So we had it all planned and yet it was flexible; we had flexibility in there.

All of the flexibility that the Coopers talked about, however, seemed to evaporate as Linda described the experience of having their first child:

> We had really, really planned for Luke, he was a pretty much well planned child! We used to laugh that that really was what "family planning" should mean – like you really *plan* a family – it's all nicely laid out and makes sense when you will have it, what you'll be doing or have done career-wise, etc. Anyway, all that changed when we had Evan. Evan was our second child and we always thought we'd have a second, but we were trying really hard to plan to have a second one when we could think about it better. I think we always believed that about two years or so was good timing, good spacing and we'd work around those assumptions and then, surprise! But it was hard. And I felt really rattled all the time, like having another child so soon after the first [the children are 18 months apart] was a lot, it was quite a lot and I felt ambushed. I had been sooooo well prepared and so ready for the first one that I thought the second we could just sort of slot in to the plan, to the program and it'd be fine!

Such concern with spacing and timing of children is a window into how fertility itself is in fact managed. Like other commodities and aspects of their lives, the Coopers viewed fertility (and even fecundity) as something that, while having a "life of its own," could be directed, controlled, and even willed into action at particular points in time, presumably at their convenience. Keenan explained:

> There's that one point in life when it's (unplanned pregnancy) like the worst thing that could happen. I'm not even talking about when we were kids and still in school or dating or whatever. I'm talking about

when we were first married and yet doing all the post-school stuff and getting into our lives and careers ... So we were good planners, like Linda told you. We really made sure we knew what we were doing. Our friends joke about it, how scheduled our kids were and how they just fit into our overall plan, but it's worth it, if you don't do it that way, it can make your life unmanageable.

The Coopers felt they had executed their family planning strategy well. Underlying this feeling is the expectation that the cultural norm of having a "family" – of having children – would be something unquestioned, unconsidered even, until the timing was "right." In my larger work, I describe many situations similar to Linda's and Keenan's stories, in part to point out that for many in contemporary American culture the assumption is that fecundity and family are things that one can "cash in" or draw on as they see fit, like a bank account. In some narratives, individuals even spoke about family "planning" in this sense as being akin to a retirement fund – you are building up an account, something to bank on and withdraw when the time is right (Upton, forthcoming). The Coopers' daily lives were well planned – the earlier mentioned kitchen wall calendar was constantly filled and meticulously maintained as their busy lives were documented for all to see and negotiate. In the remainder of this chapter, I turn to some of the challenges that couples and individuals pose to the cultural expectation to fulfil familial norms (Scritchfield 1995). Specifically, I examine the role of infertility and how it can be both unplanned and planned, as well as its cultural weight in contemporary society.

Unplanned Infertility

Fertility is a situational and even a cultural construct. Certainly, it has biological roots, but what is clear in this ethnographic data is just how manipulated the concept of fertility can be – and is – in the lives of contemporary Americans. The constructedness and the social fluidity of fertility can be seen quite readily through an examination of infertility and, in particular, through an exploration of the narratives and experiences of those who experience infertility. With the rise of delayed childbearing among middle-class working women, the number of couples who experience secondary infertility and even voluntary childlessness has increased in recent decades. While reproductive technologies exist to address some of these issues, they are not without considerable cost. It was clear in my own research just how powerful a stigmatizing label "infertility" can be when strategizing and attempting to plan one's family.

Teresa and Don Gleason: Banking on It

Many couples, similar to the Coopers in the earlier section, rely on a notion of fertility as something they can access and call on when needed. For many, however, unplanned and unexpected obstacles emerge along the path to conception. Teresa and Don Gleason, a dual-earning couple in their late thirties who live in the Midwest, explained how unexpected and unplanned their fertility struggles had become. Don said:

> You go along and think that it's something inherent and innate – that you will simply be able to "call upon" fertility when you need and want it and it can be devastating when it seems that it is not something one can simply draw upon when needed. We were totally shocked at how much work this is.

As Don explained, their fertility had become something of a bank account, which they thought they could draw on freely when the time came. However, instead they found themselves constantly thinking about what Teresa called their "big fertility cloud, always looming above us" and not being able to access it. She said: "It's like someone took away all the money you were saving up without telling you they were going to do it. We were totally surprised." Confronted with real problems in becoming pregnant, Teresa and Don finally sought the help of a fertility specialist and talked about their assumptions with respect to what Don called the "default" setting of fertility:

> It's not like we had put anything away specifically, we weren't like sperm bankers or something, but it was that sense that we could just withdraw a kid when we needed to; instead we found ourselves with nothing in the bank, you know? There was nothing there – totally dried up. Awful. I felt like Teresa had really counted on being able to have kids when we wanted to and it was totally like I had been secretly taking money out of some account without telling her, not providing [for] her or something.

For the Gleasons, the idea that their fertility (both of theirs in fact) was something to be saved and drawn on at will was pervasive. Both talked about how they had carefully planned their family and children. When things went unexpectedly awry, it was highly disruptive and contrary to how Teresa and Don saw themselves. They were in fact incredulous at the unplanned pregnancies that they saw around them, and this perception emerged in discussions about their frustrations with what Teresa described as "willy nilly childbearing" where couples or individuals simply had children because that was "what they were supposed to do." As Don suggested when I asked about their careful planning and timeline for childbearing prior to the discovery of fertility problems: "Nothing will change your life as much as having a child, so why wouldn't you plan it carefully?" When describing the "looming fertility cloud" that simply would not "rain down on them" despite their best efforts, Teresa suggested fatalistically that perhaps it was not "up to them." At some point, both she and Don suggested that when they tried to coax out their presumably reticent fertility they found themselves with nothing and so had to pursue a more aggressive means of addressing their physiological concerns and challenges. Ultimately, the Gleasons sought hormone therapies and eventually in vitro fertilization, which allowed them to complete their image of their ideal selves and family but required ironically that they draw on their literal financial savings account to supplement the presumed fertility account.

Jeffrey and Anne Dodson: Bargaining with It

Jeffrey Dodson and his wife Anne have struggled with infertility for several years – attempting a variety of infertility treatments. They always assumed they would have children. As Anne put it, "we just did not think we'd be in a situation where this was suddenly a 'problem.' All the time we were young, in school, planning our lives and careers, well, the 'problem' would have been having children – that is the ultimate irony for us now." While not as "public" as pregnant bodies, infertile bodies occupy a great deal of space and symbolic discourse in contemporary society on what it means to be not just a productive person in society but also a reproductive person. There is an ever-increasing discourse in academic as well as popular literature on how to "make one's body baby-friendly" or how to "conquer infertility" (Domar and Kelly 2004; Beer, Kantecki, and Reed 2006), and the majority of these studies place the ultimate onus of responsibility on individual personal bodies and selves. Again, the Dodsons are hardly unique in their struggle. Many couples who have delayed childbearing find themselves confronted with the reality of perceived infertility. Anne described the public reaction to their seemingly personal lives in this way:

> It was pretty unbelievable. People don't even think, they just ask, things like, "So when are you two going to have children?" or "Don't you like kids?" Pretty awful when you think about it. But what are we supposed to do, wear signs around our necks that say, "Hi, we're infertile but boy

are we trying hard"? I mean come on ... I would trade places any day with one of those women who complain about people touching their pregnant bellies, you know ... Let them walk for a moment in my shoes where everyone has something to say about why we haven't reproduced ... The worst part of it all ... it becomes a total joke and nobody needs to respond to it because you can just laugh at the sex innuendo, you know?

When I first met the Dodsons, the most striking thing in each of their narratives was the idea that they could bargain with their fertility – that they could negotiate with "it" or about it. Such a reaction is evidence of the very real reification of fertility and the concurrent cultural expectations that Americans have for it. Jeffrey spoke often of how he had "counted on it" just being there, something to rely on and, as the Gleasons talked about it, something to cash in on when the time was right.

The longer I knew the Dodsons, the more and more their language was littered with reference to "trading" – Anne would gladly have traded places with someone pregnant to bear the public scrutiny and Jeffrey would gladly have traded places with his colleagues who he said "were always asking if we could shuffle around the work deadlines so they could make it home on time to their families." In every instance, the Dodsons found themselves negotiating a cultural expectation and the public scrutiny in this pro-natalist society. Both of them would have happily traded the lesser of two evils – the social annoyances of having strangers touch a pregnant body and the familiar trope of taking up the slack at work for those with families – in order to stop suffering their similarly public, yet simultaneously relatively unseen, stigma of childlessness.

Planned Infertility: Having Only Children or "Singles Is Just Plain Selfish"

In a different context, the idea of childbearing as akin to being not just a reproductive, but also a productive, member of society is clear. One need not be in southern Africa to realize the power that fertility holds in society. While fertility has power, so too does infertility. Or, perhaps more correctly, one does not want to veer too much to the side of infertility as to arrive at an end point. One should not intend or want to "manage it too much" and have it end up as a kind of permanent state of being. Whereas childhood and childbearing are meant to end at some point, the ability to bear children is always interesting in its perceived limitations. As opposed to being seen as a passive recipient of one's reproductive status, the study of infertility helps the ethnographer to use narratives in new ways to combat such stigma. Ethnography points to the salience of linguistics and the power of language in the construction of events. Looking at the standpoint of interviewees in this study such as Debbie and Stan Streiber, I consider for example how I first came to understand the significance of being "seen" as though I were engaged in a battle "for" fertility and not actively opposed to it.

Debbie and Stan Streiber: Making It by Faking It
At a conference in San Francisco, where I was talking about the substantial changes in couples' lives in the United States when they had two children, I was approached by a man who had some questions. As we got talking, Stan asked whether in the course of my research on the cultural expectation to have two children in the United States I had ever heard of people who "faked" infertility? At the time, I replied that I had not, but I was intrigued and we talked at length about some of what was going on in Stan Streiber's and his wife Debbie's life and home. What emerged from that conversation was a compelling description of the strategies that people employ to shift the onus and stigma of reproductive decisions with which they were engaged. Specifically, as Stan's and Debbie's story unfolded, it was clear that they were knowledgeable about the cultural imperative to have two children. In his first conversation, Stan described to me the situation:

Have you ever heard of people "faking" infertility? I mean, if they are happy having one child and really don't want to have any more, have you ever heard of them faking problems? My wife Debbie, she and I are really happy with one child, we don't really want to have any more, both of us are in agreement about that. But it's amazing how when our daughter Beth turned about a year and a half or so, we got all these questions! Like, "When are you going to have another?" and "When are you going to give Beth a playmate?" That sort of thing ... Sometimes, and mostly our families say this, but we'll get the question like, "You're not just going to have just one, are you?" as if that's like the worst possible choice? Have you heard of this?

At the time, I was well aware of the notion of the pregnant body as public body and of the fact that, in particular, the pregnant body is seen as something that is open to public ownership and critique. (It is of course a truly American rite of passage, as Robbie Davis-Floyd [1992] points out.) However, I had yet to fully consider the weight behind public constructions of "family" and how this notion gets created and recreated in public discourse. Eventually, tired of being grilled by well-meaning friends and family members (who often turned hostile when told that there would be just one child by choice!), Stan and Debbie began to intimate to others that they were having problems becoming pregnant again. Stan explained:

> Well, I think it started after a really bad incident with a total stranger! If you can imagine, this woman, we were at one of Beth's play dates at the park, this woman, she was talking to Debbie and I was kinda hanging around. It was a nice day, at least it started that way – nice to spend the whole time as a family. Well, this woman, she was about Debbie's age, in her mid-thirties I'd say and she was talking and asking us which children were ours on the jungle gym, and I heard Debbie say that just one, we had Beth, who was still pretty little and was just playing around in the sand nearby with some of the other smaller kids. Well, eventually this woman was saying things like, "Oh but you better get started on her little brother or sister, hmm?" and "So are you trying to get pregnant again soon?" It was crazy! I mean who asks stuff like that? Neither of us could believe it. We sort of got in a small argument with this lady. I think Debbie had had it. We had just come from a family get-together where a lot of this stuff goes on and this woman was like the last straw. So we were all walking back to the car later and Debbie was so mad and hurt and says to me, "I swear I'm just going to start saying that we're trying and can't get pregnant. All those people get sympathy! We just get criticized."

The cultural imperative to have a second child was clear to both Stan and Debbie. The frustration they experienced became so powerful that they soon found themselves lying to others about their desire to have a sibling for Beth. The social reward for actively trying to have a second child, even if they were not successful, far outweighed the social stigma of suggesting they were content with one child.

Mark and Angie Dickson: Trying So Hard – The Rewards of Non-Efforts

Certainly, not all who "fake infertility" come to this decision as consciously as Debbie and Stan Streiber did. For many, the decision comes about much more tacitly – often the situation and state of infertility are implied and not explicitly stated. For Mark and Angie Dickson, the idea that they were experiencing a kind of secondary infertility took on a life of its own among their family and group of friends. I first met them through Angie's sister Danita, whom I knew from work. In talking about my work and interests, Danita mentioned that her sister and her husband were trying hard to have a second child and were experiencing trouble getting pregnant again. At the time, I was largely interested in how couples planned and fulfilled cultural expectations to have a second child, but this example proved to be an interesting and fruitful spring-board for these data on the faking of infertility.

As Danita explained to me, "Angie and Mark have been trying really hard, it's so sad. The whole family supports them and we're always try-ing to be there and help them and they have such a lovely little girl. She is four now, almost five, they really want her to have a sibling." Interestingly, Angie's, and later Mark's, stories were quite a bit different from the one that Danita and the rest of the family were invested in. As Angie explained,

> I'm laughing, sort of! Not too much though because it's kind of sad ... and I don't know really what to tell you, like how we got started doing this, but it's like we just sort of agreed that this was so much easier! We were at some family holiday dinner and everyone kinda joking about the second kid thing again. It seemed like we always got this and nobody else got hassled. Of course all my siblings have at least two children and the others on Mark's side are all still too young, so we were really in the spotlight. Anyway, it came up again and I guess I just was exasperated and was in the kitchen and kinda sighed to my sister-in-law and made it seem like we were "trying so hard" or I said something along those lines and she was like *instantly* sympathetic! And I can clearly remember thinking to myself how much easier it was to let them think that we were trying and it wasn't like they all thought that we were these hor-rible people. Like instead of being totally selfish, we could be the good guys! We were "trying"! And that changed everything.

Mark agreed, when I was talking to him later. On a stroll with their daughter, he described the way in which their "infertility" problems came to be part of their family narrative and the ways in which it became woven into explanations about family size:

> The awkwardness and weird silent moments were gone – unless there was somebody new in the crowd, you know, somebody who didn't know ... and then, boy, did they feel bad! [laughs]. We felt kinda guilty

sometimes, like we were letting people believe this awful thing. But you know, after a while, you almost believe it. You think, well, "Maybe ... maybe there really is something in us that makes it impossible to have any more children." And I think you just get to a point where it makes more sense to say that than it does to say what's really going through your mind, that you internalize this idea that there is something wrong with you if you don't want to have any more.

For the Dicksons and Streibers, planned infertility demonstrates both the weight of importance of fertility and just what "family" means. Mark Dickson, for example, pointed out that "family-sized" items or images in stores and media rarely depict couples or couples with just one child. However, their narratives are still grounded in the assumption that more than one child is desired. For others, agency and control over fertility pushes the boundary between permanence and more flexible fertility.

Roy and Nancy Crane: Defining Flexible Fertility – More Planned Infertility

When to start and when to stop having children are not strategies that are generally marked or linguistically labelled as periods of infertility in everyday language. With the rise of contraceptive options and technologies, fertility is taken out of the realm of something "taken for granted" or even "natural" and can be seen as something "manageable" – both for those individuals seen as fertile and those who might be infertile. Roy and Nancy Crane offer an example of a very powerful challenge to all these flexible boundaries between who is fertile and who is not.

At the age of thirty-four, Roy had a closed vasectomy (as opposed to open-ended, which allows for some easier kinds of reversal) but did not mention it to any friends or family. He and Nancy had fulfilled their "cultural obligation" and had two children, Lisa and Laurel, currently aged eight and five respectively. He described the public nature of the vasectomy in family life:

The ironic thing for us was this really intimate thing – it became totally and completely public, the topic of conversation at family gatherings later after everyone found out and we really discussed it. But before that it was really hidden and, to be honest, I felt kind of ashamed and a little bit embarrassed, dishonest really. I didn't choose this option lightly [laughing]. I'm not sure any man really does! But in some ways it just made so much sense. We were like, "Why wouldn't we do this?" when you are done having your kids, when you want to just have sex and enjoy it and not necessarily be worrying about, why wouldn't you do this? I guess you have to know you are done [having children] and that's all you want, that part is kind of a gamble. But for us, it was a no-brainer. It was cheaper and easier for me to just go in and have it done.[2] Nancy had had all the kids, so this seemed kind of, I don't know, more fair maybe? It made total sense to us, as I said, but boy, when this came out to our families – it was like "Whoa now ... what's going on here?!" Like they thought we were messing around or something, like I was going to go out and sleep around or as one of Nancy's cousins said, "We were tampering with God's will." Oh boy, that was a tough one, because suddenly it wasn't an argument about being safe, careful and responsible. It was totally the opposite.

The Cranes were criticized by friends and family alike when it became clear that they actively sought to take control and carefully "plan" their fertility – in this case, limiting it any further. Roy was teased about "being less of a man," and Nancy was repeatedly asked whether or not she "worried that this gave Roy a free pass" for extramarital affairs. Both told me how surprised they were with some of these reactions to their planned and careful decision making with respect to their fertility and family size, and yet both suggested, as Nancy said, "that it really does show you how powerful the idea of having children is in this country. If you don't do it, there must be something wrong with you. If you stop doing it, and there's surgery involved [laughs] there must really be something wrong with you!" For the Cranes, their future non-fertile sex lives were appealing, desirable, and deserved, and yet despite having fulfilled the cultural expectation to have children, to complete the family ideal, they were treated as suspect.

Using Fertility, Useful Infertility?

So what do these examples tell us about the "end of children" and the uses and usefulness of fertility? While it is certainly not unusual to talk about shifting values of children, particularly in the United States, the value of children has changed in light of contemporary reproductive technologies. Where once individuals who were unproductive and unreproductive were seen as witches – as betwixt and between statuses – they are now seen as potentially normative. In practice, fertility is useful, but infertility becomes more useful. Infertility becomes very pragmatic. And yet few demographic studies elucidate just how this may be the case. Ethnography can help unpack the complicated narratives and imperatives behind fertility and family planning.

In the Western context, there remain cultural expectations to have children. While the number of children per family has actually dropped over the course of the last several decades, couples still experience the palpable expectation to complete a "family" ideal of having two children. In conjunction with these expectations and norms, there also exists a tension between balancing work expectations and familial ones. Men and women are expected to be able to "do it all" and to create that perfect balance while being dual-earning families with less time for each obligation (Garey 1999).

Increasing employment by women outside of the home over the last few decades in addition to having children at an older age have contributed to some of the stressors that families experience. Despite all of these concerns and competing desires and obligations and expectations, however, fertility itself is a bit of a wild card. It cannot be "counted upon" nor is it wholly and forever flexible. It eventually diminishes, and, at times, we are confronted with examples of willing and voluntary infertility. To this end, I have attempted to begin to provide insight into the various ways in which contemporary couples negotiate and literally reconfigure their reproductive status – in both public and private contexts.

In other work, I weave together ethnographic data such as the vignettes in this chapter to highlight understandings of how national and international imperatives on and of fertility can be manipulated by individuals for particular reasons and to create an overall social tapestry of how fertility can fit their lives at the same time that they are struggling to fit their lives around fertility. I focus, through these stories, on pulling such imperatives together to help address some questions about the management of identity through timing, outcomes of fertility, and the life course. What remains elusive, however, is the very essence of fertility as something that is assumed yet unmeasured or unproven, negotiated yet intangible. Ethnographic data can certainly shed light on how and why constructions and understandings of fertility and infertility might be manipulated and where, when, and why some forms of fertility and infertility might be useful. We can keep track of total fertility rates, but from this ethnographic work I suggest that perhaps it is more useful to look at local narratives about why rates of fertility are important to begin with and just how and why we might go about using and imagining infertility rates in any study of population processes and dynamics. From the Coopers to the Gleasons, from the Streibers to the Dodsons, and from the Dicksons to the Cranes, ethnographic narratives on the use and usefulness of in/fertility abound and should help to point out the very salience of cultural constructions of perceived physiological categories.

Notes

1 Research for this project has been an approximately ten-year longitudinal study with over fifty couples in the United States who identified themselves as middle-class working families and who were expecting a second, or were willing to discuss decision making surrounding a second child.
2 Vasectomy is in general less expensive and less invasive surgery than the parallel tubal ligation in women, although, ironically and perhaps not surprisingly, rates of tubal ligation are higher in most Western countries than rates of vasectomy.

References

Anderson, B. 1983. *Imagined Communities*. London: Verso.

Axinn, W., M. Clarkberg, and A. Thornton. 1994. "Family Influences on Family Size Preferences." *Demography* 31: 65-79.

Beer, I., J. Kantecki, and J. Reed. 2006. *Is Your Body Baby Friendly?* Windsor, ON: AJR Publishing.

Davis-Floyd, R. 1992. *Birth as an American Rite of Passage*. Berkeley, CA: University of California Press.

Domar, A., and A. Kelly. 2004. *Conquering Infertility*. New York: Penguin Books.

Garey, A. 1999. *Weaving Work and Motherhood*. Philadelphia: Temple University Press.

Hochschild, A. 1997. *The Time Bind*. New York: Metropolitan Books.

Hochschild, A., and A. Machung. 1989. *The Second Shift*. New York: Avon Books.

Schor, J. 1992. *The Overworked American*. New York: Basic Books.

Scritchfield, S. 1995. "The Social Construction of Infertility: From Private Matter to Social Concern." In J. Best, ed., *Images of Issues: Typifying Contemporary Social Problems*, 131-46. New York: Walter de Gruyter.

Townsend, N. 2002. *The Package Deal*. Philadelphia: Temple University Press.

Upton, R. [forthcoming]. *The Next One Changes Everything: Having a Second Child in the American Middle-Class Family*. Ann Arbor, MI: University of Michigan Press.

4

The Performance of Motherhood and Fertility Decline: A Stage Props Approach

Nathanael Lauster

In this chapter, I introduce a stage prop approach to understanding fertility decline. This approach relies on a different set of assumptions from that of other approaches most commonly used to understand demographic change. In particular, I argue that parenthood is best understood as a role acted out in daily life. As such, performances of parenthood are staged, and feeling prepared to stage a successful performance requires certain props. The stage props for successfully performing parenthood change over time and within specific contexts, responding to patterns of inequality. Finally, those with greater access to the stage props for performing parenthood are more likely to take on the role. I illustrate this approach with reference to collected US census data from the Integrated Public Use Microdata Series (IPUMS) project, covering the years from 1900-2005.[1] Overall, I argue that the stage props approach encourages a more nuanced and meaningful analysis of cultural change than most other approaches.

As discussed by Philip Morgan and Miles Taylor (2006), and in Chapters 1 (by Mira Whyman, Megan Lemmon, and Jay Teachman) and 2 (by Nathanael Lauster, Todd Martin, and James White) in this volume, there are many theories for understanding fertility decline. However, underlying most of these theories are usually the same basic understandings of human behaviour. At the macro level, the meaning of children is often established with respect to their functionality within larger social and economic structures. John Caldwell (1982) provides perhaps the most striking example of a structural functional theoretical foundation for understanding fertility decline. In his analysis, changes in the mode of economic organization create conditions where children are more or less useful, altering the costs and benefits of childbearing. As a result, in modern society, the benefits of children (as agricultural labourers or caregivers for the aged) decline, while their costs (especially in education) rise (Caldwell 1982). In this approach, there may be ancillary functions of children, such as the provision of emotional connection or benefits to happiness, but to the extent that these functions operate they do not necessitate more than one child (Kohler, Behrman, and Skytthe 2005).

Similarly, at the micro level, potential parents are almost uniformly viewed as rational decision makers responding to the costs and benefits of children (which are linked to their usefulness, as determined by structure) (Morgan and Taylor 2006). In certain "weaker" versions of rational choice, underlying preferences for children can also vary from person to person (Hakim 2003). Rational decision making works through the proximate determinants of fertility, especially influencing entry into sexual partnerships, contraceptive use, and abortion, to determine childbearing behaviour.

The grounding of demographic theory in structural-functional and rational choice perspectives has often provided insight but also obscured alternative explanations that might be derived from different perspectives. In particular, cultural change tends to be ignored, as the costs and benefits of childbearing change somewhat mechanically in response to changes in the mode of economic production. Alternatively, cultural change is exogenized and reconfigured as an external influence resulting in changing preferences for children. The causes of cultural change in standard formulations are often left nebulous, and an analysis of cultural change remains mostly descriptive, employing the vague language of modernization or individuation (Lesthaeghe 1998).

A Stage Prop Approach

In this chapter, I attempt to build a theory for understanding fertility decline from alternative perspectives that are more rooted in conflict and symbolic interactive traditions and that are more directed at the study of cultural change. Following Thorstein Veblen (1992), I argue that children are not useful in functional terms (for example, as labour) so much as in symbolic terms, embedded within an evaluative status system. In particular, children can serve as the means to invidious comparison, establishing relative social status, which could operate in a direct, linear fashion so that more children enhance status – for example, where children come to symbolize virility or wealth, differentiating one person from another (Veblen 1992). In this context, the more children one has, the better. Alternatively, children could come to symbolize a relationship to self-control, including sexual self-control, in which case limiting the number of one's children to a particular, respectable range could become a symbolic means of differentiation. In this way, the presence and number of children (as well as the gender of children, in many contexts) could influence status. In turn, people may attempt to act in such a way as to alter the number of children in order to gain or avoid losing status. This approach extends the consideration of what children mean to people beyond simple provision of labour and consumption of resources. As ornamental status symbols in their own right, children can mean more in the context of social interaction (Katz 2008). Their meaning tends to be set by their position as markers of social achievement, symbolically separating the privileged from the non-privileged, rather than by some underlying function they serve for society as a whole.

This logic establishes the circumstances in which a stage prop approach might fruitfully be applied. The position of children within an evaluative status system is itself dependent on how actors relate to one another along the lines of ascribed and achieved status demarcations. To the extent that strong distinctions are made on the basis of ascribed status, mobility is severely limited, and the motivation for the marginalized to alter their childbearing behaviour in order to gain status is curtailed. In situations where distinctions based on ascribed status are weak, mobility is deemed more possible, and the motivation to alter childbearing behaviour in response to the activities of the privileged becomes much more powerful. Hence, the use of children as status markers for the aristocrat would not necessarily influence the childbearing behaviour of the peasant, if the ability of the peasant to climb in status is inherently limited by the lack of lineage at birth. Strong ascribed distinctions between racialized groups could also reduce the influence of meanings for the privileged on the behaviour of the marginalized. Overall, the presence of strong ascribed status boundaries limits the ability of symbols, which come to represent achievement, to alter the behaviour of the marginalized.

A further nuanced consideration reveals that childbearing is not simply a one-time decision, enabling "conspicuous consumption" of children thereafter. Instead, childbearing offers an entrance into the social role of parenthood. As in Erving Goffman's (1959) dramaturgical theory, parenthood is a social performance, enacted for various audiences, including those with higher status, peers, and those with lower status (Turner 1956). Yet parenthood is also an intimate performance, enacted for children, and a deeply embodied performance, with heavy emotional investment. Hence, evaluations of performances of parenthood influence both social status and self-conception. In simple terms, positive evaluations of the parental role attach social status and reduce cognitive dissonance. Negative evaluations attach social stigma and increase cognitive dissonance. Actors considering or taking on the role of parent face pressure to perform the role in a proper fashion. This fashion is determined by the performances of those with privilege (Bourdieu 1984; Lamont 1992; Veblen 1992). This group defines its own performances of parenthood against those with lesser privilege or without privilege altogether. In turn, to the extent that they are not limited by ascribed status, the masses attempt to emulate those with privilege, leading to a cultural "arms race" of sorts. Through their performances of the social role of parenthood, the privileged attempt to distance themselves from the population as a whole, while the masses attempt to draw themselves closer to the privileged.

This perspective on understanding childbearing behaviour as being linked to the meaning of children and the performance of parenthood can produce multiple ways of studying cultural change. A prominent approach is to focus on changes in the way that performances of parenthood are carried out and received. Ethnologists and ethnographers attempt to directly study the performance of parenthood across different social strata, as drawn from memoirs, letters, observation, and interviews (see, for example, Frykman and Löfgren 1987; Gillis 1996; Hays 1996; Garey 1999; Townsend 2002). However, attempts to understand cultural change could also focus on changes in the way that performances of parenthood are staged. I describe this approach as a "stage prop" approach.

Stage props include the set of other roles and acquired symbols one might evoke in support of the performance of parenthood. Some roles and acquired symbols may conflict with performances of parenthood, stigmatizing those who would take on parenthood simultaneously (for example, the role of a high school student). Other roles and acquisitions may be desirable or necessary for individuals to take on in order to perform parenthood properly. These roles I term stage props. Prominent stage props for performing parenthood "correctly" might include heading your own household, being married, being out of school, being employed (especially for fathers), being able to stay at home (especially for mothers), and owning your own home. A series of narratives develop to tie these props to the performance of parenthood within different cultural contexts. As Nicholas Townsend (2002) points out, these stage props might also be considered roles that need to be performed together, creating a package deal of successful (and gendered) adulthood. Taking on multiple roles can create tension, or role strain, but the simultaneous occupation of roles is often necessary if individuals want their performances of parenthood to be well received. Such are the internal contradictions of parenthood (Hays 1996).

Studying culture by using this approach enables the examination of new possible mechanisms by which fertility limitation might occur and become linked to various stage props. In this chapter, I discuss two such mechanisms, which I term stage management and stage fright. Stage management is the process by which individuals put together all of the staging material needed to perform a role in the correct fashion. For privileged groups, stage management is, in part, about establishing symbolic distinction from the masses. For those aspiring to privilege or just attempting to be good parents, stage management is about keeping up. In this way, stage management is strategic and can occur both before and after taking on a social role such as parenthood. Before taking on a role, stage management is likely to reduce stage fright. After taking on a role, stage management is likely to reduce the social stigma and cognitive dissonance resulting from not performing a role in the correct fashion. Either way, the process of stage management for the role of parenthood is likely to involve a lot of work, potentially competing with the work that is involved in performing parenthood, at least until all of the stage props have been collected to perform parenthood in the correct fashion.

Stage fright is the paralysis attached to the consideration of taking on and performing a social role incorrectly. It is characterized by a fear of performing a role poorly and by receiving and internalizing negative evaluations of one's performance. Just as stage fright in acting might be associated with the feeling of walking onto a stage naked, stage fright in parenting might be associated with taking on parenthood without all of the right props. As a mechanism influencing fertility, stage fright can prevent and delay one's entry into the role of parenthood, based on both embodied emotional and rational considerations (for example, weighing the costs of social stigma), but it can also be reduced by strategic stage management. In effect, I am making here a normative argument linking stage management and stage fright to perceptions of what privileged performances look like. The privileged establish cultural norms about what props are needed to perform parenthood in the correct fashion. These norms influence the rest of the population, either by serving as positive role models of what the optimal performance of parenthood might desirably look like or by serving as prescriptive instruction on what parenthood should look like.

Following Margaret Marini's (1984) critique of simplistic normative arguments, the distinction between optimal norms and prescriptive norms is potentially important since different paths link the perception of privileged performance to the behaviour of the masses in each case, and each case should be further distinguished from observed, statistical norms.[2] The assumption I am making is that the statistical norms associating privileged groups with various stage props are observable by the masses (indeed, they are meant to be observed) and, hence, are transformable into both optimal and prescriptive norms. In conjunction with narratives meaningfully linking these stage props to the achieved success of privileged groups, statistical norms become either optimal norms (generating positive associations for conforming) or prescriptive norms (involving sanctions and stigma for failing to conform). Privileged women who have completed their childbearing activity generate, by virtue of their current stage props, an optimal norm of what motherhood might ideally look like in order to conform. It is in this case where the total number of children born by the privileged might become a stage prop, translating into an optimal or desired number of children for the masses. By contrast, privileged women who are entering into motherhood through a first birth generate, by virtue of their current stage props, a prescriptive norm of what motherhood should look like in order to avoid social stigma. To the extent that first-time mothers of privileged backgrounds would not perform motherhood without acquiring a set of stage props, other prospective mothers should not do so either. Both sorts of norms can work through staging mechanisms but with differing strengths. Optimal norms theoretically have a weaker effect on staging mechanisms since they are not backed up by the threat of sanctions or stigma, but they may independently shape childbearing by influencing desires, especially for completed family size. Prescriptive norms theoretically have a stronger effect on staging mechanisms (stage fright and stage management), influencing both the entrance into parenthood and subsequent childbearing in response to the threat of sanction, stigma, and negative self-conceptualization.

Both the simplistic and nuanced stage prop versions of the status-centred approach that I suggest earlier identify the differentials between the privileged and the rest of the population as key for understanding cultural change. The real strength of this alternative theory is in elucidating the cultural processes taking place within the groups that are distinguished by achieved status differentials. Building on Thorstein Veblen (1992), Pierre Bourdieu (1984), and Jonas Frykman and Orvar Löfgren (1987), cultural change is assumed to be driven by the interplay between privileged groups and the masses. The privileged attempt to symbolically demarcate themselves, distinguishing their performances from the rest of the population. The masses attempt to emulate the performances of the privileged (at least to the extent that they are not barred from achievement by ascribed status distinctions). Emulation is viewed as a path toward upward mobility and also, in many cases, as a path toward positive self-conception. This scenario clearly lays out the processes by which cultural change is likely to occur and places cultural change at the heart of understanding fertility change.

These preceding paragraphs have sketched out a stage prop approach to understanding the possible relationships between cultural change and fertility change. Throughout the rest of this chapter, I attempt to illustrate the ways that staging mechanisms operate within a framework of cultural change. I define a privileged group in reference to a larger population containing minimal ascribed status distinctions. I define a series of possible stage props to see how they are associated with the privileged performances of parenthood over time. I explore two sorts of privileged performance, separating out optimal norms of likely "completed" parents from prescriptive norms generated by first-time parents. In the former case, I pay special attention to how the total number of children for privileged parents might influence the desires of the masses. In the latter case, I pay special attention to how stage props might prepare prospective parents for performing parenthood in the correct fashion. Finally, I consider stage fright as a mechanism limiting fertility in response to the difficulty of stage management.

Data

In order to illustrate the processes that I described earlier, I used historical census data from the United States, as collected by the IPUMS project (Ruggles et al. 2004), running from 1900 to 2005. This set of data provides a broad period of time for the study of cultural change. I focused on the historical staging of motherhood in this chapter, limiting my sample to women between the ages of fifteen and forty-nine. This age range roughly mirrors the biological limits to fertility and is commonly used by demographers interested in childbearing. I further limited the sample to non-Hispanic White women in order to focus on the symbolic meaning of children within an achieved status system. I remain wary that the meaning of children may differ across ascribed status boundaries, which may include racialized boundaries in this chapter – a position supported by the work of Carol Stack and Linda Burton (1994).

After delimiting my sample to non-Hispanic White women aged fifteen to forty-nine, running from 1900 to 2005, my next step was to separate out the privileged. This privileged group should set the meaning of children and the staging of parenthood for the rest of the population. Multiple ways of distinguishing the privileged might have been attempted. In this chapter, I separated out a high-status professional class, including women who were either working as, or married to, a doctor, lawyer, accountant, or engineer. I considered these women to be likely role models for how other women should perform the role of motherhood. It is worth noting that the results that follow are similar to those obtained using other formulations – for instance, counting women heading the top income decile households as privileged (Lauster 2010). For comparison purposes, I also distinguished a lower-status labourer class based on women who were working as labourers or married to labourers.

Two fertility variables are constructed from the census data. I used the household data gathered in the IPUMS project as the "number of own children" present to count children. From this data, I first estimated completed family size for non-Hispanic White women aged thirty-five to thirty-nine from 1900 to 2005. I noted patterns for privileged women and for the population as a whole. I picked this age range not only because these women were likely to have finished nearly all of their childbearing but also because they were likely to have nearly all of their children still living at home. As a result, they best represented the differences in completed family size for privileged women relative to the population as a whole. Nevertheless, some biases remain. In eras where women delay childbearing especially late, completed family size will be underestimated. In eras where children are both born to very young women and leave home especially early, completed family size will also be underestimated.

Aside from estimating completed family size, I also used the "number of own children" in conjunction with the "age of youngest child" to establish the presence of a woman's own infant (age of zero) in the household. The presence of an infant represents recent childbearing behaviour. As I describe later in this chapter, this information is useful on two accounts. The presence of a first-born infant in a household can be used to identify new parents and to understand how first-time privileged new parents might have stage-managed their parenthood. The presence of any "own" infant in a household can also be aggregated for groups and used to estimate age-specific birth risks, or probabilities, for a given population. These, in turn, can be transformed into a total fertility rate estimate.

There are two qualifications to all fertility estimates using this census data. First, the data used do not record all births. They record only living children remaining in the parental household. Other data, including data on the "number of children ever born," are available for some years, but not for others. These data correspond closely to the "number of own children," but not perfectly. Child mortality greatly influences the match between the current "number of own children" and "children ever born." Adoptions also influence the matching process. Both adoptions and child mortality have tended to decline over time. Arguably, this trend does not greatly influence the reliability of "completed family size" as a variable since this variable is a measure of visible family members, and child mortality and adoption are largely invisible. However, total fertility estimates will be downwardly biased corresponding to infant mortality rates, to multiple birth rates, and, likely to a lesser extent, to corresponding adoption rates. The second qualification, which influences total fertility rates (TFR), is that while data on children in the family are collected with reference to a single date (1 April in recent census years, 1 June in some earlier years), the age of children is typically referenced with respect to the age at their last birthday. Since the age of children is recorded whenever the census is filled out (always after the reference date), this results in an underestimate of the number of children below the age of one as of the reference date. Both child mortality and the underestimate of the infant population due to methods of tabulation and multiple births are likely to result in an underestimate of TFR. In the first case, biases due to child mortality are likely to decline across census years. In the second case, the underestimation of fertility due to methods of tabulation or multiple births is likely to be somewhat more random across census years.

Illustrating the Stage Prop Approach

First, I looked at how the optimal norms for what completed motherhood might ideally look like have changed over time. Privileged women are motivated to distinguish themselves from the masses, and their completed family size is one way to do that. The creation of a perceivable difference in family size between the privileged and the masses (especially when coupled with a Malthusian narrative tying small family size to responsible parenthood) sets up the privileged as different and conceivably better than the masses. However, within a context where privilege can be achieved, this hierarchy merely serves to set the aspirations for other mothers in terms of how many children serve as the best stage prop for motherhood. The number of children privileged women have when completing their childbearing is likely to shape the desires for completed family size of other women. Hence, the privileged may

Figure 4.1

Percentage of non-Hispanic White mothers, aged thirty-five to thirty-nine, with between one and three children, by privileged status, 1900-2005

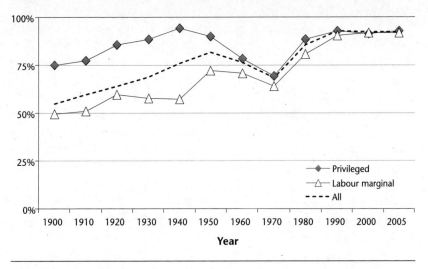

be likely to lead the decline in number of children as a way to distinguish their families, but eventually the rest of the population will catch up.

To illustrate this theory, I explore in Figure 4.1 what percentage of non-Hispanic White mothers, aged thirty-five to thirty-nine, have between one and three children. I note the patterns for privileged women and for the population as a whole. This number begins at 75 percent for privileged mothers (professionals or the wives of professionals) and 55 percent for the population of mothers as a whole in 1900. The number is even lower, at 50 percent, for mothers in the labouring class. Privileged women were more likely to have one to three children than non-privileged women, and, as a result, it is likely that the number of children that one had became associated with privilege. In the absence of ascribed status differentials, this should set up a dynamic where the non-privileged attempt to emulate the privileged. The completed fertility expressed by the privileged is likely to become an optimal norm, influencing the desired completed fertility for the population as a whole. As the population begins to act on these new fertility targets, the differences between the privileged and the population as a whole should diminish, and this sort of distinction strategy should eventually become obsolete. This scenario arguably took place in the United States between

1900 and 1950. As privileged mothers became ever more likely to limit themselves to having one to three children up until 1940, it seems as if the rest of the population gradually attempted to do the same. By 1940, the percentage of the population of mothers as a whole with one to three children reached 76 percent, exceeding the level for the privileged population in 1900. Between 1940 and 1950, even the lower-status, labouring class of mothers began to follow the patterns of the privileged. At this point, it seems, the limitation on childbearing to one to three children lost its distinctive appeal for the privileged, who became less likely to limit childbearing between 1940 and 1950. As the number of children ceased to significantly differentiate the advantaged from the disadvantaged by 1950, completed family size trends converged, from the baby boom all the way to 2005. From 1950 onward, the privileged would have to find a different way to demonstrate distinction in childbearing.

The number of children one has serves as a fundamental stage prop to the performance of motherhood, but a variety of other stage props can also distinguish the privileged from the non-privileged. As mentioned previously, prominent stage props for performing motherhood "correctly" are likely to include being married, having an employed "breadwinning" husband, heading your own household (as a couple), being out of school, being able to be a stay-at-home mother, and owning your own home. In Figure 4.2, I demonstrate the percentage of first-time mothers possessing these stage props for the privileged population. To the extent that a high percentage (at least 75 percent) of privileged first-time mothers have a stage prop, it is likely to become a prescriptive norm or something that you should have in order to become a good mother. In 1900, it is clear that being married to a breadwinner, being out of school, and being able to stay at home were all exceptionally important stage props for performing motherhood correctly. In total, 100 percent of privileged women who were first-time mothers in 1900 shared these stage props. Heading one's own household was also an important stage prop, with 86 percent of privileged first-time mothers in 1900 heading their own households (that is, not living with a parent or in someone else's household). Yet home ownership was not particularly important. Only 36 percent of privileged first-time mothers lived within an owner-occupied home. This pattern, where the stage props of motherhood included marriage to a breadwinner, being an out-of-school, stay-at-home mother, and heading one's own household, but did not include home ownership, became, if anything, more stable between 1900 and 1940. Heading one's own household became even more common for privileged

Figure 4.2

Percentage of privileged non-Hispanic, White first-time mothers, aged fifteen to forty-nine, possessing relevant stage props for motherhood, 1900-2005

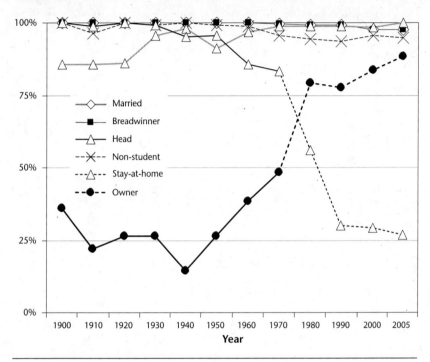

first-time mothers, while ownership of one's own housing became some-what less common. However, from 1940 onward, especially covering the post–Second World War, baby boom era, home ownership rose rapidly for privileged first-time mothers. The percentage of privileged first-time mothers living as stay-at-home mothers also began a decline. These two trends crossed paths between 1970 and 1980, vaulting home ownership into the collection of stage props necessary for the proper performance of motherhood and removing the necessity for privileged new mothers to stay out of the workplace. Between 1980 and 2005, these trends con-tinued to stabilize into a new configuration of normatively prescribed stage props defining the prerequisites for the correct performance of motherhood. Between 1900 and 2005, the overall staging of motherhood remained relatively stable, with one important exception. Staying at home became replaced by owning a home.

Figure 4.3

The difference in the percentage of privileged mothers and labouring-class mothers with a completed family size of one to three children (mothers aged thirty-five to thirty-nine), staying at home, and owning a home (new mothers aged fifteen to forty-nine), for non-Hispanic White women

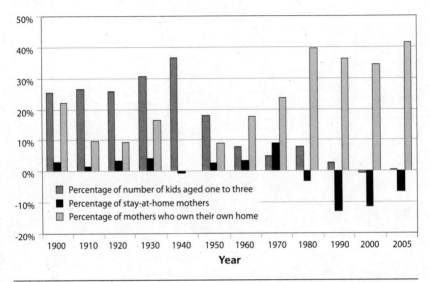

To explore the assumption that changes in the staging of motherhood might be driven, in no small part, by those of privilege searching for new ways to distinguish their performances of motherhood, I chart the differences between the privileged and the labouring class of mothers in Figure 4.3. I compare the difference in the percentage of mothers aged thirty-five to thirty-nine with estimated completed fertility of one to three children to the difference in the percentage of new mothers who are also stay-at-home mothers and/or home owners. From Figure 4.3, it is apparent that fertility limitation largely served to distinguish the privileged from the labouring class up until the Second World War. After this point, the distinctive value of the number of children a mother might have declined rapidly, yet home ownership gradually began to take on increasing importance as a source of differentiation. From 1980 onward, the vast majority of privileged mothers (78 percent to 88 percent) owned their own homes, while well under half of labouring-class mothers owned their own homes. As a result, home ownership became the primary distinction between these two groups. Strikingly, from 1980 onward, the labouring class of new mothers proved less likely to give up stay-at-home motherhood than the privileged class. The labouring class seems to have lagged behind the cultural rejection of stay-at-home motherhood in favour of own-your-home motherhood.

The last assumption behind the stage prop approach is that norms influence behaviour through stage management or stage fright. The exploration of shifts in completed family size points toward how an optimal norm might influence fertility through stage management. To the extent that mothers think that limiting their family size to one to three children will be more likely to provide them with positive reviews of their performances of motherhood, they will be more likely to stage-manage their childbearing accordingly and avoid having more than three children. However, prescriptive norms are likely to be even more powerful, evoking both stage management and stage fright as responses. Women who are bearing children are likely to work toward collecting all of the stage props necessary to perform the role of motherhood properly, hence stage-managing their performances. When they cannot collect these stage props, they are likely to avoid taking on the role of motherhood, hence experiencing stage fright.

To explore the effects of prescriptive norms regarding the perform-ance of motherhood on fertility, I consider the different childbearing experiences of those with and without all of the stage props deemed appropriate by privileged new mothers. First, I measure the proportion of those women sharing all of the stage props of privileged mothers at each age year with an own infant in the household and combine them to create a TFR estimate. This provides an estimate for what fertility would look like if all women had all of the stage props of privileged motherhood for every year in their lives between fifteen and forty-nine. The resulting TFR estimate varies widely, but it is quite high for all census years, ranging from 3.0 to 6.5 children per woman.

The actual contribution of fully staged women to the TFR for the population as a whole is complicated by the fact that most women spend many years of their lives without all of the stage props of privileged motherhood. This contribution can be estimated by multiplying the probability of having all of the stage props needed for motherhood by the probability of bearing a child for those with all of the stage props needed for motherhood for each age year, and summing the total across all age years. The actual contribution of stage-propped women to the estimated TFR ranges from 0.8 to 2.7 children per woman.

Strikingly, the years spent without stage props tend to be the younger, more fertile years. Conversely, by the time a woman is most likely in

Figure 4.4

Estimates of the potential staged total fertility rate (TFR), the actual staged TFR, and the number of years staged under thirty-five for non-Hispanic White women aged fifteen to forty-nine

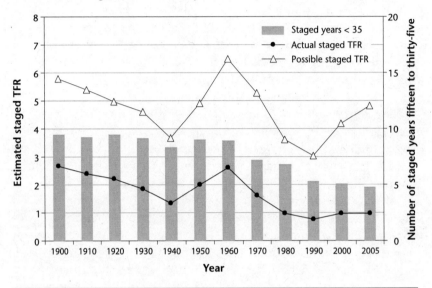

her life course to have acquired all of the stage props (over the age of thirty-five), she will have become less and less likely to have children, and, indeed, pregnancies over the age of thirty-five take on the unfortunate label of "geriatric pregnancies" in North American medical parlance. Adding up the probability of being fully staged for motherhood across all years in this age range provides an estimated sum of the average total years spent staged. Focusing just on the non-"geriatric" age range (fifteen to thirty-five), the resulting estimates of average number with all of the stage props of motherhood ranges from 4.8 to 9.4 years. This provides an estimate of the number of years of "peak" fertility during which time the average woman is likely to possess all of the stage props to perform motherhood in the "right" way.

In Figure 4.4, I demonstrate how these three estimates vary across each year from 1900 to 2005. The possible staged fertility – that is, the fertility we would expect of women if they had all of the stage props of privileged motherhood during every year of their lives from fifteen to forty-nine, varies widely, but it closely tracks the actual staged fertility during most of the time period covered. The actual staged fertility remains some two to four children less than it would be if every woman had all of the props of privileged motherhood throughout her life. This is because most women spend significant parts of their lives without all of the stage props of motherhood. The bars measure the amount of time women under the age of thirty-five have spent with the stage props of motherhood. These results remain relatively stable at an estimated average of around nine years between 1900 and 1960, but then they gradually drop to a low of less than five years in 2005. This is likely the result of the increasing difficulty people faced in obtaining home ownership at the same time that ownership was becoming increasingly important as a stage prop (Lauster 2010). Figure 4.4 demonstrates that from 1970 onward women spent less and less of their prime childbearing years with all of the stage props of privileged motherhood. As a result, actual staged fertility stopped tracking possible staged fertility. After 1990, when the fertility of women with all of the props rose again, the time women spent fully staged continued to fall. As a result, the actual contribution of staged women to TFR remained below 1.0 from 1980 onward.

As revealed in this chapter, a significant portion of total fertility in all years is fully staged fertility. It is likely that this fertility is stage-managed and, hence, "planned" in a way that fertility without stage props may not be. Nevertheless, children born to mothers without all of the stage props also contribute to the overall TFR estimates. In Figure 4.5, I estimate the total possible contribution of "unstaged" women to total fertility, which would represent the average number of children for the population of non-Hispanic White women if no one had the stage props of privileged mothers at any point in time from the age of fifteen to forty-nine. The result is well below replacement-level fertility in all census years, and only in 1960 does the estimate rise significantly above 1.0. I also estimate the average number of years women spend in an unstaged state under the age of thirty-five. This number ranges from just over ten to just over fifteen years (in all cases higher than the five to nine years spent staged).

The actual contribution of unstaged women to the TFR for the population of non-Hispanic White women is a product of the risk of childbearing in the unstaged state multiplied by the time spent in the unstaged state. The average number of children contributed to the TFR by women lacking the staging for motherhood ranges from 0.2 to 0.7 children. I argue that this low rate of childbearing for unstaged women is primarily due to the power of stage fright. Women either unable or unwilling to manage the staging for their performance of motherhood in the fashion of privileged mothers are significantly less likely to have children. As a

Figure 4.5

Estimates of the potential unstaged total fertility rate (TFR), the actual unstaged TFR, and the number of years unstaged under thirty-five for non-Hispanic White women aged fifteen to forty-nine

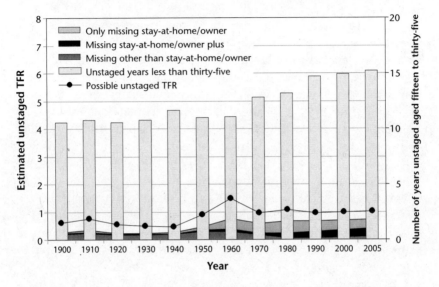

result, their contribution to total fertility remains relatively low. Nevertheless, some women still have children. These women represent either those facing difficulty in managing their childbearing (resulting in "unplanned" children) or those actively engaged in contesting the meaning of good motherhood (in effect, engaging in "experimental theatre"). Either way, these women are likely to face the social stigma of being considered bad mothers until, or unless, they manage to get all of the necessary stage props in place.

Importantly, the contribution of unstaged women to the actual TFR rises from fewer than 0.5 children before 1960 to more than 0.5 children from 1960 onward. In Figure 4.5, I attempt to break down the actual contributions of women to the TFR by how close they are to being completely staged. This result reveals that the rise in the contribution of unstaged women to the actual TFR from 1960 onward seems to be the result of women missing either "working as a stay-at-home mother" (in 1960 and 1970) or "owning a home" (from 1980 onward). The importance of these two props changed across this time period, and women may have contested their importance relative to other stage props.

Figure 4.6

Contributions of staged and unstaged women to overall total fertility rate (TFR), non-Hispanic White women, aged fifteen to forty-nine

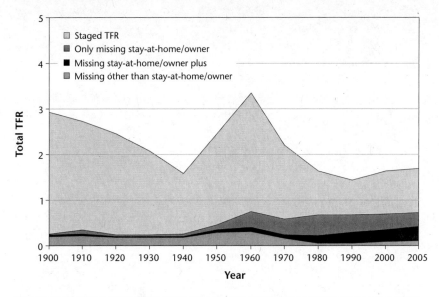

Discounting these two possibly "contested" props, the contribution of unstaged women to the TFR never rises above 0.5 children for any census year.

In Figure 4.6, I put staged fertility and unstaged fertility together, creating a rough estimate of the TFR for the population of non-Hispanic White women as a whole from 1900 to 2005. Overall, despite women spending significantly more time in unstaged states than staged states, women who are properly staged to become mothers contribute more to overall fertility in all census years and appear to be key in reaching replacement-level fertility. Put another way, stage fright in the absence of stage management would seem to be a major force determining overall fertility rates. There would likely be many more children in the United States if women had more of the stage props of motherhood.

Conclusion

In this chapter, I introduce a stage prop approach to understanding fertility change. This approach is different from other approaches commonly used in demography, relying on a foundation in conflict theory and symbolic interaction to consider the importance of cultural change. In particular, I argue that cultural change arises from the symbolic "arms race" between the privileged and the non-privileged. The privileged attempt to distinguish themselves by how their families look and by their performances in their familial roles. The non-privileged attempt to emulate the privileged so long as they are not blocked by ascribed status distinctions. Stage props serve as crucial elements in distinguishing the privileged from the non-privileged.

Stage management and stage fright link social norms generated by the privileged to the fertility behaviour of the population as a whole. I have demonstrated how stage management and stage fright might work to influence fertility, both as a means of achieving desired family size and a means of avoiding the social stigma of performing the role of motherhood poorly. Stage management and stage fright expand the range of mechanisms that might account for childbearing behaviour. Moreover, the stage prop approach to understanding fertility change seems to offer valuable insights into understanding historical patterns that are likely to be missed by other approaches. In particular, cultural change in the staging of motherhood is likely to be missed in other historical accounts. Some other approaches have recognized the importance of social inequality (Johansson 1987). However, they have largely avoided formulating a theory linking social inequality to cultural change.

The stage prop approach suggests that cultural change has the power to alter the desirable completed family size for the population as a whole, as they emulate the privileged. In this approach, family size becomes a potential prop supporting the performance of privileged parenthood in its own right. The stage prop approach also suggests that cultural change has the power to influence what other props are needed to perform motherhood in the right way, as defined by privileged mothers. Other approaches may miss the declining importance of staying at home and the increasing importance of owning a home as a means of preparing for childbearing. Other approaches may also miss the importance of differences in cultural change between places. The social norms generated by the privileged in North America might not transfer to other contexts, where different social norms have arisen.

In some ways, demography has implicitly recognized for a long time that stage props are important. The division made in this chapter between staged mothers and unstaged mothers is not so different from (and builds on) the difference between marital and non-marital fertility regularly charted by demographers. Nevertheless, the basis for the distinction between marital and non-marital fertility has rarely been particularly well theorized, especially with an explicit eye to understanding the importance of culture (as opposed to somewhat prim notions of sexual exposure).

The data used in this chapter to illustrate the stage prop approach provide unique insight into broadly representative historical changes, as captured by census records. At the same time, census data lack the richness of archival and ethnographic data, which better point toward how people come to construct, understand, and respond to social norms. Ethnographic and archival data might also explore how the particular stage props discussed here (in addition to other props) become used in the actual performance of parenthood. For instance, Townsend's ethnography (2002) offers a particularly salient example of how home ownership becomes important to the performance of fatherhood. This example might be compared to the ethnographic work of Constance Perin (1977) and Herbert Gans (1967), who demonstrate together the increasing importance of home ownership. In the case of the privileged population, such data could also demonstrate how distinction work proceeds, whereby the privileged symbolically distinguish themselves from the masses (Lamont 1992; Gillis 1996). Moreover, census records offer only cross-sectional data on how people might be staging their performances, while longitudinal data sets could offer more in the way of information on the sequencing involved (for example, the timing of transitions to fatherhood, marriage, and home ownership) as in the work of Clara Mulder and Michael Wagner (1998). Clearly, more work remains to be done.

This chapter lays out the basic framework for a stage prop approach to understanding childbearing behaviour and describes a few of the advantages for doing so. It also points toward possible keys to understanding fertility decline. It suggests that privileged mothers continue to alter the stage props needed to perform motherhood correctly. The standards keep changing, making it harder and harder for most women to feel like good mothers. In conjunction with other work (Lauster 2010), this chapter suggests that the introduction of home ownership as a stage prop for the performance of privileged motherhood was a big part of changing standards in the United States, but researchers have documented others as well (Hays 1996; Garey 1999). It seems likely that women are spending less and less of their childbearing years feeling ready to be mothers – in effect, they are experiencing stage fright. The work of Townsend (2002) suggests that men might be experiencing similar exposure to stage fright, and the weight of the stage management work required to prepare for a good performance of parenthood is growing increasingly heavy. This burden may lead a few people away from parenthood entirely since they feel it is not worth the trouble, but evidence indicates that the vast majority of people still desire children. Moreover, people frequently desire more children than they end up having, in part, I suggest, because people seem to be spending more and more time preparing before they feel ready to become parents. This response should not be interpreted as the result of a lack of commitment to the role. Instead, it suggests quite the opposite. People very much want to perform the role of parenthood properly.

Notes

1 The Integrated Public Use Microdata Series (IPUMS) project collects historical US and international census data into harmonized datasets containing individual and household records, allowing for easy, transparent data analysis (see http://www.ipums.org for details).

2 In many ways, this mirrors the reference group work of Theodore Kemper (1968), wherein he distinguishes between normative groups (prescriptive and proscriptive), comparative groups, and audience groups.

References

Bourdieu, P. 1984. *Distinction: A Social Critique of the Judgement of Taste*. Cambridge, MA: Harvard University Press.

Caldwell, J. 1982. *The Theory of Fertility Decline*. New York: Academic.

Frykman, J., and O. Löfgren. 1987. *Culture Builders: A Historical Anthropology of Middle Class Life*. Trans. A. Crozier. New Brunswick, NJ: Rutgers University Press.

Gans, H. 1967. *The Levittowners: Ways of Life and Politics in a New Suburban Community*. New York: Vintage Books.

Garey, A. 1999. *Weaving Work and Motherhood*. Philadelphia: Temple University Press.

Gillis, J. 1996. *A World of Their Own Making: Myth, Ritual and the Quest for Family Values*. Cambridge, MA: Harvard University Press.

Goffman, E. 1959. *The Presentation of Self in Everyday Life*. New York: Anchor Books.

Hakim, C. 2003. "A New Approach to Explaining Fertility Patterns: Preference Theory." *Population and Development Review* 29: 349-74.

Hays, S. 1996. *The Cultural Contradictions of Motherhood*. New Haven, CT: Yale University Press.

Johansson, S.R. 1987. "Status Anxiety and Demographic Contraction of Privileged Populations." *Population and Development Review* 13: 439-70.

Katz, C. 2008. "Childhood as Spectacle: Relays of Anxiety and the Reconfiguration of the Child." *Cultural Geographies* 15: 5-17.

Kemper, T. 1968. "Reference Groups, Socialization, and Achievement." *American Sociological Review* 33: 31-45.

Kohler, H., J. Behrman, and A. Skytthe. 2005. "Partner+Children=Happiness? The Effects of Partnerships and Fertility on Well-being." *Population and Development Review* 31: 407-45.

Lamont, M. 1992. *Money, Morals, and Manners*. Chicago: University of Chicago Press.

Lauster, N. 2010. "Housing and the Proper Performance of American Motherhood, 1940-2005." *Housing Studies* 25: 541-55.

Lesthaeghe, R. 1998. "On Theory Development: Applications to the Study of Family Formation." *Population and Development Review* 24: 1-14.

Marini, M. 1984. "Age and Sequencing Norms in the Transition to Adulthood." *Social Forces* 63: 229-44.

Morgan, S., and M. Taylor. 2006. "Low Fertility at the Turn of the Twenty-first Century." *Annual Review of Sociology* 32: 375-99.

Mulder, C., and M. Wagner. 1998. "The Connection between Family Formation and First-Time Home Ownership in the Context of West Germany and the Netherlands." *European Journal of Population* 17: 137-64.

Perin, C. 1977. *Everything in Its Place: Social Order and Land Use in America*. Princeton, NJ: Princeton University Press.

Ruggles, S., M. Sobek, T. Alexander, C. Fitch, and C. Ronnander. 2004. "Integrated Public Use Microdata Series: Version 3.0," http://www.ipums.org.

Stack, C., and L. Burton. 1994. "Kinscripts: Reflections on Family, Generation, and Culture." In E. Glenn, G. Chang, and L. Forcey, eds., *Mothering: Ideology, Experience, and Agency*, 33-44. New York: Routledge.

Townsend, N. 2002. *The Package Deal: Marriage, Work and Fatherhood in Men's Lives*. Philadelphia: Temple University Press.

Turner, R. 1956. "Role-Taking, Role Standpoint, and Reference-Group Behavior." *American Journal of Sociology* 61: 316-28.

Veblen, T. 1992. *The Theory of the Leisure Class*. New Brunswick, NJ: Transaction Publishers.

5
Parenthood, Immortality, and the End of Childhood

Nicholas W. Townsend

I first met Busi when she was visiting her birthplace, a village in South Africa, three days after the death of one of her senior kinswomen. Seventy years old when I met her, Busi was a charismatic healer and successful businesswoman with a thriving practice in a mining township near Johannesburg. In this chapter, I use Busi's life experience to illustrate my argument that one of the ends or purposes served by childhood is giving parents an assurance that they will be remembered and honoured after they die. That is to say, from the point of view of parents, one motive for having children is to grant themselves, if not immortality, at least continued existence after death.

Busi had come home to the village in order to honour her kinswoman and her lineage by making sure that the old woman had an appropriate funeral. In preparation for the event, Busi strode around her ancestral compound with unruffled self-confidence and an eagle eye for detail, supervising her assembled kin in all of the tasks, both great and small, involved in producing an important funeral. In between sending people to fetch firewood, organize chairs, and butcher cattle, Busi would pause to inspect the cook fires, the corn meal, and the awnings or to consult with others about the transport of guests, the arrangements with the burial company, and the preparation of the grave. Every few minutes she would turn away from the mundane to the essential social interactions that make a funeral significant, intercepting and acknowledging visitors and making sure that the protocol for greeting the chief mourners – the dead woman's age mates sitting wrapped in blankets in the shade of a house – was followed with the proper respect. Throughout the week between the old woman's death and her funeral, Busi's energy was completely focused on making sure that the event reflected honour and prestige on the dead woman and on her entire extended family.[1]

An appropriate funeral, one that is well attended, well performed, and recognized by the community, is the final event of a life well lived. The funeral is not, however, only the *marker* or consequence of a successful life; it is also the *guarantee* and confirmation that the life in question was indeed successful. Put differently, a funeral does not just indicate the chronological end of a life, but it is also a culminating ritual that contributes to the survivors' judgment of a person's life and to the kinds of memorials and memories that endure. In this sense, a funeral may also be a goal or end of a person's life. I argue that people may recognize that the value of their lives is vouchsafed by the celebration and commemoration they get from the survivors, that the most secure way to be sure that there are survivors who will care to commemorate them is through having children, and, therefore, that one of the ends or purposes of childhood is the validation of parents' lives and their hope for survival after death.

Ends as Events and Purposes

Births and deaths are connected in time as the beginnings and ends of individual lives, and they are connected in populations because births must outnumber deaths for a population to avoid extinction. In *Childhood's End*, Arthur C. Clarke (1987) describes how all of the children on Earth are separated from the adults as humanity evolves to its eventual end in union with the "overmind." Clarke's title expresses his own view that humanity has not reached its potential but is only at an early stage in its development. For him, union with cosmic consciousness marks the temporal end and the fulfilled purpose of humanity's childhood. As a student of social life rather than of cosmic destiny, I cite Clarke's title because of the distinction he makes between "childhood" and "children." In his depiction of the limited progress of humanity, Clarke imagines the responses of the last generation of adults on Earth after the children are removed in preparation for their apotheosis. The adults in *Childhood's End* do not evolve – they are left where they were – and Clarke depicts their lives without children as having no future and, hence, no real purpose. The children's absence marks the evolution of the species beyond its childhood, but the adults do not experience this development; they feel only the loss of their children. They are no longer parents, and the fundamental basis of social organization – the reciprocal relationship that is expressed in "parenthood" and "childhood" – has been erased.

The distinction between "children" and "childhood" is the distinction between young human beings, whose existence depends on biological reproduction and whose survival and development depend on socially organized care and nurture, and the particular social relationship that defines specific people as elements of specific parent-child dyads. This distinction is concealed in English, where both "adulthood" as a life-stage and "parenthood" as a social relationship are contrasted with the same term "childhood," just as the distinct social statuses of "adult" and "parent" are contrasted with the single term "child." This double use of "childhood" and "child" glosses over a distinction that we nevertheless recognize when we talk of "adult children" and "parents who are still children themselves." Considering childhood as a social position and relationship as well as a life stage, I argue that human births and deaths are connected in contingent – neither biologically nor logically neces-sary – webs of meanings and intentions. In particular, I contend that one primary purpose of childhood is to make sure that adults, when they die, have people to mourn them, to give them an appropriate fu-neral, to validate their lives, and to maintain their existence as memories and ancestors. For most of us, kinship is the surest way to realize this purpose. After we die, we are entirely dependent on the living for any recognition, appreciation, remembrance, and existence. To anticipate death is to recognize our total dependence on other people.

Reproduction and Replacement

It is a cliché, but no less true for being one, that children are at the same time reminders of our mortality and promises of our immortality. As a result, to speak about childhood, particularly as a parent and grand-parent, is to speak at once of both birth and death. On the one hand, children are our replacements. They remind us of our past, of our youth, of our age and our aging, and of our inevitable death. Interviewing fath-ers in the United States, I was struck by the centrality of sport in men's discussions of the relationship between fathers and sons. There is an arc to this relationship: at first, the father teaches and encourages and allows his son to win, as the son's ability grows he has to learn to lose, then the competition becomes real and the son may sometimes win based on his own merits. Eventually, the son will surpass the father, and at this point the father stops competing for he knows that he will never win again. Once his son has replaced him, time will bring only decline and eventual death. A folktale known around the world tells of a man who plans to abandon his aged father to die in the wilderness and leaves the old man with a blanket. "Wait!" says the father, "take half this blan-ket, you will need it when your son leaves *you* here." A man becomes an adult and cares for his children, but as he ages he depends on his children to care for him. And every man moves through the stages: first depending on, then replacing, his father; first raising, then depending on, his son.

On the other hand, children are also our future, our legacy, and our continuation. It is our children who will remember us, who will carry on our work, who will preserve what we have made and what we value, and who will continue our family, lineage, nation, and species. In *Childhood's End*, Clarke (1987) assumes that when all of the children are removed, and the adults realize no more will be born, their reasons and motives for living and the very point of life will disappear. Neither gratification of the senses nor lofty achievement provides satisfaction in the absence of a human future that will survive both the sybarite and the savant. For Clarke, childhood's "end" refers not only to the termination of childhood in time but also to childhood's point and purpose. In this chapter, I follow Clarke's lead and argue that the "end" of childhood is not just a chronological marker in a life course but that it may also refer to a goal or objective in a life strategy. I realize that the move from "end" as terminus to "end" as telos may be nothing but a verbal trick or a dubious metaphysical proposition, but I believe that the move is justified by the light it shines on questions about childhood.

The idea of replacement is more easily grasped at the individual, than at the species, level. "Generations," for instance, are often "good to think with," but they are confusing fictions from the perspective of demography and reproduction. We may agree on what we mean by the "baby boom generation," but because children are born in every season and in every year the boundaries we draw around it are inevitably arbitrary. Individually and collectively, the people born in a single year have children over a period of years if not decades. They do not, as a group, experience their replacement by a subsequent generation. For the individual, however, the birth of a first child is a discrete and definite event and that child is a distinct and specific person. Earlier in this chapter, I described this idea in terms of a man's life and particularly in terms of a father and his son. The fundamental dynamic is the same for women, although the relationship between mother and daughter seems to be more nuanced in cultures of European origin, perhaps because mother and daughter are felt to share substance to a greater degree than other parent-child pairs.

In addition to the general tendency to think of men's experience as normative, two features of the social organization of reproduction, especially in poor rural populations, frequently obscure our view of generational replacement in women's lives. The first such feature is that a woman's childbearing may easily overlap with that of her eldest daughters. In England and Wales, women having their first birth within marriage in 2000 were, on average, between the ages of twenty-nine and thirty, which means that, on average, women becoming grandmothers for the first time were almost sixty years old (Office for National Statistics 2003). In rural Bangladesh, the average age for married women having their first birth was under nineteen, and they could expect, on average, to become grandmothers before the age of forty (Haque and Sayem 2009). The second feature of social organization that obscures generational replacement for women is that daughters have almost universally grown up to do the same tasks that their mothers did – and still do in most cases – and mothers and grandmothers often share child care and domestic work.

For both men and women, however, if children are at the same time signs of mortality and of immortality, then their own childhood ends when they become parents. And since it is supplemented rather than superseded by "grandparenthood," parenthood is a social position and relationship that survives the children's transition into adulthood and, sadly, even their premature death.[2]

Parenthood Achieved: The Attribution of Childhood

It may seem obvious, and it is frequently assumed, that biological reproduction transforms people into parents and causes their achievement of the status of "parenthood." Child abandonment and adoption are only two instances of the many social practices demonstrating that biological reproduction is neither a sufficient nor a necessary preliminary to, or cause of, parenthood. Other examples include the levirate, in which a man's brother marries his widow and her children become the offspring and heirs of the dead brother, and "woman marriage," a practice that is widespread in Africa in which one woman marries another in order to produce children for her patrilineage (Herskovits 1937; Krige 1974). In neither case can the genitor, or biological father, be the pater or social father.

In modern cultures of European origin, the attribution of children becomes a problem not only in cases of abandonment and adoption but also when children are born from donated sperm or eggs or from surrogate mothers. The problems arise because of a cultural assumption that shared substance as the consequence of sexual reproduction is the foundation of the relationship between children and parents (Schneider 1968). This cultural assumption is by no means universal (Montagu 1937; Pulman 2004). Interestingly, in European cultures, the force of the idea that married couples share substance by becoming "one blood" has weakened. For the Tswana and many other Africans, the mixing of the blood between husbands and wives is very real and motivates the cautious behaviour and careful treatment of widows and widowers. There are, however, other ways of placing children into culturally approved statuses of childhood. Several authors in this volume refer to the principle, dating at least from Roman law, that "the husband of the wife is the father of the child." And as Rebecca Upton discusses in Chapter 3 in this volume, useful stories may be told, and accepted, to reconcile this principle with the cultural ideal of sexual exclusivity and the cultural assumption that married couples want children.

Most people do achieve parenthood through biological reproduction. The point of describing other routes to parenthood is to demonstrate that their goal is parenthood rather than mere reproduction. People conceive and bear children in order to become recognized as adults within their cultures, performing the full range of socially recognized relationships with others. If they cannot reproduce, they will often make arrangements to have children attributed to them. Having children, through biological reproduction or social attribution, is a route toward, and a way of being, the kind of person one wants to be – the kind of person who is acknowledged and respected by others and who has reason to believe that the respect of others is warranted.

Children for the Ancestors: Busi's Parenthood

Busi, whom I described at the start of this chapter as she directed the funeral of her kinswoman, was the last born of her mother's nine children. Busi's father had only one wife, and his lineage's hopes for a male heir hung on the fates of these nine children. Three of them died in infancy, and three others died before they had children of their own. The three survivors were all daughters, and the two oldest both married out of their father's family. Busi, the youngest child, was also married, but because she bore no children the marriage was dissolved. The position of a childless woman is precarious because it is usually through having children that women became fully adult and eventually become respected elders. Women who cannot bear children can become mothers by being "given" children by a kinswoman or, rarely, by marrying a man who already has children. Neither of these routes provides the woman's father with incontrovertible male heirs, and Busi did not take either of them. Instead, when she had returned from her marriage to her father's household, her deceased ancestors came to her with two purposes.[3] One was to tell her that, since she was their last chance for patrilineal descendants, she must produce children in the family name, and the other was to reveal to Busi her vocation as a healer.

Having seen Busi in action, and having observed her as she calmly regulated the affairs of her complex household from a seat in the shade of a hut, I had no difficulty imagining her as a much younger woman rising to her ancestors' challenge. She determined, guided I am sure by her ancestors and by the living members of her father's lineage, that she herself would be the father, the pater, of children who would share her name and be born into her father's lineage. She would achieve this status by marrying a woman who could bear children, and her position as her father's heir made such a marriage possible. Accordingly, Busi paid bridewealth to the parents of Rodah, a woman twenty-five years her junior, and became her husband. To guarantee her own claims to fatherhood and to ensure that no other man could make the claim, Busi also paid bridewealth to the parents of Mark, a man of her own age. I am not sure that one could refer to Busi as Mark's "husband," but she was certainly not his "wife." The important point is that Busi had married both of them in the sense that their children would be unreservedly accepted as members of her own lineage. Between 1973 and 1997, Rodah bore her four daughters and three sons.

Busi's story illustrates the intimate connection between being socially accepted as a parent in life and being recognized as an ancestor after death. Busi's ancestors will fade away less suddenly because of her parenthood, and Busi herself will surely be memorialized more ostentatiously and remembered more enduringly than if she had not had children, for she had brought about the survival of a lineage. Busi and her community accepted the rationality and psychological reality of her ancestors' desire for her to have children. They understood that the point of Busi's having children was to prevent the ending of her patriline, to avert the anger of her ancestors, and eventually to preserve their existence. The members of the community also recognized that Busi's marital arrangement had allowed her to become the head of her own household and to control her own affairs, just as her vocation as a healer had made it possible for her to have one of the few careers available to women, but I never heard either of these consequences mentioned as a possible motivation for her actions.

Parenthood, the End of Reproduction

Fear of being replaced and fear of mortality have frequently been analyzed as individual preoccupations and unconscious motivations. Freud, for instance, found clues to the complications of parenthood in the ancient Greek origin myths. The first three generations of gods – Ouranos, Cronus, and Zeus – all hid or ate their children, Cronos castrated his father, and Zeus both overthrew his father and swallowed the woman pregnant with his child, only to have Athena emerge fully armed from his forehead. For Freud, myth crystallized the individual predicament in a collective form and gave expression to fathers' fear of being replaced by their sons, to sons' desire to remove and replace their fathers, and to the centrality and even inevitability of reproduction in this process of generational succession.

Rather than search for motivation in the dark mirrors of the individual unconscious, social anthropology starts from the existence of society and understands individuals as being constituted by organized patterns of relationships between social positions defined and established prior to, and independent from, them. Anthropology's individuals are transient actors performing in roles, and on stages, that were there before they came on the scene and that will endure after their final exits. Since its emphasis has been on social reproduction – the maintenance of social institutions, patterns of activity, social groups, and social positions, as individual personalities and bodies come and go – anthropology has seen families and family relationships as embedded in a web or matrix of kinship that constitutes an always important, and frequently central, element of every society's structure. This kinship is a set of culturally specified social positions and a set of culturally specified expectations linking them with reciprocal claims and obligations. It includes living, dead, and as yet unborn (and even non-human) members, and it is described in an idiom of shared, complementary, or potentially incompatible substance. Often, though not universally, kinship is depicted in terms of the dimensions of descent and reproductive unions.

The units of analysis in kinship are not individual human beings but, rather, the relationships between the positions that they occupy. Childhood is not a developmental stage or a span of ages so much as it is one status relative to others. Fatherhood and childhood are not so much attributes of fathers and children but, instead, particular kinds of connections between people. Being connected to each other in the relationship between fatherhood and childhood is, in fact, what constitutes two people as father and child.

Good Deaths, Good Lives, Good Funerals

Once we recognize that the stages of life and their characteristic activities are situationally constructed, that the specific experiences and emotions of contemporary adolescents are not primordial but have developed historically, that the division of a man's adulthood into warrior and elder is not universal, we can legitimately ask in what sense death itself is situationally or socially constructed. We can all agree that the age distribution and the pattern of causes of mortality are social phenomena. Public health, nutrition, warfare, occupational safety, toxic pollution, disease transmission, and genocide are all social factors affecting who will die and when. However, I am less confident that all would agree that there is any meaningful sense in which death can be said to be the end, or the goal, of life. Recognizing that any such sense must be limited and will vary in acceptability between individuals and between cultures, my attempt in this chapter is to delineate a sense in which death can be both the telos and the terminus of life.

As a starting point, I assert that it is meaningful, at least in the English-speaking world, to say that there are better and worse deaths. Other things being equal, it is better to die rapidly than in a drawn-out process of decay; better to die peacefully than wracked by pain; better to die satisfied with one's achievements and with one's affairs in order than to die tormented by failed ambitions and unsettled accounts; better to die surrounded by people who are loving and familiar than to die alone or among strangers; better to die leaving one's dependents provided for than to die fearful for their future. And beyond the recognition of better and worse, it is also meaningful to accept the reality, or at least the possibility, of good deaths – deaths that are preferable to life, deaths that are sought after and prized in themselves, or deaths that are the culmination of good lives. Death in battle, or heroic death more generally, has often been seen as being preferable to the shame of living. Some deaths are deemed good because they are oriented toward previous generations – for example, death in defence of the religion, way of life, or achievements of one's ancestors. In a few frequently quoted lines, Thomas Macaulay (1842) has his hero Horatius, preparing to sacrifice himself in the defence of Rome, proclaim, as a purely rhetorical question, the value of a death oriented to the past:

For how can man die better
Than facing fearful odds,
For the ashes of his fathers
And the temples of his gods?

In all of the civilized nations that have followed Rome, parents have encouraged their sons to go to war and sons have gone and died to make their parents proud.[4]

But most good deaths, I contend, are oriented toward the future.[5] Good deaths save and preserve future generations who will not only survive but will also remember and immortalize the dead. Horatius, having invoked his ancestors, turns immediately to reproduction and future immortality and, in less-remembered lines, adds his mother, his wife, and his child:

And for the tender mother
Who dandled him to rest,
And for the wife who nurses
His baby at her breast?

When people leave their dependents provided for, or when they die to preserve a way of life, they are dying for their children, and it is this fact that makes their deaths good. Even the hope for a death that is good only in the limited sense that it is clean and reasonably rapid is often coupled with the desire to save the survivors from distress, work, expense, and sordid memories.

The proof of a good death is always in the hands of the survivors. It is the living who must retain memories of the dead, and it is they who must conduct the funerals, erect the monuments, and establish the memorials. In a famous speech encouraging the people of Britain to continue to fight, to sacrifice, and to die even though Hitler had subjugated Europe and driven the British army into the sea, Winston Churchill (1940) made explicit the relationship between heroic death and immortality: "Let us therefore brace ourselves to our duties, and so bear ourselves that if the British Empire and its Commonwealth last for a thousand years, men will still say, 'This was their finest hour.'" Churchill recognized that heroic deaths create long memories. In general, ancestors continue to exist only so long as their descendants recognize, worship, acknowledge, or remember them. If descendants neglect them, the ancestors may be angry, but if the living simply ignore or forget them then the ancestors cease to exist.

A good funeral does not only mark a death, but it can also be the culmination of a life and, by its own splendour and quality, demonstrate that the life memorialized was indeed good. The proof of a good life, in other words, is that it ends in a funeral worthy of such a life. A good funeral both signifies and certifies success, just as obituaries and monuments are not simply descriptions but also tangible tokens of worthwhile lives. The decision to grant Princess Diana, the divorced wife of the heir to the British throne, a state funeral on the scale previously reserved for reigning monarchs and such national heroes as the Duke of Wellington and Winston Churchill, was expedient in light of her popularity and of the popular discontent with the British royal family at the time of her death. Diana's state funeral, however, did not simply recognize her goodness. Its (unintended) effect was to establish her as a secular saint and affirm that her life, as a beautiful woman, a wronged wife, a loving mother, and a crusader against land mines, had indeed been good. Appreciating the validating role of a good funeral, people of all walks of life and in all societies plan for, and in a sense live for, their funerals.

Achieving Ancestorhood

There is a simple reason why children are integral to a worthy funeral and a good life. In order to die a good death for, sacrifice for, bequeath to, and have a lasting impact on one's children, one must have children who are in some meaningful and important sense recognized as one's own. In general and in the abstract, the end of childhood as a social status puts an end to meaningful death as well as to meaningful life. However, for actual people, it is not the mere existence of children that matters but, rather, the existence of children who stand to them as child to parent, whose specific attribution to the status of childhood constitutes their own parenthood. Issues around childhood and parenthood are not about particular ages or stages of life but, instead, about the attribution of people to social positions.

I have argued that childhood as a social status must exist in order to establish people as parents and full adults, in order to establish the net of kinship that places and supports people in relationship to one another, and in order to form the families, lineages, and ethnic groups that make possible the articulation of individuals and society. I have also argued that childhood, by associating particular children with particular adults, provides our best hope for immortality. These arguments are necessary foundations for my contention that the end – not only the chronological end but also the purpose – of childhood is parenthood.

People actively seek parenthood – the connection to children who belong to them – not only for the tangible and intangible benefits of children but also in order to assure themselves that they will receive posthumous validation and a place in the memories of others. The assurance that others will acknowledge one's death, praise one's life, and cherish one's memory is a crucial support to one's own conviction that one's life has been worthwhile and successful. And it is as close to being an ancestor or an immortal as any of us can get.

Busi's experience has exemplified much of my argument about the purposes or end of childhood. Her parenthood and her attention to her kinswoman's funeral demonstrated the importance of having claims on descendants in order to be validated and remembered after death. Busi's parenthood – the childhood of her children – assured her, as well as her ancestors, of the services of survivors in the kinship world of the village. Yet the concern she expressed was not about her place in the memory of her kin but, rather, about her lasting significance to the community of patients, apprentices, helpers, and their kin to whom the compound where she practised her healing was a focal point.

As she organized the funeral of her kinswoman, she was determined that everything be done right, and she was particularly eager that I photograph all of the details of the multi-day event so that she could show "her people" what a proper funeral looked like "so they will know how things should be done when I die." Busi's efforts to guarantee herself a good funeral were efforts to ensure that her life would receive validation and that, because she was remembered and admired, she, herself, would become an ancestor.

Notes

1 Extended families in this area are, according to cultural ideals, patrilineal segments of three or four generations. In reality, individual men and their descendants may become estranged and, at least for practical purposes, cease to be members. In addition, on the other hand, a good number of people trace their membership through their mothers who did not marry, or were deserted by, their fathers.

2 Several of the authors in this volume, and many elsewhere, refer to and measure the number of years or percentage of life spent "as a parent" and treat this period as having an end as well as a beginning. There is no real inconsistency between this usage and my assertion that the end of parenthood is at death. The first considers parenthood as the activity of caring for, or being responsible for, one or more children and divides that activity into parenting infants, parenting school age children, and so on. The second expresses the idea that becoming a parent is an irreversible step into a status that lasts beyond the child's chronological youth and, sadly, sometimes beyond the death of the child. Once a parent, always a parent – the relationship may end, but the status is permanent.

3 Many readers will interpret this sentence to mean that Busi had a dream, or saw a vision of her ancestors, or that she was guided by overt or internalized social pressures. The reports that I heard, however, attributed the desire for heirs, and the capacity to direct people to realize that desire, directly to the ancestors. In Busi's account, she was following their instructions.

4 Many parents have struggled to make sense of their children's deaths by insisting that they did not die in vain. They have been supported in this struggle by the language of nationalism and of war memorials. To send a son to his death, to

sacrifice him for the good of some cause, has even been portrayed as the ultimate achievement of parenthood.

5 Some good deaths are purely existential – deaths without spectators or survivors can be meaningful only to those about to die. Albert Camus (1975) argued that suicide could be meaningful in a world without meaning. In a story by Jorge Luis Borges (1998), the life of the protagonist, who is facing the firing squad, is fulfilled when he completes a poem in the time it takes the bullets to travel from the muzzles of the guns to his heart.

References

Borges, J.L. 1998. "The Secret Miracle." In J.L. Borges, ed., *Collected Fictions*. Trans. A. Hurley, 157-62. New York: Viking.

Camus, A. 1975. *The Myth of Sisyphus*. New York: Penguin.

Churchill, W. 1940. Speech delivered in the House of Commons and broadcast on BBC radio, 18 June 1940, http://www.winstonchurchill.org/.

Clarke, A.C. 1987. *Childhood's End*. New York: Ballantine Books.

Haque, Md. A., and A. Md. Sayem. 2009. "Socioeconomic Determinants of Age at First Birth in Rural Areas of Bangladesh." *Asia Pacific Journal of Public Health* 21: 104-11.

Herskovits, M. 1937. "A Note on 'Woman Marriage' in Dahomey." *Africa* 10: 335-41.

Krige, E.J. 1974. "Woman-Marriage, with Special Reference to the *Lovedu*: Its Significance for the Definition of Marriage." *Africa* 44: 11-37.

Macaulay, T. 1842. "Horatius." In *Lays of Ancient Rome,* 47-76. London: Longman, Brown, Green, and Longman, Representative Poetry Online, University of Toronto, http://rpo.library.utoronto.ca/.

Montagu, A. 1937. *Coming into Being among the Australian Aborigines: A Study of the Procreative Beliefs of the Native Tribes of Australia*. London: Routledge.

Office for National Statistics. 2003. *Birth Statistics 2000,* Series FM1 no. 29. London: Office for National Statistics, http://www.statistics.gov.uk/downloads/theme_population/Fm1_29/FM1_29_v3.pdf.

Pulman, B. 2004. "Malinowski and Ignorance of Physiological Paternity." *Revue Française de Sociologie* 45: 121-42.

Schneider, D.M. 1968. *American Kinship: A Cultural Account*. Englewood Cliffs, NJ: Prentice-Hall.

6

Leaving Home: An Example of the Disappearance of Childhood and Its End as a Predictable Set of Uniform Experiences

Adena B.K. Miller

In this volume, the theme of "Childhood's End" has been developed along three strands: the disappearance of children through declining fertility rates, the disappearance of childhood as a uniform phase in the life cycle, and the political and policy responses to changes in the physical and social presence of children. The present chapter explores the second strand of these themes, the disappearance of childhood as a predictable uniform traditional set of life-phase experiences. This examination will be done by focusing on the social stage of childhood and its end as the beginning of another life stage, adulthood. In doing so, the goal is twofold. The first is to situate the end of childhood within a discussion of the changing nature of dependency, what it means to be an adult, and the consequences that these meanings hold for the transition to adulthood. The second is to highlight how experiences in childhood are altering the experience of the end of childhood and the transition to adulthood for many young people. This will be illustrated using an empirical example of one marker of the end of childhood – the age at which individuals first leave the parental home – in relation to one family transition in childhood – parental divorce. Furthermore, to illustrate the complexity of these issues, attitudes toward marriage will also be explored as possible moderating and mediating influences between parental divorce and the age at which youth first leave the parental home. The analysis is based on a Canadian sample of young people. With these two goals in mind, it is hoped that the present chapter will illustrate the necessity of being critically aware of the disappearance of childhood and its end as a uniform and traditional set of experiences and the possible consequences that this experience has for young people's past, present, and future.

The Changing Nature of Dependency

The disappearance of childhood and its end as a uniform set of life-phase experiences can be situated within a discussion of the changing nature of dependency, of what it means to be an adult, and of the consequences these hold for the transition to adulthood. The nature of dependency and its relation to adulthood has altered within the context of late modernity. Young people today are faced with different challenges and opportunities from those of their parents' generation (Furlong and Cartmel 2007). Unlike previous generations, today's youth are faced with an uncertain economic environment with little social security and a decrease in traditional cultural markers to guide their experience through childhood and into adulthood. This situation hampers their ability to transition from dependency to independence. Hence, while childhood and adulthood were traditionally associated with dependence and independence, respectively, the sharp distinction between the two can no longer be assumed. If the end of childhood and the beginning of adulthood cannot be defined within a dichotomy of dependency and independence, how do we know when childhood is over and adulthood has begun?

Although ambiguity surrounds the definition of adulthood, becoming an adult can be understood as a complex process that includes chronological age and a series of transitions that are bound by historical and social context. Thus, the process of becoming an adult is simultaneously based on individual characteristics and societal conditions. How each individual and each generation is enabled and constrained by its individual characteristics and historical and societal environments can be seen by looking at three interconnected transitions: the school-to-work transition, the domestic transition, and the housing transition (Coles 1995). Here, the domestic transition signifies moving from the family of origin to the family of destination and the housing transition signifies moving away from the parental home. While these transitions may have been uniform and highly predictable for much of the twentieth century, the process of becoming an adult has recently become more highly differentiated. Thus, the connection between these transitional markers has become less integrated and predictable. It is the question of how broader changes in the nature of dependency and adulthood connect to the housing transition, which is conceptualized as the age when youth first leave home, that will be the focus of the present discussion.

Increased differentiation between individuals of the same generation making the transition into adulthood is occurring in the context of an extended period of dependency of youth on their families for emotional and economic support. This period of extended dependency is attributed to social and economic factors that have resulted in changes in life events traditionally associated with adulthood. Researchers in the field of youth studies have pondered the causes and consequences of youth prolonging the transition to adulthood (Côté 2000; Arnett 2004). Terms such as "emergent adult" (Arnett 2004) and "twixter" (Grossman 2005) have been developed to reflect the changing nature of youth, the life course, and the attainment of adulthood within late modernity (Furlong and Cartmel 2007). It has been documented that youth have been delaying leaving home in many countries including Germany, Denmark, France, Italy, Great Britain, Canada, and the United States (Mitchell 2006). In the United States, the transition to adulthood appears for some young adults to continue into the later twenties and even thirties (Furstenberg 2002). Similarly, one in five Canadian men, and one in ten Canadian women, still reside with at least one parent at the age of twenty-nine (Beaujot and Kerr 2007).

The implications for different launching times are unclear, and the precise consequences are difficult to decipher (Beaujot and Kerr 2007). Researchers have suggested that leaving home early can be linked to lower educational aspirations and attainment and can pose problems for establishing savings and experimenting with new relationships (Bernhardt, Gahler, and Goldscheider 2005). For children who leave home late, the consequences are even less clear. Researchers have debated whether the extension of youth is a time for exploration (Arnett 2004) or an institutionalized moratorium whereby some youth are marginalized (Côté and Allahar 2006). Thus, the implications for leaving home late depend on why youth extend their dependency. If youth are extending dependency in order to accumulate identity, social, cultural, and financial capital, then they may benefit from remaining in the parental home (Côté 2000). However, if youth remain in the parental home due to a lack of opportunity and resources, then an extended period of dependency may harm young adults, impeding them from completing other intertwined transitions, such as school-to-work and domestic transitions (Côté and Allahar 2006). While the precise consequences of different launch times are unclear, different timings contribute to the differentiation in trajectories taken out of childhood and into adulthood, reflecting both different starting points and pathways actively and passively taken.

These discussions raise debate about the ideal age to transition and the impact on youth, their families, and society for transitioning or not.

The 1950s and 1960s are often idealized as a time when transitions were uniform and swift. Gill Jones (1995) notes that during this time domestic and housing transitions occurred soon after the transition from school to work was complete. If one takes a broader historical perspective, however, this period can be seen as an aberration rather than the norm. For instance, in the United States and other industrialized nations, the parents of today's youth left home earlier than any cohort before or since (Goldscheider and Goldscheider 1998). The 1950s and 1960s cannot be used to set a normative standard on the timing and routes that today's youth should take out of the home since changes in the broader context have influenced the way in which these transitions are experienced and completed. However, they do provide a comparison from which current patterns of home leaving can be examined.

Although the context within which individuals transition into adulthood differs, the routes people take are similar. Youth leave the parental home for further education, employment, travel, military service, marriage, cohabitation, and independence. While the routes that youth take to leave the parental home are similar to those of previous generations, changes in the patterns of family formation and dissolution have altered the proportion of individuals seeking specific routes. For instance, marriage used to be one of the main routes out of the home, but with the increase in age at first marriage, higher proportions of youth are taking alternative routes (Jones 1995).

The changing nature of when and how individuals transition into adulthood can be conceptualized as a reflection of increased flexibility in the life course and family. Presently, changes in society, which are characteristic of late modernity, have led to increased flexibility and a deinstitutionalization of distinct life stages (Côté 2000; Allan 2008). Increased flexibility and a lack of standardization in the life course result in each life stage being less predictable, which has two implications for the present discussion. First, a deinstitutionalization of distinct life stages makes it increasingly difficult to judge the beginning and end of one life stage from another. The earlier discussion on the changing nature of dependency and the attainment of adulthood demonstrates a complex situation – young people who are trying to attain adulthood in contemporary society are faced with a lack of standardization. The second implication pertains to the second goal of this chapter. Specifically, increased flexibility in family dissolution has altered the family environment and the experiences that children have in childhood, contributing to the disappearance of childhood as a uniform, traditional set of experiences. This absence is of significance because experiences in childhood have the ability to alter experiences at the end of childhood and the transition into adulthood for many young people, and this process will be illustrated through an empirical example: examining the end of childhood in relation to one family transition – parental divorce. It is to this discussion that we now turn.

Leaving Home in the Context of Family Dissolution

The second goal of this chapter is to highlight how experiences of family dissolution in childhood can alter childhood and its end. This portrayal will be illustrated with an empirical example of the relationship between parental divorce and the age at which individuals first leave the parental home. The purpose of providing an empirical example is to aid in the discussion of the complex, ever-changing nature of childhood, its end, and the attainment of adulthood in contemporary society.

Parental divorce in childhood has been linked to a diverse range of short- and long-term outcomes for children. These outcomes include lower educational aspirations and attainment, poorer relationships with parents, lower psychological well-being, and an increased risk of experiencing divorce in their own marriages (Amato and Booth 2000). In regard to leaving home, researchers have found that children from non-traditional and non-intact families leave home earlier than those from intact families (Mitchell, Wister, and Burch 1989; Zhao, Rajulton, and Ravanera 1995). Specifically, living with a step-parent, coming from a divorced background, and a high-conflict family home are all associated with early departure (Bernhardt, Gahler, and Goldscheider 2005). Moreover, it has been argued that the number of people leaving home due to family problems is increasing because of the increase in divorce, reconstituted families, and single-parent families (Jones 1995). Whether individuals leave early due to childhood changes in the family structure is complicated by the increasing variation within the ways that individuals are leaving home, as discussed earlier, as well as the increased flexibility in norms and values surrounding family life.

While transitional markers of adulthood have broken down, so have normative understandings of family life, resulting in increased flexibility in ideals and practices. Demographic markers of the changing nature of family life in industrialized nations include high rates of marital dissolution, increases in the age at first marriage and parenthood, and same-sex marriage (Allan 2008). Changes in family practices have been coupled by changes in individual and social values surrounding marriage, divorce, and parenthood. In industrialized nations, there has been an increase in the acceptance of divorce (Amato et al. 2009). Increased variation in cultural ideals of marriage and family has resulted in more individual-ized understandings of family life. Competing ideologies of marriage and individualism have led to a contradiction in cultural ideals for personal life. Marriage as a lifelong commitment continues as an ideal, while divorce is acceptable and desirable if a marriage becomes detrimental to an individual's self-development (Cherlin 2009). Thus, while the majority of the population still marries, the permanence of marital unions is no longer assumed, and alternative ways of coupling and uncoupling have emerged.

Observed changes in practices, norms, and values are of consequence because they influence the number of individuals who experience family transition and their short- and long-term adjustment (Amato 2000). While parental divorce may alter individuals' life courses, the extent to which this alteration occurs as attitudes toward marriage and divorce become more permissive is unclear (Cherlin, Kiernan, and Chase-Lansdale 1995). For instance, shifts in the cultural meaning of marriage, divorce, and family life could alter negative consequences of experiencing parental divorce as a result of increased social acceptance and institu-tionalized norms and practices that support families and children through family restructuring. For these reasons, attitudes toward marriage will be included in this chapter's analysis to emphasize the complexity and unpredictability of childhood and its end. Overall, by looking at the relationship between parental divorce, leaving home, and attitudes toward marriage, changes in the family environment that have decreased the predictability of childhood and its end are emphasized.

Exploring Parental Divorce, Age at Leaving Home, and Attitudes toward Marriage

The aim of providing an empirical example is to demonstrate the com-plexity and unpredictability of childhood and its end. Through the empirical example, the ways in which experiences of parental divorce in childhood impact the age when individuals leave home for the first time will be explored. We will also see how the presence of emotional and financial resources in the family of origin accumulate and become part of the fabric that supports or hinders young people as they make their way out of the parental home.

Initial Research Questions

To explore the relationships among parental divorce, the age at first home leaving, and attitudes toward marriage, the following research questions were posed: Is there a direct effect between experiencing parental divorce and the age at leaving home? Is there a direct relationship between attitudes toward marriage and the age at leaving home? Do individuals' attitudes toward marriage moderate or mediate the relationship between parental divorce and the age at leaving home?

Data and Variables

Analysis was based on data from the 2001 General Social Survey (GSS) based on public use microdata (Statistics Canada Manual 2003). The GSS is a sample survey with a cross-sectional design aimed at providing researchers and policy makers with information about changes in Canadian families. Data collection occurred from February 2001 to December 2001. The target population was non-institutionalized persons who were fifteen years of age or older, living in the ten provinces of Canada. A subsample of individuals ranging in age from seventeen to thirty was taken (N = 788) to minimize generational and cohort issues during interpretation.

Dependent Variable

A single indicator was used to measure the age at which respondents first left home. During this analysis, the age at first home leaving was recoded to represent three groups of home leavers: early (fourteen to seventeen), on time (eighteen), and late (nineteen to thirty). The criterion for early, on-time, and late home leaving was established based on conceptual and practical justifications. Conceptually, young people are increasingly being seen as beginning their transition into adulthood at the age of eighteen, with the first transition typically being leaving the parental home (Arnett 2004). Furthermore, the perception of young people becoming or beginning to become adults at the age of eighteen is supported by institutional configurations in Canada that structure school-to-work transitions and citizenship rights. Practically, on examination of the data, the median age at which individuals left the parental home was eighteen years of age.

Independent Variables

Parental divorce was measured using a single indicator in which respondents were asked whether they had experienced parental divorce during childhood. Attitudes toward marriage were similarly measured by a single indicator in which respondents were asked how important being married would be to their overall happiness. Gender, the number of siblings that a respondent grew up with, the mother's education, the closeness of the mother and father, and the perception of a happy childhood were also entered into analysis.

Analysis

Logistic regression analyses were performed separately for each of the three categories: early, on-time, and late home leavers, with eight predictors: gender, mother's education,[1] total number of siblings, closeness of mother and father, happy childhood, parental divorce, and attitude toward marriage. Three separate models were created for each group to eliminate issues with findings from early home leavers and late home leavers cancelling each other out. Overall, 788 cases were available for analysis. Within the sample, 235 individuals left home on time, 248 individuals left home early, and 305 individuals left home late. Table 6.1 shows regression coefficients and odds ratios for each of the three models and their eight predictors.

A test of the full Model 1, early home leavers, with all eight predictors against a constant-only model was statistically significant – X^2 (8, N = 788) = 184.89, p < 0.001 – indicating that the predictors, as a set, reliably distinguished between early home leavers and all other home leavers. According to the Wald criterion, mother's education, number of siblings, closeness to father, happy childhood, parental divorce, and importance of marriage reliably predicted early home leaving. The odds ratios demonstrated that individuals whose mothers had some university or more were 52 percent less likely to leave early than those whose mothers had high school or lower. For every increase in the number of siblings, individuals were 15 percent more likely to leave home early. Individuals who reported being very close to their fathers were 31 percent less likely to leave home early than those who reported low closeness to fathers. Individuals who reported having a very happy childhood were 47 percent less likely to leave home early than those who reported not having a very happy childhood. Individuals who experienced parental divorce were 68 percent more likely to leave home early than those who did not experience parental divorce, and individuals who reported that marriage was important to their overall happiness were 43 percent less likely to leave home early. These findings are consistent with Barbara Mitchell's (1994) argument that suggests that those with fewer family emotional and economic resources leave the parental home earlier.

A test of the full Model 2, on-time home leavers, with all eight predictors against a constant-only model was statistically significant – X^2 (8, N = 788) = 42.21, p < 0.001 – indicating that the predictors, as a

Table 6.1

Final models for early, on-time, and late home leavers

Model Variables	Early home leavers β	Early home leavers Odds ratio	On-time home leavers β	On-time home leavers Odds ratio	Late home leavers β	Late home leavers Odds ratio
Gender	0.17	1.18	0.39	1.47*	-0.49	0.61***
Mother's education	–	0.84	0.12	1.13	0.05	1.05
	-0.18	0.48***	–	0.98	0.57	1.78**
	–		-0.02			
	-0.73					
Number of siblings	0.14	1.15*	0.02	1.03	-0.15	0.86*
Closeness to father	-0.53	0.59**	0.62	1.86**	0.05	0.96
Closeness to mother	-0.24	0.78	0.20	1.22	0.15	1.16
Happy childhood	-0.64	0.53*	0.20	1.22	0.61	1.83*
Parental divorce	0.52	1.68**	-0.08	0.93	-0.44	0.64*
Importance of marriage	-0.56	0.57***	0.02	1.02	0.48	1.62**
Constant	0.36	1.43	-2.01	0.13	-0.86	0.42

Notes: * $p < 0.05$, ** $p < 0.01$, *** $p < 0.001$

set, reliably distinguished between on-time home leavers and all other home leavers. According to the Wald criterion, gender and father closeness reliably predicted on-time home leaving. The odds ratio for gender indicates that women were 47 percent more likely to leave home on time than men. For father closeness, the odds ratio demonstrated that individuals who reported that they were very close to their fathers were 86 percent more likely to leave home on time than those who reported low closeness. These findings suggest that on-time home leavers may have the emotional and financial resources to begin transitioning into adulthood despite the risks that youth face.

A test of the full Model 3, late home leavers, with all eight predictors against a constant-only model was statistically significant – $X^2 (8, N = 788) = 127.12$, $p < 0.001$ – indicating that the predictors, as a set, reliably distinguished between late leavers and all other home leavers. According to the Wald criterion, gender, mother's education, number of siblings, happy childhood, parental divorce, and importance of marriage reliably predicted late home leaving. The odds ratios demonstrate that women were 29 percent less likely to leave home late than men. Individuals whose mothers had some university or more were 78 percent more likely to leave home late than those whose mothers had high school or less. For every increase in the number of siblings, the odds of leaving home late decreased by 14 percent. Individuals who reported having a happy childhood were 83 percent more likely to leave home late than those who did not. Individuals who experienced parental divorce were 36 percent less likely to leave home late, and individuals who reported that marriage was very important to their overall happiness were 62 percent more likely to leave home late. Findings for Model 3 suggest that late home leavers perceive the advantages of having more family economic and emotional resources than other home leavers. This is consistent with previous research that sees late home leaving as a privilege of those who are able to draw on family resources, while they try to make their way through education, employment and housing transitions in difficult times (Côté and Bynner 2008).

Possible moderating and mediating effects of attitudes toward marriage were also explored. Attitudes toward marriage are of consequence because they may change the way in which parental divorce impacts home leaving and thus indicate the complexity of the home-leaving process. A moderator can be defined as an interaction effect, where the relationship between two variables changes when the third variable is entered into the regression (Baron and Kenny 1986). The interaction terms of parental divorce and the importance of marriage were entered into the regression for all three models. No moderating effect was found. However, a mediating relationship between parental divorce, the importance of marriage, and the age at leaving home was found.

A mediator can be defined as an indirect or chain relationship, where there is a statistically significant relationship between each of the three variables (Baron and Kenny 1986). Table 6.2 shows the regression coefficient and odds ratio for parental divorce as a predictor of attitudes toward marriage. The odds ratio for parental divorce indicates that individuals whose parents divorced or separated were 44 percent less likely to view marriage as being important, when compared to individuals from intact families. There is not, however, a perfect mediator because parental divorce still affects the age at first home leaving when the importance of marriage is controlled. Thus, the importance of marriage is just one out of many possible mediating factors.

Findings suggest that individuals who view marriage as being important to their happiness are less likely to leave home early and more likely to leave home late than those who view marriage as not being important to their happiness. Individuals who view marriage as being important may be taking different routes out of the home from those who do not

Table 6.2

Parental divorce as a predictor of attitude toward the importance of marriage

Variables	β	Odds ratio
Divorce	-0.59	0.56*
Constant	0.99	2.71

Note: * p < 0.001.

view it as being important to their happiness. As well as indicating alternative routes out of the home, attitudes toward marriage can also be an indicator of how much of an effect parental divorce may have on an individual's adjustment. While the present analysis does not allow for inference about the specific pathways that differing attitudes toward marriage influence, it provides evidence that future research is needed to unravel the pathways through which individual and broader social attitudes are of consequence to children's short- and long-term adjustment to divorce.

Discussion
The aim of this chapter was two-fold: to situate childhood's end within a discussion of the changing nature of maturity and dependency and to demonstrate how increased unpredictability in childhood can alter the end as well as the beginning of adulthood. Demonstrating how childhood family transition is connected to adulthood is just one example of how individual experiences of childhood and its end are becoming increasingly differentiated. With this in mind, leaving home, parental divorce, and the relationship between the two have been used as tools through which to discuss the complex nature of childhood and its end as an increasingly unpredictable time in one's life.

To this effect, direct, moderating, and mediating relationships were explored between parental divorce, the importance of marriage, and the age at first home leaving. Three models were produced to explore the direct relationships within the sample for each group of home leavers. Results from the logistic regression suggest that parental divorce and the number of siblings increased the odds of leaving home early, women and individuals who reported feeling close to their father were more likely to leave home on time, and individuals who reported having a mother with some university or more, who had had a happy childhood, and who placed high value on the importance of marriage were at increased odds of leaving home late.

The findings are consistent with previous research that sees the age at which youth take their first steps toward adulthood as being influenced by the financial and emotional resources available to them through their family of origin (Mitchell 1994). A mother's education, parental divorce, number of siblings, and the perception of parental closeness and a happy childhood are all indicators of positive or negative family economic and emotional support. For early home leavers, greater numbers of siblings and parental divorce can decrease the availability and transference of financial resources. In contrast, findings from on-time home leaving suggest that it is women, along with people who reported feeling close to their fathers, who were more likely to leave on time. For this latter group, being close to one's father is likely to act as an indicator of his availability and readiness to provide financial and emotional support. Similarly, findings for late home leavers suggest that individuals who have remained in the parental home perceive there to be more family economic and emotional resources than those who are leaving earlier. Situated within the debate over whether the extension of youth serves as a time for exploration or an institutionalized moratorium, findings support the notion that the extension of youth as a time for exploration is a "middle-class" phenomenon that may mask the difficulty of attaining adulthood today (Arnett 2004; Côté and Allahar 2006). This finding suggests that experiencing "emerging adulthood" is more available to youth who have a familial safety net (Côté and Bynner 2008).

Whether individuals leave early or late, however, the consequences of being off time in a primary transition – from childhood to adulthood – may ripple through to subsequent transitions. Situated within a life-course framework, individual and family characteristics accumulate, some acting as advantages and others acting as disadvantages that youth can use or need to overcome, as they move through subsequent life-transitions. Parental divorce and its influence on the age of home leaving and educational attainment is one example of how individual, family, and social conditions compound as individuals move through different life stages. Young people who experience more than one adverse situation are at greater risk. For instance, parental divorce is associated with leaving home early; individuals who leave home early are at risk for lower educational attainment (Bernhardt, Gahler, and Goldscheider 2005); and family dissolution has been found to be related to lower educational investment by parents (Goldscheider and Goldscheider 1998) as well as an unwillingness or inability of youth to return to the parental home when support is needed (Mitchell 2006). Consequentially, if individuals who experience parental divorce leave the parental home earlier, they may be at higher risk of lower educational attainment than those who have not experienced parental divorce or those who remain in the parental home longer. Therefore, parental divorce may stimulate an alternative life-course pattern beginning at the age when they first leave home and rippling through to subsequent transitions, with the consequences of leaving home early being compounded by the increased obstacles that young people who experience parental divorce may face.

As a result, the end of childhood is further complicated by the uncertainty and ambiguity of family life. While direct analysis suggests that parental divorce is significantly related to the age at which youth first leave the parental home, with attitudes toward marriage functioning as a mediator, the extent to which parental divorce impacts outcomes in young adulthood and the way in which these will persist or change as individual and broader societal values change require further investigation (Cherlin, Kiernan, and Chase-Lansdale 1995). Individual and social values affect the way in which individuals experience parental divorce as well as reflecting changes in institutional structures that support individuals and families through restructuring. Much of the existing literature, thus far, has focused on the ways in which marriage and divorce are changing in industrialized nations, particularly in the United States (for example, Hackstaff 1999; Cherlin 2009). There are, however, significant differences in the proportions of Americans and Canadians experiencing specific patterns of family transition (Cherlin 2009). For these reasons, Canadian research is needed both to understand the consequences of these differences for individuals experiencing these events and to examine the impact of Canadian cultural ideals of marriage, divorce, and family life. With an understanding of the cultural context within which individuals are experiencing and adjusting to parental divorce, a more holistic understanding of the consequences can be explored. This is of particular relevance in a social world that is characterized by fluidity and increased differentiation. For while normative markers of the end of childhood have become more negotiable, so have the understandings of family life. Understanding the individual and social experience of becoming an adult in the context of the changing nature of dependency, maturity, and family life will provide an interesting foundation for future work.

Childhood and its end is a complex socially constructed process that depends on individual characteristics and societal conditions. As Bob Coles (1995, 6-7) has suggested, "there is no clear end to the status of childhood and no clear age at which young people are given full adult rights and responsibilities." With this notion in mind, future research should be directed at conceptualizing home leaving as a process with efforts made to track individual subjectivities and pathways through which different time-varying covariates influence young people's life trajectories and everyday experiences. The growth of interest in youth studies will undoubtedly fuel researchers to pursue these exciting lines of inquiry.

As researchers move forward in explaining the end of childhood and the transition to adulthood, theoretical and analytical flexibility will prove to be essential (Allan and Crow 2001). The ambiguity that surrounds age-specific constructions of normatively prescribed life events is inherent in the tendency to see increasing differentiation within late modernity (Wallace and Kovatcheva 1998). As the context within which individuals leave home continues to change and normative timetables begin to shift, the concept of being on or off time may no longer capture the lived experiences of individual home leavers (Jones 2009). Although increasing differentiation can be seen as defining and structuring individuals' experiences in late modernity, it is essential not to let the perception of choice mask underlying longstanding social inequalities that still shape individuals' lives (Furlong and Cartmel 2007). Thus, continually questioning the causes, consequences, and meaning behind youths' experiences is necessary in order to be critically aware of the disappearance of childhood and its end as a uniform and traditional set of experiences and the possible consequences that this process has for young people's past, present, and future.

Acknowledgments
The author would like to extend special thanks to Graham Allan for his guidance and supervision as well as to Nathanael Lauster, Carrie Yodanis, and James Côté for comments and suggestions on earlier drafts.

Notes
1   The father's education was also available in the dataset. However, there was high multi-collinearity between the mother's and father's education. A comparison between a full model with the mother's education and a full model with the father's education – $X^2 (8, N = 788) = 0$, $p > 0.25$ – resulted in no statistical difference in prediction. Therefore, the mother's education was used in the final model production.

References
Allan, G. 2008. "Flexibility, Friendship, and Family." *Personal Relationships* 15: 1-16.
Allan, G., and G. Crow. 2001. *Families, Households and Society.* New York: Palgrave.

Amato, P. 2000. "The Consequences of Divorce for Adults and Children." *Journal of Marriage and Family* 62: 1269-87.

Amato, P., and A. Booth. 2000. *A Generation at Risk: Growing Up in an Era of Family Upheaval.* London: Harvard University Press.

Amato, P., A. Booth, D. Johnson, and S. Rogers. 2009. *Alone Together: How Marriage in America Is Changing.* London: Harvard University Press.

Arnett, J. 2004. *Emerging Adulthood: The Winding Road from the Late Teens through the Twenties.* New York: Oxford University Press.

Baron, R., and D. Kenny. 1986. "The Moderator-Mediator Variable Distinction in Social Psychological Research: Conceptual, Strategic, and Statistical Considerations." *Journal of Personality and Social Psychology* 51: 1173-82.

Beaujot, R., and D. Kerr. 2007. "Emerging Youth Transition Patterns in Canada: Opportunities and Risks." Discussion Paper. Policy Research Initiative Project: Investing in Youth, http://ir.lib.uwo.ca/.

Bernhardt, E., M. Gahler, and F. Goldscheider. 2005. "Childhood Family Structure and Routes out of the Parental Home in Sweden." *Acta Sociologica* 48: 99-115.

Cherlin, A. 2009. *The Marriage-Go-Round: The State of Marriage and the Family in America Today.* New York: Alfred A. Knopf.

Cherlin, A., K. Kiernan, and P. Chase-Lansdale. 1995. "Parental Divorce in Childhood and Demographic Outcomes in Young Adulthood." *Demography* 32: 299-318.

Coles, B. 1995. *Youth and Social Policy.* London: University College London Press.

Côté, J. 2000. *Arrested Adulthood: The Changing Nature of Maturity and Identity.* New York: New York University Press.

Côté, J., and A. Allahar. 2006. *Critical Youth Studies: A Canadian Focus.* Pearson: Educational Publishing.

Côté, J., and J. Bynner. 2008. "Changes in the Transition to Adulthood in the United Kingdom and Canada: The Role of Structure and Agency in Emerging Adulthood." *Journal of Youth Studies* 11: 251-67.

Furlong, A., and F. Cartmel. 2007. *Young People and Social Change: New Perspectives.* New York: Open University Press.

Furstenberg, F., ed. 2002. "Early Adulthood in Cross-National Perspectives." *The Annals of the American Academy of Political and Social Science* 580. Thousand Oaks, CA: Sage.

Goldscheider, F., and C. Goldscheider. 1998. "The Effects of Childhood Family Structure on Leaving and Returning Home." *Journal of Marriage and the Family* 60: 745-56.

Grossman, L. 2005. "Grow Up? Not So Fast." *Time,* 24 January, 26-35.

Hackstaff, K. 1999. *Marriage in a Culture of Divorce.* Philadelphia: Temple University Press.

Jones, G. 1995. *Leaving Home.* Buckingham, UK: Open University Press.

–. 2009. *Youth.* Malden, MA: Polity.

Mitchell, B. 1994. "Family Structure and Leaving the Nest: A Social Resource Perspective." *Sociological Perspectives* 37: 651-71.

–. 2006. "The Boomerang Age from Childhood to Adulthood: Emergent Trends and Issues for Aging Families." *Canadian Studies in Population* 33: 155-78.

Mitchell, B., A. Wister, and T. Burch. 1989. "The Family Environment and Leaving the Parental Home." *Journal of Marriage and the Family* 51: 605-13.

Statistics Canada Manual. 2003. *2001 General Social Survey, Cycle 15: Family History. Housing, Family and Social Statistics*. Doc. CAT#12M0015GPE. Ottawa: Ministry of Industry Ottawa.

Wallace, C., and S. Kovatcheva. 1998. *Youth in Society: The Construction and Deconstruction of Youth in East and West Europe*. New York: St. Martin's Press.

Zhao, J., F. Rajulton, and Z. Ravanera. 1995. "Leaving Parental Homes in Canada: Effects of Family Structure, Gender and Culture." *Canadian Journal of Sociology* 20: 31-50.

7

The Disappearance of Parents from Children's Lives: The Cumulative Effects of Child Care, Child Custody, and Child Welfare Policies in Canada

Edward Kruk

> The true measure of a nation's standing is how well it attends
> to its children – their health and safety, their material security,
> their education and socialization, and their sense of being
> loved, valued, and included in the families and societies into
> which they were born (UNICEF 2007).

This chapter examines the "disappearance of children" by foregrounding the issue of parental disengagement from the lives of children in three contexts:

- child care – children spending less time in their parents' care and more in non-parental care, associated with federal and provincial child care policies that discourage parental involvement;
- child custody – the legal exclusion of "non-custodial" divorced parents from the daily routines of children's lives, linked to policies that re-move custodial rights and responsibilities from one parent after parental divorce; and
- child protection – the disengagement of parents of children in state care, connected to policies that emphasize child removal over family preservation and discourage ongoing parental contact and family reunification.

I will argue, first, that these factors have contributed to a significant reduction in parental time with children; second, that declining parental involvement levels are associated with increased dissatisfaction among parents in regard to their parental role; and, third, that the social policies that discourage parental involvement are significant contributing factors to the "disappearance of children" in Canada, as reflected in the declining fertility rate (see Chapter 1 by Mira Whyman, Megan Lemmon, and Jay Teachman and Chapter 2 by Nathanael Lauster, Todd F. Martin, and James M. White in this volume). Current Canadian federal and provincial government policies discourage parental involvement in children's lives and reflect a pervasive devaluing of the role of parents in children's lives.

Current levels of parental involvement in children's lives in Canada fall short of what parents actually desire, as parents want to spend more time with their children but encounter a multitude of constraints (Bibby 2003). Canadians continue to report that their families are more important to them than their political convictions, religious beliefs, jobs, and wages. For most Canadians, family life is about relationships in which they are taken care of, in which they assume the responsibility to take care of others, and in which parents' responsibility to their children remains paramount (Bibby 2003). Involvement in child care has been shown to reduce parental depression. Ranae Evenson and Robin Simon (2005) conclude that the primary benefits of active parenting are a sense of purpose in life and personal gratification, with the highest level of depression occurring among adults who have a child under the age of eighteen with whom they are not living or actively involved.

Yet with rising levels of parental role strain, role overload, and role conflict, as well as a lack of adequate state support for parental involvement, children are bearing the brunt of decreased parental involvement. In the 2007 United Nations Children's Fund (UNICEF) report on the well-being of children in the economically advanced nations, Canada ranked relatively high in regard to children's material and educational well-being. However, it ranked extremely low – eighteenth out of twenty-one countries – in regard to the same children's family relationships, particularly with respect to spending time with their parents. At the same time, Canadian children scored high on problematic behavioural and risk measures such as substance abuse, violence, and risk taking. In regard to the subjective factor of well-being, Canadian children ranked very low – the rate of youth suicide in Canada and depression in children is of particular concern. The problem of youth suicide is most acute among Aboriginal youth, for whom the suicide rate is seven times higher than the national average, and among Inuit youth, for whom it is eleven times higher. Although "child poverty" continues to be defined primarily in economic terms by Canadian child advocacy groups such as Campaign 2000, the "poverty of parental involvement" is increasingly being recognized as central to children's compromised emotional well-being, particularly in terms of youth depression and suicide, early engagement in sexual activity, addiction, and youth crime (National Center on Addiction and Substance Abuse 2005; Statistics Canada 2007).[1]

Child Care Policy

The 2002 *National Work-Life Conflict Study,* which was a Health Canada-sponsored project examining the balance of work and life in a sample of 33,000 Canadians across the country, noted a "precipitous decline" in the amount of time that parents are spending with their children over a ten-year period, 1991-2001 (Higgins and Duxbury 2002). The decline was most marked among mothers. In ten years, mothers' time with their children had declined by 33 percent, primarily the result of increased time spent in paid work outside the home. However, despite the prevailing rhetoric that fathers are increasing their parenting time, fathers' time in paid employment also increased, and their time with their children also declined by 15 percent. A study of time usage by Statistics Canada (2005a) revealed that in 2005 Canadian workers spent forty-five minutes less per day with family members than they spent with them in 1985.

According to Reginald Bibby (2003), although 90 percent of Canadian adults report that a two-parent home in which parents are able to raise their children is the ideal child care arrangement, they believe that a broad array of child care options should be available within a society of diverse values and heterogeneous family forms. Most parents of dependent children would prefer part-time paid work to the full-time arrangements they actually have in order to allow them the time they would like (and say they need) for the care of their children as well as other dependents. In Bibby's study, after at-home parental care, parents' second child care preference was grandparent care; then care by another relative; and, finally, child care in a home setting. Yet the child care debate in Canada has focused almost entirely on financially supporting the out-of-home regulated daycare option. Many Canadian parents thus feel derailed in regard to achieving their ideal child care arrangement, as they find themselves having to subcontract care to third parties outside the home.

The province of Quebec has been held up as a model jurisdiction with respect to child care provision, with substantial subsidies for daycare centres but reduced direct financial benefits to parents themselves. With the introduction of the Quebec daycare program in 1997, the provincial government removed many of its universal benefits for children, including its generous family allowance, which in 1997 was $8,000 after the birth of a third child. The non-refundable credit for dependent children under the age of eighteen and the tax reduction for low-income families were scrapped. Instead, the daycare program provides over $32 per day per child in daycare (paid to providers) so that parents need only pay $7 per day. The imbalance between those individuals getting financial help and those who are not has been a common criticism by home care activists in Quebec, since only 48 percent of the province's children use subsidized daycare, although all parents are obliged to pay for it.[2] Anti-poverty groups argue that the state's subsidy of daycare is unfair since the wealthy get the same tax break as do the poor, as long as they use daycare. The current cost of the Quebec daycare plan is $1.5 billion per year. Norma Kozhaya (2006) found that the families who benefited most from the Quebec subsidized daycare system were those that earned a higher income: 58 percent of the children who got subsidized daycare were from homes with incomes over $60,000, although in total only 49 percent are from that income sector. Philip Lefebvre (2002) also found that children who attended daycare in Quebec were from more privileged backgrounds than children who did not, with only 22 percent of the very poorest children in the province being in daycare. Both Lefebvre and Kozhaya concluded that, administratively, daycare is very costly, with the expense to the state being $11,600 per child in Quebec.[3] In the United States, the RAND Corporation, who along with the World Bank have strongly supported preferential government funding for daycare, surveyed the various costs associated with daycares (Datar 2005). Excluding capital, rent, major repairs, and food, costs averaged $15,217 per year for infants, $11,827 for two-year-olds, and $9,678 for three- to five-year-olds.

The benefits of daycare provision for preschool children's cognitive development have been documented by several studies, yet the major finding of the United States–based National Institute of Child Health and Development (NICHD) was that children who were cared for exclusively by their mothers did not develop differently from those who were also cared for by others (Friendly 2008; Mustard 2008). Lynda Gagne's (2003) analysis of the influence of parental labour market participation and the use of substitute child care on the cognitive development of preschool children in Canada found little effect on the school readiness scores of most preschool children. Children from higher-income families in substitute care exhibited better cognitive outcomes than children from lower-income families, possibly because children in higher-income families were exposed to a higher quality of substitute care or because of the advantages of growing up in a family with greater resources.

Sarah-Eve Farquhar (2008) expressed concerns with problems of bias in many daycare-based studies based on non-representative samples. She found that good outcomes at a daycare may not be caused by the daycare given the many home-based educational experiences that those children have. She concluded that parents have a far greater impact than early childhood education experiences on children's developmental outcomes. While children may exhibit cognitive gains (at least in the short term), their social and emotional development has been consistently found to be negatively affected by the daycare experience, particularly in regard to behavioural problems and aggression.

Michael Baker, Jonathan Gruber, and Kevin Milligan's (2005) analysis of the Quebec daycare system found the impact on children to be dramatic. On a variety of behavioural and health outcomes, ranging from aggression to motor skills to social skills to illness, daycare children fared worse than stay-at-home children. Bruce Fuller (2007) found a slower pace of social development and higher incidence of lack of sharing among daycare children. Bernardine Woo (2007) found that children cared for at daycare centres were twice as likely to develop mental health problems as children cared for by their parents. Susanna Loeb et al. (2005), in a study for the US National Center for Education Statistics, reported serious negative social and emotional effects associated with the daycare experience, compared to home-based care. The NICHD (2006) found that children attending daycare for over thirty hours per week had three times as many behavioural problems as children in third-party care for under ten hours per week. In a follow up to the NICHD study, Steve Biddulph (2006) discovered that cortisol is secreted at twice the rate when preschool children are in third-party care, and he concluded that children under the age of one need a one-to-one relationship with a caregiver. Lise Dubois and Manon Girard (2005) found that daycares expose children to more disease and put children at risk of infection and that daycare children are prescribed a much higher level of antibiotic medication. Similarly, Norman Doidge (2007, 287) concluded that what works best for children's brain development is a "one-on-one exposure in a warm emotional bath of parent-child connection." Jay Belsky (2007) concludes that in the first five years of life, the more hours a child spends in third-party care, the higher the levels of future problem behaviour.

Directions for Child Care Policy Reform

There is no question that a national daycare program would be a support to Canadian parents and would serve to relieve some of the role strain, conflict, and overload that parents experience (Friendly 2008). However, a child care program that funds only one option of care – the regulated daycare sector – overlooks the needs of families who provide, or wish to provide, more in-home family-based care for their children and is a disincentive to the parental care of children. The establishment of a national daycare program, providing a network of accessible "high quality" non-profit daycare centres across the country, is the culmination of a policy trend that has steadily decreased and removed direct child care benefits to parents, such as universal family allowances, which is a significant factor in reducing parental child care involvement.

A national strategy that featured parental child care involvement would proceed in a very different fashion from a national daycare program since it would seek to provide incentives for parents to spend more time with their children as well as giving them autonomy over their child care options and providing a universal benefit that is inclusive of a broad array of parenting choices, including children in regulated daycare settings, in informal family day homes, or with trusted neighbours, children in the care of relatives such as grandparents, and children raised at home by their parents.

Lefebvre's (2002) analysis of the costs and benefits of state funding for various arrangements for the care of children concluded that the most efficient system would be a universal family allowance, suggesting annual amounts of $2,500 per child aged zero to three, $2,000 per child aged four to five years, and $1,500 per child aged six to seventeen years, which are similar to the amounts available in the United Kingdom. A figure that many child care advocates are now holding out as a baseline is a direct parental subsidy of $4,000 per year per child, which is more in keeping with the Scandinavian nations' funding patterns.[4] Finland, for example, has provided for many years a flat-rate child allowance to all children up to the age of three who are not in the daycare system, which amounts to $4,300 per year. An additional $238 per month is given to low-income families, totalling $595 per month or $7,104 per annum. Sweden's government has announced funding changes for its child care. Parents who use daycare will continue to receive state funding of $1,600 a month, and those who use home-based care, who have not received any government benefits before, will now get funding of $570 per month or $6,840 per year.[5]

Child Custody Policy
Child custody is another arena in which parental care of children is undermined by current social policy, with the removal of legal custody

from one parent in litigated cases and the absence of court-determined shared parenting arrangements. Divorcing parents who cannot agree on the post-separation living arrangements for their children are forced to rely on a judicial determination, and the "winner-take-all" "sole custody" approach removes child care responsibility from one parent, resulting in less overall parental involvement for children, as the "non-custodial" parent is granted periodic "access" to his or her children. Regardless of whether parents shared child care responsibility while living together, judges routinely limit and constrain the contact of the parent deemed "non-custodial" in favour of the "custodial" or "residential" parent. Despite evidence that shared parenting is a viable option to the sole custody system, the alternative of shared parental care after a conflictual parental separation is assumed by the Canadian judiciary to be unworkable and not in children's best interests (Kruk 2008). Although recent research on Canadian child custody outcomes in contested cases is lacking, court file analysis data reveal that in 77 percent of contested custody cases child custody is awarded solely to the mother, and solely to the father in only 8.6 percent of cases, with shared physical custody arrangements being virtually non-existent (Department of Justice 1990; Millar and Goldenberg 2004). Sole custody is enshrined in provincial child and family legislation, such as British Columbia's Family Relations Act.[6] Although section 27(1) of the act states that, "whether or not married to each other and for so long as they live together, the mother and father of a child are joint guardians," on separation, according to section 27(2), "the one of them who usually has care and control of the child is sole guardian of the person of the child."

The sole custody model, prevalent in Canadian courts, flies in the face of recent research on child and family outcomes, which indicates that the most salient factor in children's adjustment to the consequences of their parents' divorce is the protection and continuation of parental involvement in children's lives and that shared parenting arrangements are most likely to shield children from parental conflict (Kelly 2000; Bauserman 2002; Kruk 2008). Further, the notion that children's interests will best be served by sole custody is not in accord with child development theory – children form primary attachment bonds with each of their parents, and their well-being primarily depends on maintaining these relationships (Kelly 2000).

A recent large-scale US study of young adult children who have lived through parental divorce concludes that most children want to spend roughly equal amounts of time with each of their parents after separation and consider such "shared parenting" to be in their best interests

(Fabricius 2003). Further, a recent meta-analysis of the thirty-three major North American studies comparing outcomes in joint versus sole custody arrangements reveals that children in joint arrangements fare significantly better than children in sole custody arrangements on every measure of adjustment, both general and divorce-specific (Bauserman 2002). The study also found that conflict between parents in shared custody arrangements lessens over time, and increases in sole custody arrangements, as parents threatened by the loss of their children and their parental identity continue to battle years after their actual physical separation. Half of first-time serious family violence occurs after separation, within the current adversarial "winner-take-all" sole custody system (Corcoran and Melamed 1990; Statistics Canada 2004). Canada lags behind several US jurisdictions, Australia, France, Sweden, and other countries in reforming child custody law and practice in a manner that positions children's needs for the active involvement of both parents in their lives at the forefront of child custody legislation.

Directions for Child Custody Policy Reform

Contrary to current practice and dominant socio-legal discourse in Canada, new evidence suggests that when parents disagree over the living arrangements of their children after parental separation, the children's positive post-separation adjustment is best achieved by means of a legal shared parental responsibility presumption. This is defined as children spending at least 40 percent of their time with each parent, rebuttable when a child is in need of protection from a parent (Kruk 2005). The current framework of sole physical custody in contested cases is associated with high rates of father (and sometimes mother) absence, increased inter-parental conflict, and a marked reduction in children's standard of living (Kelly 2000). The standard of living of non-residential parents is even lower than of custodial parents, and an adversarial battle over child custody can easily drain a family's financial resources (Braver and Stockburger 2005). A presumption of equal time for children with each parent after divorce, where parents share child care responsibilities and each continue to play an active role in their children's lives, would not only have immediate and beneficial consequences for the children but would also provide a powerful symbol of the importance of continuing parent-child relationships and their immunity to the termination of the marital or cohabiting relationship.

For the minority of separations involving serious family violence, criminal sanctions against those family members who perpetrate the violence are necessary, and, in such cases, the courts need to retain their traditional role in the determination of custody. Further, a system that draws a clear line between criminal law and child custody determination would hold accountable those who falsely allege abuse in custody cases as well as those who perpetrate abuse.

A legally rebuttable presumption of shared parental responsibility (rebuttable in cases of established violence) would establish a legal expectation that existing parent-child relationships will continue after separation. In cases of dispute, shared parenting, defined as children spending roughly equal time with each of their parents, would be the legal presumption in the absence of family violence or child abuse. This would provide judges with a clear guideline and would preserve meaningful parental relationships between children and both of their parents, encourage parental involvement, increase cooperation, and reduce conflict. In diverting parents from a destructive court battle over their children's care, it would provide an incentive for parents to engage in therapeutic family mediation focused on the development of shared parenting plans. Such shared parental responsibility is in keeping with current caregiving trends as fathers are increasingly sharing responsibility for child care in two-parent families (Higgins and Duxbury 2002; Marshall 2006), and joint physical custody has emerged as the norm in non-litigated child custody cases (Statistics Canada 2005b).

Child Protection Policy
Canadian child protection policy and practice is a third arena in which parental involvement in children's lives is increasingly discouraged and devalued. This is evident in dramatically increased rates of children in state care, and child welfare agencies' continuing emphasis on child removal, at a time when other jurisdictions are directly focused on family preservation, supporting parents in the fulfillment of their parental responsibilities. A large increase in children apprehended and taken into government care has occurred since the mid-1990s in Canada. In Ontario alone, a 56 percent increase occurred in a five-year period, with 11,609 children in care in 1998, rising to 18,126 in 2003 (Swift and Parada 2004). The number of children in care across Canada increased from 40,000 in the early 1990s to 76,000 in 2000 (Child Welfare League of Canada 2003). Whereas in New York, which implemented a family preservation policy, the number dropped from 49,365 in 1992 to less than 19,000 in 2002 (Office of the Public Advocate of New York 2002), and the overall number of child abuse complaints declined by 52 percent.

Nico Trocme et al. (2005) noted a 125 percent increase in substantiated child abuse in Canada from 1998 to 2003, within the context of increased rates of child removal.

It is clear that a family preservation and support approach to child protection is associated with decreased child abuse rates, whereas rising rates of child apprehension, originally intended as a last resort, are not. Physical abuse is not the primary reason that children are removed from parental care in Canada. According to Trocme et al. (2005), physical harm to children occurred in only 10 percent of cases of substantiated maltreatment, with only 3 percent of cases requiring medical intervention. Apprehensions are generally the result of parents' struggles with poverty, addiction, and mental health problems (Eamon and Kopels 2004), with Aboriginal children being nearly ten times more likely to be in government care than non-Aboriginal children (Pivot Legal Society 2008).[7]

Most Canadian child protection agencies have embraced the use of standardized risk assessment tools, which have been heralded as providing an objective, standardized method to assess risk of abuse and neglect. There is no research, however, that has demonstrated the effectiveness of such risk assessments as predictors of future harm to children (Callahan and Swift 2007), and numerous concerns have been expressed about relying on such "deficit-based" approaches to assessment. Focusing on the past rather than on the present, parental weaknesses rather than strengths, and individual faults rather than structural factors contributing to parents' struggles, have been cited as fundamental flaws of the risk assessment approach (McKenzie, Palmer, and Barnard, 2008; Pivot Legal Society, 2008).

Once children are in state care, little emphasis is placed on reunification planning, as social workers have too many cases and too few resources to address underlying social and economic problems. The prescription of psychotropics for children in government care is a widespread practice, parental visits with children are not prioritized by social workers, and "supervised visits" discourage contact for parents whose children are in state care (Pivot Legal Society 2008).[8] The outcomes for children in the foster care system have been described as "devastating," with 73 percent of youth offenders in British Columbia coming from the child protection system, and only 21 percent of these children managing to graduate from high school, compared with 78 percent of the general population (Pivot Legal Society 2008).

Directions for Child Protection Policy Reform

Clearly, Canadian child protection policy and practice has strayed far from the goals of family preservation, support, and reunification as central to the child protection mandate, particularly in cases where physical or sexual abuse are not primary concerns. Parents are being removed from children's lives due to social problems such as poverty, addiction, and mental health struggles. Family preservation programs, respite care, and shared parenting, all of which motivate parents to take voluntary action toward reducing the risk of harm to their children, are not being utilized to the same degree as in other jurisdictions. The lack of funding parity between foster caregivers and family caregivers is also a major problem, as the financial resources made available to struggling family members caring for children are minimal.[9]

There are a number of collaborative alternatives that promote responsible parental involvement in children's lives via a family preservation approach to child protection: family group conferencing, child protection mediation, traditional circles, and family development responses. When parents require respite care for their children, "shared parenting" foster care models between birth parents and foster parents provide an alternative to parental removal from the children's lives. These alternatives focus on respite care support and emphasize co-parenting alliances between foster carers and birth parents, who are sometimes given the option of continuing to reside with the child, with a respite carer or "mentor family" available when needed. The key to such programs is encouraging parents to be actively involved in their children's care while building supportive and trusting relationships with child protection social workers. Parents retain primary responsibility for their children but are able to approach parenting as a team with a foster family.

When children are in state care and parents demonstrate a commitment to making changes to address child protection concerns, it is imperative that their commitment be recognized and supported by means of facilitating a family reunification process as quickly as possible, with required supports made available. The current impasse of inadequate resources to support parents in the fulfillment of their parental responsibilities must be addressed. Part of this initiative involves addressing the emotional consequences to the parent of child apprehension, which when unaddressed presents a significant barrier to successful family reunification. Finally, "risk assessment" models to child protection have come under scrutiny and been found wanting. New assessment tools are needed that take into account both family strengths and the systemic barriers that make it difficult for parents to be able to effectively address their children's needs.

Conclusion

Canadian child care, child custody, and child protection policies and systems represent significant barriers to parental involvement in children's lives. The absence of parents undermines children's psychological, emotional, and social well-being. In particular, the lack of state support for parental involvement is a disincentive to having children, and steps must be taken to reverse this trend. The unasked question in current debates in child care, child custody, and child protection policy remains: What are the responsibilities of government institutions to support parents in the fulfillment of their parental responsibilities?

Canadian families are experiencing increasing levels of work-family strain, conflict, and overload, and studies are showing a widening gulf between children and their parents, a sense of disconnection (Higgins and Duxbury 2002; Alexander 2008), with family ties not only undervalued but also actively discouraged in a system where loyalty to the free market takes precedence (Alexander 2008; Maté 2008). Family responsibilities are a major encumbrance to free-market societies. Thus, it is no surprise to find, in the preamble to Bill C-303 – a federal daycare funding initiative that has been inactive since the 2008 election – that the primary objective of Canadian child care policy is neither maximizing parental involvement nor the well-being of children but, rather, supporting "the participation of parents in employment or training and community life."[10] In such a climate, it is not surprising to find that 35 percent of parents do not take any paid or unpaid leave after having a birth or adoption in Canada (Lero 2007).

As Gary Teeple (1995) notes, child care, child custody, and child protection policy in Canada has changed dramatically within the social and economic context of neo-liberalism, which supports both the expansion of transnational corporate interests and the concomitant retrenchment of national welfare structures in the interests of facilitating corporate agendas. A program of legislative and policy change designed to reduce social spending and to dismantle programs aimed at supporting parents in addressing children's needs has been in effect since the mid-1990s. Programs designed to assist parents have been particularly hard hit, and the disappearance of parents from children's lives has been most evident after the introduction of measures to reduce the social safety net.

Does reducing the social safety net, and focusing on ensuring that parents are in paid employment and away from children, serve the best interests of children, and is this a universal principle the public endorses? Survey results reveal the opposite. Most parents want to see the current federal grant of $1,200 per child per year enriched to the point where it is "sufficient to have an impact upon parents' [child care] choices" (Ipsos Reid 2007, 5). Parents want to spend more time with their children.

The key to addressing the disappearance of parents from children's lives is a matter of the state directly supporting parents in the fulfillment of their parenting responsibilities. Such a "parental-responsibility-to-children's-needs" approach would, first and foremost, clearly acknowledge the central place of parents in children's lives. It would provide, in the realm of child care, direct family allowance payments to parents as well as other incentives for parents to spend more time with their children. In the area of child custody, it would provide legislative reform in the form of shared parental responsibility to protect parent-child relationships and parental reunification for children estranged from one of their parents via a sole custody decree. Finally, in the context of child protection, it would provide family preservation and support programs as well as greater family reunification efforts for children in government care.

A final note on the main theme of this volume – the disappearance of children. How will addressing the problem of the disappearance of parents from children's lives address the problem of the disappearance of children? Canada's declining fertility rate, which is currently at 1.66 – with the "replacement rate" of 2.1 children needed to adequately maintain the tax base, health care, and pension plan systems – has serious implications for social programs and the government's ability to provide needed human services (Statistics Canada 2009). If trends continue, by 2015, there will be more people in Canada over the age of sixty-five than those under the age of fifteen, and, by 2021, deaths will outnumber births.

The remedies to the "birth dearth" that have been traditionally suggested in Canada include having people earn longer and retire later, having teens in paid employment earlier, and having immigrants come to fill the void of taxpayers. What is rarely suggested is to encourage births. With many countries concerned about a declining birth rate, attention is beginning to focus on how to entice couples to become parents. Providing incentives for parents to spend more time with their children, since this seems to be a major consideration for parents in their decision to have children, is critical in this regard. In recognizing that households raising children have a reduced ability to pay tax, other nations have begun to introduce birth bonuses, deductions for the care of children, and vouchers for care costs. These initiatives help make having children more affordable and provide incentives for parental involvement. In Australia, birth grants of $4,133 per child have led to birth-rate increases, and, in Europe, generous tax breaks for parents have also had some success (Brusentsev and Vroman 2007). France reversed its birth-rate drop in 1996 with the introduction of a parental allowance of $800 a month for a parent to be home with a child for three years. The French birth rate is now close to replacement rate and, in this respect, is noteworthy among Western nations (Letablier 2005). Russia has announced several policies to reverse its birth drop including monthly funding per child equivalent to the minimum wage ($55 per month for a first child, $110 per month for a second child, and the minimum-wage level for a third child), the extension of maternity leave from three years to as much as seven years, and an immediate cash bonus on the birth of a second child of $11,000 (Motiejunaite and Kravchenko 2008).

In Quebec, the birth rate in the 1980s was the lowest in the West. When the Quebec government introduced its provincial daycare program, the birth rate did not increase. However, the birth rate increased significantly in 2007 – the largest one-year surge since 1909. The introduction, one year earlier, of parental leave with up to 75 percent of one's salary for thirty-two weeks, which was much larger than the previous federal payment, was seen as the main factor in the increased birth rate. Nearly 100,000 parents claimed the new benefit, including 36 percent of fathers, which was up from the 18 percent that had been previously demonstrated.[11]

If, indeed, the true measure of a nation's standing is how well it attends to its children, then it is imperative that as a nation we value the parental care of our children. A national child and family policy with parental care being at the centre of a network of care could be a symbol of how important supported parental care is to what children most need in their formative years. Canada's "birth dearth" is tied in with the expectation that having children will not be supported or valued by the society and culture within which people live. Supporting parents in the fulfillment of their parental responsibilities is a collective social responsibility. In Canada, we are seriously negligent in this regard. There are beginning reforms underway, but much needs to be done in the way of increasing state support to parents to fulfil their parental responsibilities. Funding parenting itself, so that children can spend more time in parental care and fewer children are removed from the care of either or both of their parents, is critical. Encouraging shared parenting responsibility between fathers and mothers so that both parents can work outside the home and actively parent their children is another step. A national daycare program to support parents should be made available within a broader universal framework of direct financial supports to children and families – funding that "flows with the child." Notwithstanding the recent rulings to the contrary, state institutions do have a duty of care to support children and families.[12] No less than the future of children is at stake.

Notes

1 The report by the United Nations Children's Fund (UNICEF) ranked Dutch children the highest for overall well-being. Psychologist Paul Vangeert of the University of Groningen stated that the primary reason for the high ranking is that young parents in the Netherlands remain at home for an extended period to care for their children to give them a strong start in life.

2 Despite the existence of these groups, government most often consults daycare advocacy groups on the issue of child care. In Canada, some of these groups include the Association of Early Childhood Educators of Ontario, the Canadian Child Care Federation, First Call, Early Childhood Educators of British Columbia, the Child Care Advocacy Association of Canada, the Canadian Child Care Federation, the Child Care Human Resources Sector Council, the National Children's Alliance, the Child Care Resource and Research Unit (funded by Social Development Canada), the Child Care Policy Net, and a number of Centres of Excellence for Early Childhood Development. Home care activist groups such as the Kids First Parent Association of Canada, the National Family Child Care Association, and Équité Soins de Garde have rarely been consulted.

3 Daycare funding includes fee subsidies, below market/free rent at public buildings such as universities and schools, administration costs, regulatory costs, wage subsidies, research, training costs, grants, capital expense subsidies and grants, equipment subsidies and grants, non-profit treatment, charitable status tax treatment, promotion, lobbying, and advertising. The $11,600 figure does not include these costs. Were Canada's two million children aged zero to five actually in a daycare setting funded by the government, the cost to the state and the taxpayer would be over $23 billion per year, far more than government parties have been promising for a national child care program. The cost of operating daycares for every child would be so high it would bankrupt the state.

4 Suggested by the National Association of Women and the Law, the Citizens for Public Justice, and Campaign 2000.

5 The Swedish government some time ago created a tax policy to preferentially treat parents who work outside the home and to penalize those who stay in the home taking care of their own children. Canadian daycare lobbyists have often

cited the Swedish public daycare system as a model, but many Swedish child care advocates have cautioned against doing so. Since the ruling party fell in the 2006 national election, the previous child care funding structure has been replaced by one that provides cash incentives for parental care.

6 Family Relations Act, R.S.B.C. 1996, c. 128.

7 Fewer than 16 percent of these children are placed with an Aboriginal caregiver. These children, in particular, suffer "cultural devaluation."

8 Supervised visits are not ordered in cases where there are safety concerns. A common reason for supervised access is to allow social workers the opportunity to observe the interaction between parent and child. Such supervision creates an unnatural environment that negatively affects the parent-child relationship. It is only one part of the larger "web of surveillance" to which parents of children in care are subject.

9 Foster care rates are set at $800-$900 per child per month, with additional supplements for special needs. They are $250-$450 for children in the home of a relative (Pivot Legal Society 2008).

10 An Act to Establish Criteria and Conditions in Respect of Funding for Early Learning and Child Care Programs in Order to Ensure the Quality, Accessibility, Universality and Accountability of Those Programs, and to Appoint a Council to Advise the Minister of Human Resources and Skills Development on Matters Relating to Early Learning and Child Care, 39th Parliament of Canada, 2006-7.

11 It is heartening to see that parents have babies when they can spend time with them, not just when there is an easy government incentive to not spend time with them.

12 The Supreme Court of Canada ruled in 2007 that the child welfare system can take and keep children in government care without a finding of abuse or unfitness, saying that there is no general basis in Canadian law under which a family can claim that a "duty of care" is owed to them by child welfare agencies or their employees. *Syl Apps Secure Treatment Centre v. B.D.*, 2007 SCC 38, [2007] 3 S.C.R. 83.

References

Alexander, B. 2008. *The Globalization of Addiction*. Toronto: Oxford University Press.

Baker, M., J. Gruber, and K. Milligan. 2005. *Universal Childcare, Maternal Labor Supply, and Family Well-Being*. National Bureau of Economic Research: Working Paper no. W11832, Social Science Research Network, http://ssrn.com/abstract=875708.

Bauserman, R. 2002. "Child Adjustment in Joint Custody versus Sole Custody Arrangements: A Meta-Analytic Review." *Journal of Family Psychology* 16: 91-102.

Belsky, J. 2007. "Recent Child Care Findings." *Pediatrics for Parents* 23: 2-4.

Bibby, R. 2003. *The Future Families Project: A Survey of Canadian Hopes and Dreams*. Ottawa: Vanier Institute of the Family.

Biddulph, S. 2006. *Raising Babies: Should Under-Threes Go to Nursery?* London: Harper Collins.

Braver, S.L., and D. Stockburger. 2005. "Child Support Guidelines and the Equalization of Living Standards." In W. Comanor, ed., *The Law and Economics of Child Support Payments,* 91-127. New York: Edward Elgar Publishing.

Brusentsev, V., and W. Vroman. 2007. "Compensating for Birth and Adoption." Paper presented at the Canadian Economic Research Forum, Halifax, 1 June.

Callahan, M., and K. Swift. 2007. "Great Expectations and Unintended Consequences: Risk Assessment in Child Welfare in B.C." In L. Thomas Foster and B. Wharf, eds., *People, Politics and Child Welfare in British Columbia,* 158-83. Vancouver: UBC Press.

Child Welfare League of Canada. 2003. *Children in Care in Canada.* Ottawa: Child Welfare League of Canada.

Corcoran, K., and J.C. Melamed. 1990. "From Coercion to Empowerment: Spousal Abuse and Mediation." *Mediation Quarterly* 7: 303-16.

Datar, A. 2005. *Delaying Kindergarten: Effects on Test Scores and Child Care Costs.* Santa Monica, CA: RAND Corporation.

Department of Justice Canada. 1990. *Evaluation of the Divorce Act, Phase II: Monitoring and Evaluation.* Ottawa: Minister of Justice.

Doidge, N. 2007. *The Brain That Changes Itself.* New York: Penguin.

Dubois, L., and M. Girard. 2005. "Breast-Feeding, Day-Care Attendance and the Frequency of Antibiotic Treatments from 1.5 to 5 Years: A Population-based Longitudinal Study in Canada." *Social Science and Medicine* 60: 2035-44.

Eamon, M.K., and S. Kopels. 2004. "'For Reasons of Poverty': Court Challenges to Child Welfare Practices and Mandated Programs." *Child and Youth Services Review* 26: 821-36.

Evenson, R.J., and R.W. Simon. 2005. "Clarifying the Relationship between Parenthood and Depression." *Journal of Health and Social Behavior* 46: 341-58.

Fabricius, W.V. 2003. "Listening to Children of Divorce: New Findings That Diverge from Wallerstein, Lewis, and Blakeslee." *Family Relations* 52: 385-96.

Farquhar, S. 2008. *Assessing the Evidence on Early Childhood Education/Childcare.* Auckland: Child Forum.

Friendly, M. 2008. "Early Learning and Child Care: Is Canada on Track?" In R.B. Howe and K. Covell, eds., *A Question of Commitment: Children's Rights in Canada,* 45-72. Waterloo: Wilfrid Laurier University Press.

Fuller, B. 2007. *Standardized Childhood: The Political and Cultural Struggle over Early Education.* Stanford, CT: Stanford University Press.

Gagne, L. 2003. *Parental Work, Child-Care Use, and Young Children's Cognitive Outcomes.* Catalogue no. 89-594-XIE. Ottawa: Statistics Canada.

Higgins, C., and L. Duxbury. 2002. *The 2001 National Work-Life Conflict Study.* Ottawa: Health Canada.

Ipsos Reid. 2007. *Focus Groups on Issues Surrounding Child Care: Final Report.* Ottawa: Human Resources and Skills Development Canada.

Kelly, J. 2000. "Children's Adjustment in Conflicted Marriage and Divorce: A Decade Review of Research." *Journal of the American Academy of Child and Adolescent Psychiatry* 39: 963-73.

Kozhaya, N. 2006. *$7-a-Day Childcare: Are Parents Getting What They Need?* Montreal: Montreal Economic Institute.

Kruk, E. 2005. "Shared Parental Responsibility: A Harm Reduction–Based Approach to Divorce Law Reform." *Journal of Divorce and Remarriage* 43: 119-40.

–. 2008. *Child Custody, Access and Parental Responsibility: The Search for a Just and Equitable Standard.* Guelph, ON: Fatherhood Involvement Research Alliance, Social Science and Research Foundation of Canada.

Lefebvre, P. 2002. "The Effect of Childcare and Early Education Arrangements on Developmental Outcomes of Young Children." *Canadian Public Policy* 28: 159-85.

Lero, D. 2007. "Research on Parental Leave Policies and Children's Development: Implications for Policy Makers and Service Providers." In *Encyclopedia on Early Childhood Development,* 1-9. Montreal: Centre of Excellence for Early Childhood Development.

Letablier, M. 2005. "Fertility and Family Policies in France." *Journal of Population and Social Security* 1: 245-61.

Loeb, S., M. Bridges, D. Bassock, B. Fuller, and R. Rumberger. 2005. *How Much Is Too Much: The Influence of Preschool Centers on Children's Social and Cognitive Development.* Working Paper no. W11812. Cambridge, MA: National Bureau of Economic Research.

Marshall, K. 2006. "Converging Gender Roles." *Perspectives on Labour and Income* (Statistics Canada) 7(1): 5-17.

Maté, G. 2008. *In the Realm of Hungry Ghosts: Close Encounters with Addiction.* Toronto: Alfred Knopf.

McKenzie, B., S. Palmer, and W.T. Barnard. 2008. "Views from Other Provinces." In L. Foster and B. Wharf, eds., *People, Politics, and Child Welfare in British Columbia.* Vancouver: UBC Press.

Millar, P., and S. Goldenberg. 2004. "A Critical Reading of the Evidence on Custody Determinations in Canada." *Canadian Family Law Quarterly* 21: 425-35.

Motiejunaite, A., and Z. Kravchenko. 2008. "Family Policy Emphasis and Gender Role Attitudes: A Comparison of Russia and Sweden. *Journal of European Social Policy* 18: 38-49.

Mustard, J.F. 2008. *Investing in the Early Years: Closing the Gap between What We Know and What We Do.* Adelaide: Government of South Australia.

National Center on Addiction and Substance Abuse. 2005. *Family Matters: Substance Abuse and the American Family.* New York: National Center on Addiction and Substance Abuse.

National Institute of Child Health and Development. 2006. *The NICHD Study of Early Child Care and Youth Development: Findings for Children up to Age 4 ½ Years.* Washington, DC: National Institute of Child Health and Human Development.

Office of the Public Advocate of New York. 2002. *Families at Risk: A Report on New York City's Child Welfare Project.* New York: Child Welfare Fund.

Pivot Legal Society. 2008. *Broken Promises: Parents Speak about B.C.'s Child Welfare System.* Vancouver: Law Foundation of British Columbia.

Statistics Canada. 2004. *Family Violence in Canada: A Statistical Profile.* Ottawa: Minister of Industry.

–. 2005a. *General Social Survey – Time Use.* Ottawa: Minister of Industry.

–. 2005b. *Divorce in Canada: A Statistical Profile.* Ottawa: Minister of Industry.

–. 2007. *Crime Statistics.* Ottawa: Minister of Industry.

–. 2009. *The Daily: September 22, 2009*. Ottawa: Minister of Industry.

Swift, K., and H. Parada. 2004. "Child Welfare Reform: Protecting Children or Policing the Poor?" *Journal of Law and Social Policy* 19: 1-17.

Teeple, G. 1995. *Globalization and the Decline of Social Reform*. Toronto: Garamond.

Trocme, N., B. Fallon, B. MacLaurin, J. Daciuk, C. Felstiner, T. Black, L. Tonmyr, C. Blackstock, K. Barter, D. Turcotte, and R. Cloutier. 2005. *Canadian Incidence Study of Reported Child Abuse and Neglect 2003: Major Findings*. Ottawa: Minister of Public Works and Government Services Canada.

United Nations Children's Fund (UNICEF). 2007. *Child Poverty in Perspective: An Overview of Child Well-Being in Rich Countries*. Florence, Italy: UNICEF Innocenti Research Centre.

Woo, B. 2007. "Emotional and Behavioural Problems in Singaporean Children Based on Parent, Teacher, and Child Reports." *Singapore Medical Journal* 48: 1100-6.

8
Navigating the Pedagogy of Failure: Medicine, Education, and the Disabled Child in English Canada, 1900-45

Mona Gleason

> Experience has taught that a Mental Defective has good manual possibilities if trained early to make the most of this ability. If the unstable qualities are suppressed, and suitable environment for work and recreation is provided, the chances are good for this type of individual surviving and being an asset to the community. It is the uneducated and uncontrolled feebleminded population that is dangerous.
>
> – Eric Kent Clarke, Associate Medical Director, Canadian National Committee for Mental Hygiene, and Psychiatrist of the Department of Public Health, Toronto, 1925.

Children in Western societies, argues Viviana Zelizer (1985), became emotionally "priceless" in the industrial age as their sentimental value grew and their economic value waned. As the twentieth century dawned, childhood was redefined as a distinct developmental stage of life characterized by nurture, pleasure, play, protection, and potential. North American social reformers heartily endorsed Swedish reformer Ellen Key's (1900) call for the twentieth century to be, as the title of her influential book proclaimed, "the century of the child."

Indeed, the twentieth century ushered in new beginnings for many children. It was an era of reform and child saving as well as of growing acknowledgment of children's rights.[1] At the state level, supplementing the important efforts of private philanthropic organizations such as Ontario's Children's Aid Society (1891), early initiatives included Canada's Royal Commission on the Relations of Labour and Capital (1889), which devoted much attention to child labour, and the first

American White House Conference on Dependent Children (1909), which supplied the impetus for the establishment of the US Children's Bureau (1912). Reformers also focused on institutional "care," including orphanages and industrial schools, the kindergarten movement, compulsory schooling, and new hygienic measures to preserve children's health (Gléason et al. 2010). Overall, concern for children was a central tenet of the developing social welfare apparatus in North America and the West more generally.

The century of the child, and the new beginnings that it presaged, necessarily traded on the end of other, less desirable, childhoods. Children who ran afoul of the law, whose parents were addicted, absent, criminalized, or impoverished, or who were fatherless or racialized as non-White became particular targets of intervention and remediation (Sutherland 1976; Jones and Rutman 1981; Myers and Sangster 2001; Myers 2006). Children with disabilities, as Eric Kent Clarke's (1925) opening quotation suggests, presented uniquely difficult challenges to efforts dependent on the reformation of behaviours, circumstances, attitudes, and values. Disability, presented in professional discourse as physical or intellectual differences in need of serious attention, did not readily or easily yield to change.[2]

In this chapter, I explore how medical and educational professionals represented disability, particularly disability in childhood, in their professional writing.[3] Through a small number of oral history interviews with adults who grew up with the physical disability label, I attempt also to understand how these professional representations were navigated in everyday life.[4] While medical and educational professionals were not the only experts whose attention turned to people with disabilities, they possessed considerable power in this regard. Thoroughly medicalized and pathologized in this period, disability came under the purview of the medical establishment. The role of education in the containment, and, where possible, recuperation, of children with disabilities was also seen as paramount. Medical and educational professionals were not alone in shaping attitudes toward disability and, in particular, toward children with disabilities. Their opinions and judgments in this regard were nonetheless influential.[5] Solidifying a powerful partnership, medical and educational professionals utilized "dividing practices," in Michel Foucault's (1986) phrase, to identify, categorize, and improve bodies and minds judged outside the tight boundaries of "normal." (Anita Garey also examines the role of professionals in shaping understandings of "normal" childhoods in Chapter 9 of this volume.)

I argue that medical and educational professionals, despite their good intentions, represented disability as precluding both a "normal" and a "socially acceptable" childhood. While significant shifts in medical understandings of disability took place over the decades, underpinned by sympathetic intentions of improving and sustaining lives, doctors, nurses, teachers, and curriculum specialists nevertheless contributed to a eugenic-inspired "pedagogy of failure" regarding the disabled child well into the 1940s.[6] By casting disability as a moral and developmental failure in need of amelioration, medical and educational professionals helped make children with disabilities "abnormal." While this knowledge production may not have strictly represented an end of childhood, the central theme explored in this book, it helped entrench clear boundaries around the constitution of the "normal" child and the "abnormal" child. Physical and behavioural difference was believed to threaten not only the health and happiness of individual children and their families but also public health and a stable citizenry. For children labelled disabled, the "century of the child" was thereby more ambivalent than celebratory. As evidence from oral histories suggests, some children and their families closely adhered to advice geared toward "normalizing" their differences. Others followed their own paths, honing their coping strategies that had been forged within their families and defying the advice of professionals.

Disability in the Era of Child Saving and Eugenics

Running through the numerous reform efforts intended to improve society and protect children at the turn of the century was an undercurrent of anxiety about threats to social order and stability. Mental and physical "deficiency" mobilized medical and educational experts in multiple national contexts, including Canada, at the dawn of the new Century (Simmons, 1982; MacLaren, 1990). Uncertainty about the stability of the present and the future crystallized in the figure of the unproductive, morally suspect, dependent, physical, or mental "defective." Children were not exempt from such representations or anxieties.

In the early decades of the new century, professionals delivered the eugenicist message that "inferior heredity" was the principle cause of "degeneracy." Poor environments exacerbated what inheritance had begun. Children who were declared "abnormal" and left unmanaged, experts argued, would see little improvement. Segregated and supervised training, however, could contain and manage the failures associated with their disabilities. Lamenting the neglect of these "defectives," concerned medical and educational professionals called for increased surveillance and segregation.

To accomplish these measures, several key messages about the fate of children labelled "defective" found repeated expression in the professional writing of medical and educational experts. Motivated by their belief in eugenics, leading medical figures such as Charles Kirk Clarke, dean of the Faculty of Medicine at the University of Toronto and cofounder of the Canadian National Committee for Mental Hygiene, Helen MacMurchy, Ontario's leading public health expert and inspector of the "feeble-minded," and David Brankin, superintendent of British Columbia's Provincial Department of Neglected Children, discussed the causes of abnormality and advocated identifying, classifying, and ultimately segregating children with disabilities.

A public lecture delivered to high school students in 1899 by Charles Kirk Clarke (1899) elucidated the approach.[7] Entitled "The Evolution of Imbecility," Clarke's lecture served two purposes. First, it offered a detailed accounting of the current medical understanding of the etiology and characteristics of "mental abnormality." Second, and importantly, Clarke encouraged the teachers to do more to help "defectives" by identifying their deficiencies and differentiating among their students. "The more one studies heredity," Clarke asserted, "the more one is satisfied that the progressive teacher will adopt a system of teaching founded on the capabilities of the individual pupils rather than on the theory that all children are alike and able to develop in the same direction" (1899, 6). For proponents of the institutionalization of "defectives," such as MacMurchy, Clarke, and Gordon S. Mundie, a psychiatric specialist at the Royal Victoria Hospital in Montreal, etiological discussions supported arguments for segregation and institutionalization. In his essay "The Mentally Defective," which was published in the *Canadian Medical Association Journal (CMAJ)* in 1914, Mundie (1914, 397) made his disposition very clear:

> In Canada very little has been done for the mental defective, and in our own province of Quebec, it does not need the trained eye of the expert to see that there are large members of these poor unfortunates who are a menace to the stability of the country, and I have no hesitation in saying that it would be cheaper for the province to have institutions to look after them than to have them roam at large as at present.

For Mundie, like other eugenic-minded health reformers, few options were reasonably available to "poor unfortunates," given conventional wisdom about the causes of mental deficiency. As David Brankin (1920, 6), superintendent of the Provincial Department of Neglected Children, told his audience of women from the Girl's Central School in Victoria, British Columbia, in 1920: "The problem of defective children is due to several main causes, not the least amongst these is the unjust legacy handed down by unwise parents." Thus, deficiencies were believed to be the result of either a primary cause, "inferior heredity" being the most important example, or a secondary cause from unfavourable environmental conditions, such as birth injury, tuberculosis, fever, or syphilis. In either instance, but especially in the case of "inferior heredity," little change in an otherwise bleak outlook for the afflicted was to be reasonably expected. Given such negative assumptions embedded in eugenic discourse, anxieties about the declining birth rate of upper- and middle-class families and the increasing birth rate of the "lower orders," including non-White immigrants, were sufficient to spark fears of "race suicide" among elites (MacLaren 1990).

By the 1930s, supporters of eugenics, increasingly weary of unchecked immigration in the era of the Great Depression, aggressively defended the sterilization of "defectives" as the most logical preventative measure against "defects."[8] Although the eugenics movement reached its zenith in the United States and the rest of Canada in the 1930s, hospitals for the "feeble-minded" in the Western province of Alberta continued their program of forced sterilizations into the 1950s and 1960s. Eugenic sterilization in most parts of English Canada, however, was an increasingly defensive discourse as medical professionals questioned its effectiveness and, as the atrocities of the Nazi holocaust emerged, recoiled from its horrific implications (MacLaren 1990, 146-48).

Jessa Chupik and David Wright (2006) have shown that, from the perspective of families, the institutionalization of "defective" children was often the last resort for families. For some parents whose children were recommended to the Orillia Asylum in Ontario, for example, "idiocy" was a curable and treatable condition requiring energy and patience. Families refused to see their children as "hopeless" and instead availed themselves of a range of treatment and supervisory options. Orphanages, philanthropic organizations, industrial schools, and Children's Aid Societies took in children on both a limited and ongoing basis in order to relieve exhausted and financially strapped parents.

Evidence from oral histories makes clear that in the case of physical disabilities, parents routinely supplemented sanctioned medical practices with other kinds of treatment for their children. Conventional medical wisdom was important, but not all families felt compelled to rely on it exclusively. Florence Drake was born in Vancouver, British Columbia, in 1908. When she was two years old, she contracted poliomyelitis. The disease affected her leg muscles, often rendering her unable to walk. Florence remembers a woman coming to her house to treat her with mild electrical shock therapy on her legs when she was around four years old. "She used to come on the street car, and she had a black box with her, and it was full of wires," Florence recalled, "and I was scared to death of it."[9] As she recounts,

> I hated it, and I used to run and hide when she came. And she would wind this all around my leg and then she would plug it in – into the electricity. And it was all pins and needles and everything all up and down my leg.

Despite warnings from conventional medical professionals regarding the dangers of "quackery," families made their own decisions about how to proceed (Halpenny and Ireland 1911, 174; Lucas 1926). Surgical attempts to "normalize" Florence's uneven gait, an option that was more in keeping with medical advice, were never successful. She took advantage instead of orthotic shoes available at Pierre Paris's orthotic shoe store on Hastings Street: "He made me a pair of shoes and he built one boot a way up with cork. It was quite light in weight, but it was sure ugly looking."[10]

Promoting Prevention in the Preschool Years

The identification, classification, and segregation of "defective" children advocated by medical and educational professionals early in the century gave way to a preventative orientation in the interwar period as more finely calibrated "dividing practices" gained legitimacy. Doctors, in particular, began the search for any abnormalities long before the child was school age. Pediatric practitioners were encouraged to diagnose "degeneracy" in infants and to put the spotlight on faulty parenting (particularly on the part of mothers) as a possible causal or exasperating factor. Infants, suggested Hector Charles Cameron (1931, 240), bore the stamp of "inherited neuropathy" in unpleasant physical characteristics that the doctor should readily problematize: "Thin, meagre, and tense, with rigid face and limbs ... the response to the approach of a friendly face is not a smile, but a cry or frown." Lloyd P. MacHaffie (1937, 498), school medical officer for Ottawa's public schools, chastised parents and fellow doctors alike for the neglect of "preventative pediatrics." "I am convinced," MacHaffie wrote, "as the result of several years' examinations of thousands of school children, that a great many children enter school saddled with defects which should never have developed if adequate attention and supervision had been given during the preschool period."

The number and orientation of nation-wide child health centres testified to increasing surveillance of the young. Ontario's minister of health, Dr. Charles Hastings, opened the first child health centre in 1915 in Toronto to provide mothers without a family physician the "benefits of regular medical supervision" (Sutherland 1940, 17). By 1940, the city boasted twenty-three centres, while "practically every city and town throughout the dominion had set up similar agencies for the care of the Canadian child" (Sutherland 1940, 17). Far beyond simply providing accessible health care, however, the centres joined public schools as important surveillance sites: "Defects are caught in over forty-five percent of the children between the ages of two and five attending the centres, which otherwise, unless corrected, might handicap them for life" (1940, 22). The fact that many "handicaps" could be caught and corrected put the onus squarely on those in positions of authority to act decisively. "Now," Harris McPhedran (1929, 659) declared in the *CMAJ* in 1929, "a new era is dawning and the physician of the future will be regarded chiefly as one called upon to prevent disability and disease." Rather than concentrating merely on identifying "defective" children, medical and educational professionals concentrated instead on preventing and eliminating "defects."

Many parents were eager to take up new treatments and technological advancements to improve the life changes of their children. Like many other polio victims, for example, Florence Drake's legs developed at an uneven pace – in spite of the elaborate electric therapy she had endured in her childhood – and she was eventually fitted with "irons." Irons were braces that fit around the foot, inside the shoe, and extended up the side of her leg to her knee where they were fastened. She wore this brace for a number of years. In 1919, at the age of eleven, her parents sent her to Vancouver General Hospital (VGH) for a series of operations that would take place over the next two years. A doctor at VGH, Florence recalled, promised that he could help her gain back some of her physical mobility. "Well," she recalled her father saying to the doctor, "you go ahead because she has never had anything done for any of it ... I will just leave it in your hands and you do what you think you can do for her." The operations on her feet were at least partially successful, but they left behind scars that ran from her toes around the front of her foot to her ankles. When the doctor proposed more operations to correct "weak knees," Florence recalled that she refused to co-operate. "I would have to lay on my back for one year while he put weights attached to my leg at the bottom of my bed ... this I refused," she said. She had missed two years of school by this time and would eventually end her schooling when she reached Grade 8.

Learning Disability in Schools

By the beginning of the First World War, schooling in the form of manual training was held out as an important bulwark against the threats associated with unmanaged "abnormal" youngsters. The arrival of large numbers of non-White immigrants, particularly at the end of the First World War, was seen as a threat to the country's dominant British identity. Public schools, as they had done in the case of physical and mental "abnormality," were called on to inculcate "healthy citizenship" by promoting assimilation. Alberta school medical inspector Dr. J. Dunn (1918, 932), echoed widespread sentiment in this regard:

> We are educating a nation. It rests with us to say whether ... the race shall advance or retreat. [In the] public schools ... the children come together and mingle ... here they begin to understand the nature of British citizenship. If, therefore, we wish to produce and perpetuate a nation of strong, virile, intellectual, and normal men and women, let us see to it that our public schools are in every way of the best possible character.

Physical and mental "defectives" or "cripples," as they were described in professional discourse, were at the very centre of debates and contestations regarding public health and school reform as they evolved over the early to mid-decades of the century. As Angus MacLaren (1990), Gerald Thomson (2002; 2006), and Nic Clarke (2004/5) have shown, Canadian medical and educational professionals, influenced by eugenic theories on race betterment, routinely looked to schools and other major social institutions as partners against unidentified and, more importantly, untreated and untrained "feeble-minded" and physically "defective" youngsters. Perfectly positioned to disseminate new curricular information about physical and mental "hygiene," schools emerged as comprehensive human-sorting stations. Large numbers of children, compelled to attend, could then be tested, examined, and sorted into "normal" or "abnormal" categories, and treatment, if indicated, could be pursued.

Concern for the proper surveillance of "defective" children was shared by those more directly involved in the public schools, such as school medical inspectors, curricula developers for teachers and students, and teachers themselves. Influential leaders such as Vancouver's supervisor of subnormal classes, Josephine Dauphinee, were preoccupied with imparting lessons in health and hygiene, particularly in targeting abstinence from alcohol and tobacco, as critical ways to address suspected causes of "abnormality."[11] Curriculum specialists prioritized lessons regarding heredity as key to improving health. Dr. Archibald P. Knight (1910, 229), professor of physiology at Queen's University in Kingston, Ontario, and author of *The Ontario Public School Hygiene* wrote:

> If you have followed the teachings of this book thus far, it must be clear to you now that our lives from birth until old age are shaped largely by two great influences: (1) by what we inherit from our parents, grandparents, or other ancestral relatives, and (2) by our environment, that is, by our surroundings.

Gordon S. Mundie argued that while parental inheritance was no doubt important, inferior environments could have equally tragic and regrettable effects on children's health. Much was at stake for advocates of improved standards of public health and hygiene. "A condition of ill health, actual disease, or starvation of the mother," Mundie (1914, 399) reminded his readers, "cannot but be injurious to the growing embroyo [sic], and the same may be said of improper food, impure air, deficient light and inadequate sleep, which are so often the lot of young children in our city slums." Regardless of causation, outcomes were similar. "Mental deficiency is a defect of the higher centres, not a disease," Mundie made clear, "therefore, there is no cure for it" (404).

In his 1916 address to the Alberta Medical Association, Dunn (1918, 928) spoke from his additional experience as medical inspector of schools in Edmonton. In Dunn's experience, physical "defects" were just as troublesome, both for individual children and society as a whole, as mental "defects." Bad teeth, for example, set in motion a costly chain of unfortunate, and ultimately preventable, events. He warned:

> Decayed teeth mean aching teeth, aching teeth mean germ-ridden mouths and germ-saturated food favouring the propagation of contagious diseases, poor mastication and digestion, impaired nourishment and bodily resistance, intestinal and general toxic absorption, all of which prevent proper intellectual advancement, and favour the various forms of physical disturbances and degeneration.

For Dunn, like other professionals, the primary benefit of compulsory public schooling was as a sorting station for "normal" and "abnormal" children. "Normal" youngsters progressed through their grades; "abnormal" youngsters were, depending on their distance from "normalcy," either treated and improved or segregated into special classes or institutions. The segregation of "subnormal" children in special classes had begun in earnest first in France with the work of Edward Sequin, onward to Germany, and by the turn of the twentieth century had become established practice in Cleveland, Chicago, and New York (Armstrong 2002; Read and Walmsley 2006). By 1910, authorities in Toronto were identifying and segregating "subnormal" children. Two pieces of Canadian legislation further facilitated the impulse to identify, classify, and segregate the "abnormal": the Special Class Act of 1911 and the Auxiliary Class Act of 1914 (Thomson 2006, 55-56; see also Trent 1994).[12] Helen MacMurchy (1915, 86), a leading proponent of the legislation, praised the main provisions of the act, which allowed not only for special classes in the public school buildings but also empowered school boards to build separate institutions, such as "industrial training schools" and "farm colonies for the mentally defective." The latter were particularly important, in MacMurchy's estimation, for they "provide protection for the mentally defective and renders them happy and as useful they can be; it also protects the community and the nation."

School and public health work satisfied two interrelated impulses: to protect and enhance the welfare of children labelled "deficient" and to protect society from the dangers such children were assumed to represent. Laying the foundations of an enduring pedagogy of failure, experts in this period characterized physical and mental disability as the irrevocable corruption of body and moral fibre. In 1915, Mundie (1915, 405) underlined this enduring link between "defects" and costs to the community:

> Crime, like all conduct, is an attribute of mental life and this being so, in order to get at the cause of crime we must study the mental life of the criminal. Very little has been done in developing this science, but what has been done has clearly shown that most criminals are physically and mentally inferior.

Children thus afflicted and not properly dealt with, warned MacMurchy (1915, 86), "cannot make good in the community ... and are a source of evil and a burden of expense."

While leading medical professionals such as Mundie and MacMurchy characterized the segregation of "defectives" as beneficial to the interests of the nation, teachers working in public schools acknowledged more personal benefits. An Ontario teacher, writing to fellow intermediate grade teachers in 1915, pointed out that the Auxiliary Class Act made possible the temporary segregation of a whole range of students thought both ill-served in classrooms for "normal" youngsters and destined to hold back the progress of their peers:

> These [auxiliary classes] may be established under the Act for foreigners: handicapped by language, manners, habits – better be taught by an expert who could more rapidly pass them on as they are often possessed of mature ability; Japanese, Chinese, Russian, Italian, semi-deaf, semi-blind, physically defective, crippled, some so much so that they have to be carried or have to climb long flights of stairs on their knees. (Kerr 1915, 620)

The conflation between racialized "handicap" ("foreigners" handicapped by language, manners, and habits) and physical "handicap" suggests the extent to which "normalcy" was socially constructed to serve particular interests.[13]

The central importance of public schooling for the promotion of loyal British subjects, a familiar refrain in the rhetoric of educational professionals, tended in practice not to apply to all children. Jean Tierney, born in 1908 in Vancouver, British Columbia, was struck with poliomyelitis in 1910. Between the ages of eleven and fourteen, she spent most of her time in hospital undergoing painful treatments and a series of operations in hopes of "normalizing" her condition. Her lack of conventional mobility rendered her unable to attend school for years at a time. Laura Trent, who developed a "limp" also as a result of poliomyelitis, recalls that a helpful neighbour and a sympathetic principal were key to her success at school. Born in 1920 in Parry Sound, Ontario, she did not attend school until she was ten years old and only then with considerable effort. "I remember living in the country," she recalls, "and in winter it was very slippery – I couldn't get to school – I couldn't balance myself." She continues:

> And there was a boy next door who was from a big family and do you know that every morning when it was slippery he would bring his sleigh and try to get me to school ... I was never counted late by the principal

if I got there and it was slippery. Because he knew I couldn't manage like the rest of them, and I couldn't keep my balance like the rest of them.[14]

In an era before accommodation imperatives, children with disabilities relied on a network of allies – including families, neighbours, and school officials – to help them get to, and remain at, school. If good will was not forthcoming or available, regular attendance at school could prove elusive. In the case of children who underwent surgical interventions, school attendance was further compromised.

Testimony from oral histories and autobiographies also reminds us that peers, inside and outside school, acted as powerful agents of exclusion. Within the culture of children and youth, the pedagogy of failure could impinge on experience in profound ways. As a student at North Vancouver High School in British Columbia in the late 1930s, Robin Williams (1997, 199) remembers that "brains and a winning personality were valued, but among boys prowess at sports was probably number one." Athletic competition was seen as the quintessential way to display those attributes perceived to be the rightful domain of young and virile male bodies – strength, speed, agility, and muscularity (Vertinsky 1994). Williams was acutely aware of the importance of sports since he was for the most part excluded from them. Having survived poliomyelitis, he spent much of his childhood judged unable to compete with his brothers and friends. They, unlike him, easily satisfied gendered expectations about the physical abilities of "normal" boys.

Girls were not exempt from such gendered discussions. Conventional understandings of "beauty" precluded bodies that were considered in any way "abnormal." "Good looks are intrinsically bound up with health," wrote a columnist in *Chatelaine* magazine, Canada's premier women's magazine, in 1932:

If we develop sound, strong bodies, beauty will follow of its own accord, and there will be only a little "finishing" to do. Babies nowadays have far more opportunity to grow into beautiful women than their grandmothers did, or even their mothers did. (Lee 1932, 26)

In a 1939 health textbook approved for use in Canadian schools, health was similarly linked with "good looks" via strong, tall bodies in the case of girls. "Mary is a healthy girl," students were taught, because "she stands straight and tall ... she gains in weight and grows taller ... Mary is a pretty girl because she is such a healthy girl" (Andress, Goldberger, and Dolch 1939, 49). Laura Trent, who was a victim of polio, learned as she grew up in Ontario in the 1930s that she would simply never be considered an attractive mate. The social economy of heterosexual dating and marriage, assumed to be a part of every "normal" adolescent's experience, was considered closed to her. "Because I never thought," she explained, "that anybody – deep down in my heart – I never thought that anybody would take me because I was lame. I had that idea." Certainly the actions of her father, in conjunction with a larger culture of prejudice, reinforced her feelings as an undesirable, even imperilled, outsider:

> My dad always had the idea that because I was lame, that someone would take advantage of me. And he was very strict. I remember right up until I was 16, I could only go out on Friday night and I had to be in by 9:00 and if I wasn't in by 9:00 my Dad was out looking for me.

While girls in general were often held to close account by adults, based on their liability for domestic labour as well as assumptions about their sexual vulnerability, those labelled with a disability were doubly burdened.

The approved health curriculum on the eve of the Second World War made schools both implicit and explicit contributors to the failure associated with physical and mental "defects." While the explicit emphasis on eugenics and heredity no longer took centre stage, potent links between "normal" bodies and civic pride and purpose were forged. Good health, which was signalled most immediately by "normal" vigorous young bodies, demonstrated democratic citizenship. A "failed" body continued to signal a "failed" nation. The significantly titled book *New Ways for Old* placed self-conscious emphasis on the connections between "normal" bodies and behaviours, health, civic pride, and belonging to the nation:

> New beliefs about what education should do have made great changes in schools. Learning the three R's was the chief activity of the old schools, but the aim of the new schools is learning to live ... "Learning to live," in a modern school, means that each boy and girl may grow strong and sturdy, in mind and body, and may become the best person possible for him to be, for his own sake, and for his home and community. (Wood, Lerrigo, and Lamkin 1938, vi)

Although the progressive health curriculum prided itself on being innovative and cutting edge ("the aim of the new schools is learning to live"), the long-standing elements of a pedagogy of failure endured. Self-control continued to influence how children and young adults were encouraged to think about their embodied selves. "No matter what you wish to do in the world," suggested J. Mace Andress and Elizabeth Breeze in *Health Essentials for Canadian Schools* (1938, 242), "your ability to control your own mind and muscles must be the basis of your success." Health, according to Andress and Breeze, was a commodity easily won if students were willing to "first, have a desire to be healthy; secondly have the determination to undergo training in order to win health." "Most people," students were taught, "could win health if they only knew how and tried" (6). In a 1939 textbook vignette involving an exchange between a student named Martha and her teacher, Miss Long, internalized discipline of a compliant body was implicitly connected to success in life:

> "I heard the bell in the hall and I just jumped," said Martha. "I wanted to run. But the rule for a fire drill is "Walk, don't run." So I told my muscles to make me walk." "Your muscles wanted to run," said Miss Long, "but you told them not to run. Good muscles will do what you tell them to do." (Andress, Goldberger, and Dolch 1939, 121)

As Miss Long's approval of Martha's embodied restraint insinuates, disciplined, compliant bodies housed good children. Students able to master and control their bodies, to benefit from "good muscles," were on the road to successful adulthood, which was the ultimate goal of childhood in the eyes of many adults. The implications of this kind of discourse for children with bodies or behaviours that marked them as "abnormal" was, however, very problematic.

Psychologizing Disability

As the Second World War continued, psychology became an increasingly influential force in the medical treatment of children labelled with physical and mental differences. Particularly as a result of military-oriented research on the suitability of recruits, battle fatigue, and the "problem" of the returning soldier, psychological reasoning increasingly shaped professional attitudes and treatment.[15] The increasing popularity of psychology as a medical tool signalled a growing sensitivity to the social and emotional needs of children. By the 1950s, for example, hospital practice was shifting to acknowledge "the beneficial effects of daily visiting and a play program on the mental health of young children" (Young 1992, 1424). Children with physical and/or mental differences were often assumed, rightly or wrongly, to suffer negative psychological ramifications. Treatment was thus aimed at bringing bodies in line with conventional expectations regarding "normalcy." Dr. Hamilton Baxter (1941, 217), a plastic surgeon at the Children's Memorial Hospital in Montreal, argued in 1941, for example, that

> the most important effect of protruding ears on children is psychological, and may be expressed either in a feeling of inferiority which may cause the child to avoid personal contacts, or perhaps to develop a super-abundance of self-expression in an effort to compensate an injured ego.

In either case, Baxter suggested to his colleagues, early detection of the "defect" on the part of parents enabled corrective surgery to be carried out before any psychological damage could occur. "Children have a keen ability to detect the usual," Baxter pointed out, "and any abnormality in a playmate is the object of frank curiosity and ridicule" (217).

Margaret Roberts, born in Terrace, British Columbia, in 1945 remembered undergoing operations to correct her flat feet. She wore plaster casts on her legs for six months and endured painful infections as a result. In her experience, surgery significantly worsened her physical mobility:

> People could see me from a mile away ... as soon as they saw me they knew who I was because of the way I walked right after that operation because things weren't right ... my parents really felt that doctors were gods then. You know that's where they put them – up on a pedestal.[16]

The status and power of medical science, the high social cost attached to embodied difference, and the deference given to medical doctors, as her experience made clear, tended to encourage compliance.

Conclusion

I have argued in this chapter that medical and educational professionals in English Canada over the first half of the twentieth century equated disability with the impossibility of a normal and socially acceptable childhood. Children who lived with the disability label, while they certainly did not disappear during this time period, became the objects of professional interventions. These interventions effectively drew strict boundaries around the "normal" and the "abnormal." Efforts to root out disability were forged on children's bodies and included various attempts to change, improve, "normalize," or simply contain intellectual and physical differences. Between 1900 and the end of the Second World War, doctors and educational specialists in English Canada had much to say about "defective" children. This very preliminary examination reveals that while considerable shifts took place, powerful ideas about the constitution of "normal" saturated the professional discourse, drove attitudes, and shaped practices. Disability was presented through a pedagogy of failure that operated within much of the professional discourse over the period under study and, indeed, well beyond. While wartime doctors and educationalists no longer emphasized "inferior heredity," they continued to cast "difference" in terms of tragedy and mistake.

The oral histories of adults who grew up over the period give us another perspective on professional efforts to end what was understood as unfortunate and unhealthy circumstances. While medical and educational professionals were undoubtedly motivated by a strong desire to improve the lives of children, the consequences of their efforts solidified oppressive associations between disability and "abnormality." In some cases, the surgical solutions advocated by medical professionals had the opposite effect: they compounded disabilities rather than "fixing" them. Children with disabilities and their families actively navigated these often choppy waters and, despite their desires to conform to social expectations, did not always heed professional advice deemed too invasive, impractical, or unhelpful.

In more contemporary times, attitudes that align disability with the end of childhood continue to be expressed and, with equal tenacity, refuted. Canada, despite signing both the 1989 UN Convention on the Rights of the Child and the 2006 UN Convention on the Rights of Persons with Disabilities, has yet to fulfil commitments that ensure full participation in all aspects of Canadian life for children with disabilities and their families.[17] As a discussion paper commissioned by the National Children's Alliance for the First National Roundtable on Children with Disabilities in 2002 argued, "despite all the policy attention going to children in recent years, children with disabilities have been overlooked ... and for some children with disabilities – for example, for Aboriginal children with disabilities and their parents – the situation is even more pronounced" (Hanvey 2002, 7). From the perspective of contemporary advocates and allies, adequate and equitable support for children with disabilities and their families remains elusive. Increased and consistent funding for improved educational opportunities, affordable, assisted housing, adequate health care resources, and income assistance for caregivers are the targets of constant battles (see, for example, Kierstead and Hanvey 2001; Ferguson 2002; Enns and Neufeldt 2003).

Despite these disappointments, parents and other advocates have a long history of demanding equity for children whose bodies and behaviours make them vulnerable to social exclusion.[18] Their efforts have born fruit, exemplified by accommodation and inclusion efforts in public schools, a vibrant disability rights movement, shifts in legal protections, and cultural demands for more than simply "tolerance" of disability. To counter an enduring pedagogy of failure that continues to cast disability as an end of childhood, parents call instead for attitude shifts and equitable treatment that bespeak new beginnings for their children: "[People] just need educating," argues a British Columbia mother of a son with cerebral palsy. "We just don't believe in a limit," suggested another BC mother of disabled siblings. "My sons have proved that they can learn, given the right opportunity and support" (Bendell 2008).

Acknowledgments

This research was made possible by a grant from the Spencer Foundation. I am grateful to Shaista Patel and Satnam Chahal for research assistance.

Notes

1 Canadian scholarship includes Sutherland (1976), Rooke and Schnell (1983), and Comacchio (1990). With respect to American literature, see, for example, Lindemeyer (1997) and Sealander (2003).

2 A note about the language I employ. Although considered derisive to modern ears, the terms I use in this chapter such as "defective," "degeneracy," "crippled," and "feebleminded" are those used by the professionals in the past and require careful historical unpacking. By also employing the phrase "children labelled disabled" at various points in this chapter, my intention is to signal the contextual and social tentativeness of this designation. Not all children labelled disabled in the past would be labelled thus contemporarily and vice versa. Ultimately, by employing quotation marks around particular words and phrases, it is my intention to trouble them, suggest their social construction, and open them up to critical inquiry.

3 I surveyed leading professional medical journals for doctors and nurses including the *Canadian Medical Association Journal* and the *Public Health Journal* over the first decades of the twentieth century. I also used health textbooks that were approved for use in English-Canadian schools over the same period.

4 I use four oral history interviews in this chapter gleamed from sixty-two oral history interviews conducted by myself and two graduate students, Lori MacFadyen and Natalie Chambers, between 2001 and 2004. Cited here as part of the Child Health Project, interviewees were selected primarily through word

of mouth and some limited advertising in retirement homes in Vancouver and Penticton, British Columbia; and Montreal. We relied primarily on a snowball effect in which those interviewed told friends and family who, in turn, contacted us. The interview was intentionally open ended and asked participants for their childhood recollections of anything to do with health, health care, learning to be healthy, illness, and medical treatment. We asked only that participants be raised in Canada and born before 1960. Historians are well aware of the problems and limitations associated with oral histories. They counsel caution in using memories that can be unreliable, fallible, and that tend to "re-construct" rather than "re-collect" a life. See, for example, Sutherland (1992) and Thompson (1994).

5 Scholars such as Gerald Thomson (2002, 2006), Nic Clarke (2004/05), Jessa Chupik (2006), David Wright (Chupik and Wright 2006), and Veronica Strong-Boag (2005) have focused on judgments of various educational, medical, and social work professionals regarding disability.

6 David Mitchell and Sharon Snyder (2003) have encouraged historians to pay more interpretive attention to the role of eugenic science – the belief that social problems could be ameliorated by limiting the "breeding of undesirables" – in expressions of mass violence, genocide, and marginalization of "otherness" from the late eighteenth century to at least the end of the Second World War.

7 Charles K. Clarke was the father of Eric Kent Clarke.

8 As Deborah Park and John Radford (1998) have shown, judgments of the hospitals' Eugenics Board and allied professionals guided individual decisions to sterilize.

9 Child Health Project, Interview no. 023, transcript, 1.

10 Names of interview subjects have been changed to protect anonymity.

11 On Josephine Dauphinee's contribution to the institutionalization imperative surrounding children labelled mentally "defective," see Thomson (2006).

12 Special Class Act, Government of Canada, 1911; Auxiliary Class Act, Government of Canada, 1914.

13 In the interwar period, equations between what were judged "failures of development" with racial inferiority were perhaps most explicitly exemplified by professional characteristics of "Mongolism" or Down syndrome. Hegemonic ideas about race dictated that the "races of mankind" were arranged hierarchically with "Caucasians" at the top and "Mongolians" and "Ethiopians" near the bottom. Other groups, such as "Malaysian" and "American (American continent)" occupied middle positions. Human embryos, scientific thinking held, retraced or recapitulated the phases of the evolutionary history of its race as it developed in the womb. Thus, Langdon Down, the British doctor who provided the first comprehensive description of this "deficiency," labelled the physical features associated with the syndrome as representing "Mongol" – lower race – features. See, for example, the discussion in Warner (1935, 495-500). Useful historical critiques are offered in Volpe (1986) and Gould (1980).

14 Child Health Project, Interview no. 10, transcript, 3.

15 In the 1940s, British and American medical researchers advocated for more humane treatment of hospitalized children, building on British psychologist John Bowlby's work on the deleterious effects of "maternal deprivation" on children in orphanages. See Young (1992).

16 Child Health Project, Interview no. 017, transcript, 6-7.
17 UN General Assembly, *Convention on the Rights of the Child*, 20 November 1989, United Nations, Treaty Series, vol. 1577, 3, http://www.unhcr.org/; United Kingdom: Parliament, Joint Committee on Human Rights, UN *Convention on the Rights of Persons with Disabilities*, 4 January 2009, HL Paper 9/HC 93 [incorporating HC 1204-i of Session 2007-08], http://www.unhcr.org/.
18 For a historical example of this advocacy in practice in the Canadian context, see Clarke (2004/5) and Chupik (2006).

References

Andress, J.M., and E. Breeze. 1938. *Health Essentials for Canadian Schools*. Boston: Ginn.

Andress, J.M., I. Goldberger, and M. Dolch. 1939. *Growing Big and Strong*. Boston: Ginn.

Armstrong, F. 2002. "The Historical Development of Special Education: Humanitarian Rationality or 'Wild Profusion of Entangled Events'?" *History of Education* 31: 437-56.

Baxter, H. 1941. "Plastic Correction of Protruding Ears in Children." *Canadian Medical Association Journal* 45: 217-20.

Bendell, L. 2008. "Attitudes towards Children with Disabilities Need Improvement, Parents Say," CBC News, http://www.cbc.ca/.

Brankin, D. 1920. "Defective Children: Product of Neglect." *Victoria Daily Times*, 14 May, 6.

Cameron, H. 1931. "Sleep and Its Disorders in Childhood." *Canadian Medical Association Journal* 24: 239-44.

Chupik, J. 2006. "Fires Burning: Advocacy, Camping and Children with Learning Disabilities in Ontario, 1950-1990." In D. Mitchell, R. Trautadottir, R. Chapman, L. Townson, N. Ingham, and S. Ledger, eds., *Exploring Experiences of Advocacy by People with Learning Disabilities*, 119-27. London: Jessica Kingsley.

Chupik, J., and D. Wright. 2006. "Treating the 'Idiot' Child in Early Twentieth-Century Ontario." *Disability and Society* 21: 77-90.

Clarke, C.K. 1899. "The Evolution of Imbecility." *Queen's Quarterly* 6: 297-314.

Clarke, E.K. 1925. "The Role of the Department of Public Health in the Education of the Adolescent Mentally Defective Child." *Public Health Journal* 16: 436-38.

Clarke, N. 2004/5. "Sacred Daemons: Exploring British Columbian Society's Perceptions of 'Mentally Deficient' Children, 1870-1930." *BC Studies* 144: 61-90.

Comacchio, C. 1990. *"Nations Are Built of Babies": Saving Ontario Mothers and Children, 1900-1940*. Montreal and Kingston: McGill-Queen's University Press.

Dunn, D.J. 1918. "Medical Inspection of School Children." *Canadian Medical Association Journal* 8: 925-32.

Enns, H., and A. Neufeldt, eds. 2003. *In Pursuit of Equal Participation: Canada and Disability at Home and Abroad*. Concord: Captus Press.

Ferguson, P. 2002. "Notes towards a History of Hopelessness: Disability and the Places of Therapeutic Failure." *Disability, Culture, and Education* 1: 27-40.

Foucault, M. 1986. "The Subject and Power." In H.L. Dreyfus and P. Rabinow, eds., *Michel Foucault: Beyond Structuralism and Hermeneutics*, 208-26. Brighton, UK: Harvester.

Gleason, M., T. Myers, L. Paris, and V. Strong-Boag. 2010. "Introduction." In Gleason, M., T. Myers, L. Paris, and V. Strong-Boag, eds., *Lost Kids: Negotiating Disadvantage for Children and Youth in Canada, Australia, and the United States, 1900 to the Present*, 1-12. Vancouver: UBC Press.

Gould, S. 1980. "Dr. Down's Syndrome." *Natural History* 89: 142-48.

Halpenny, J., and L. Ireland. 1911. *How to Be Healthy*. Toronto: W.J. Gage.

Hanvey, L. 2002. *Children with Disabilities and Their Families in Canada: A Discussion Paper*. Ottawa: National Children Alliance for the First National Roundtable on Children with Disabilities.

Jones, A., and L. Rutman. 1981. *In the Children's Aid: J.J. Kelso and Child Welfare in Ontario*. Toronto: University of Toronto Press.

Kerr, Mrs. M.H. 1915. "Defective Children." *Public Health Journal* 6: 620.

Key, E. 1900. *The Century of the Child*. New York: Putnam.

Kierstead, A.G., and L. Hanvey. 2001. "Special Education in Canada." *Perception: Journal of the Canadian Council on Social Development* 25: 1-6.

Knight, A. 1910. *The Ontario Public School Hygiene*. Toronto: Copp Clark.

Lee, A. 1932. "The Beginnings of Beauty." *Chatelaine*, 26 September.

Lindemeyer, K. 1997. *A Right to Childhood: The US Children's Bureau and Child Welfare, 1912-46*. Urbana, IL: University of Illinois Press.

Lucas, C.N. 1926. *Public Health Education in the Schools*. Vancouver: BC: Provincial Board of Health.

MacHaffie, L. 1937. "Preventative Paediatrics as Seen by the School Medical Officer." *Canadian Public Health Journal* 28: 498-504.

MacLaren, A. 1990. *Our Own Master Race: Eugenics in Canada, 1885-1945*. Toronto: Oxford University Press.

MacMurchy, H. 1915. "The Mentally Defective Child." *Public Health Journal* 6: 85-86.

McPhedran, H. 1929. "The Pre-School Child." *Canadian Medical Association Journal* 20: 659-61.

Mitchell, D., and S. Snyder. 2003. "The Eugenic Atlantic: Race, Disability, and the Making of an International Eugenic Science, 1800-1945." *Disability and Society* 18: 843-64.

Mundie, G.S. 1914. "The Mentally Defective." *Canadian Medical Association Journal* 4(5): 396-405.

–. 1915. "Juvenile Delinquency." *Canadian Medical Association Journal* 5: 405-10.

Myers, T. 2006. *Caught: Montreal's Modern Girls and the Law, 1869-1945*. Toronto: University of Toronto Press.

Myers, T., and J. Sangster. 2001. "Retorts, Runaways, and Riots: Patterns of Resistance in Canadian Reform Schools for Girls, 1930-1960." *Journal of Social History* 34: 669-98.

Park, D., and J. Radforth. 1998. "From the Case Files: Reconstructing a History of Forced Sterilization." *Disability and Society* 13: 317-42.

Read, J., and J. Walmsley. 2006. "Historical Perspectives on Special Education, 1890–1970." *Disability and Society* 21: 455-69.

Rooke, P., and R.L. Schnell. 1983. *Discarding the Asylum: From Child Rescue to the Welfare State in English-Canada, 1800-1950*. Lanham, MD: University Press of America.

Sealander, J. 2003. *The Failed Century of the Child: Governing America's Young in the Twentieth Century*. New York: Cambridge University Press.

Simmons, H. 1982. *From Asylum to Welfare*. Toronto: National Institute on Mental Retardation.

Strong-Boag, V. 2005. "'Today's Child': Preparing for the 'Just Society' One Family at a Time." *Canadian Historical Review* 86: 673-99.

Sutherland, H. 1940. "Health of the Baby Becomes Increasingly Important." *Saturday Night,* 23 March, 17-22.

Sutherland, N. 1976. *Children in English-Canadian Society: Framing the Twentieth Century Consensus*. Toronto: University of Toronto Press.

–. 1992. "When You Listen to the Winds of Childhood, How Much Can You Believe?" *Curriculum Inquiry* 22: 235-326.

Thompson, P. 1994. "Believe It or Not: Rethinking the Historical Interpretation of Memory." In J. Jeffrey and G. Edwall, eds., *Memory and History: Essays on Recalling and Interpreting Experience,* 1-13. Lanham, MD: University Press of America.

Thomson, G. 2002. "A Fondness for Charts and Children: Scientific Progressivism in Vancouver Schools 1920 to 1950." *Historical Studies in Education* 12: 111-28.

–. 2006. "'Through No Fault of Their Own': Josephine Dauphinee and the 'Subnormal' Pupils of the Vancouver School System, 1911-1941." *Historical Studies in Education* 18: 51-73.

Trent, J.W., Jr. 1994. *Inventing the Feeble Mind: A History of Mental Retardation in the United States*. Berkeley, CA: University of California Press.

Vertinsky, P. 1994. "The Social Construction of the Gendered Body: Exercise and the Exercise of Power." *International Journal of the History of Sport* 11: 147-71.

Volpe, P. 1986. "Is Down Syndrome a Modern Disease?" *Perspectives in Biology and Medicine* 29: 423-36.

Warner, E. 1935. "A Survey of Mongolism, with a Review of One Hundred Cases." *Canadian Medical Association Journal* 33: 495-500.

Williams, R. 1997. *A Vancouver Boyhood: Reflections of Growing up in Vancouver, 1925-1945*. Vancouver: Peanut Butter Publishing.

Wood, T., M. Lerrigo, and N. Lamkin. 1938. *Adventures in Living: New Ways for Old*. New York: Nelson and Company.

Young, J. 1992. "Changing Attitudes towards Families of Hospitalized Children from 1935 to 1975: A Case Study." *Journal of Advanced Nursing* 17: 1422-29.

Zelizer, V. 1985. *Pricing the Priceless Child: The Changing Social Value of Children*. New York: Basic Books.

9
Pathologizing Childhood
Anita Ilta Garey

As a life stage, "childhood" is a social construction. The years that it covers, the rights and responsibilities that are assigned to it, and its "fit" within the larger social system to which it belongs have varied across cultures, over time, and by race, class, and gender. Thus, "childhood's end," or purpose *(raison d'être),* also varies in these ways. What, then, is childhood's end in the contemporary United States? That is the question explored in this chapter – a question that turns on its head the more typical approach to looking at aspects of childhood. Instead of examining the way in which society deals with a presumably fixed and natural childhood, such as Mona Gleason's portrayal in the previous chapter, I start from the perspective that the way children are treated illuminates the way that childhood is constructed and, thereby, the social ends of childhood within a particular culture.[1]

Childhood in the United States, which now covers infancy to about eighteen years of age, has evolved from a life stage that was integrated into a productive family economy to one that has become "economically useless" to non-agrarian families in a wage-labour society (Zelizer 1985, 6). Social historian Steven Mintz (2004, x) notes that, "unlike children in the past, young people today have fewer socially valued ways to contribute to their family's well-being or to participate in community life." Children have not only become occasions for consumption by parents and other family members, requiring large investments of time, labour, and money for their maintenance and development, but are also consumers in their own right, constituting a target market for product advertisers (Schor 2004; Pugh 2009).[2] In economic terms, childhood has become primarily a life stage of consumption rather than of production.

It is a prevailing belief that the investments made in one's offspring during their childhood, adolescent, and early adult years will reap benefits to the older generation and to the society as a whole when those children reach full adulthood and become economically productive and socially useful members of society. I argue, however, that, although today's children do not, in general, produce goods, they do fulfil an economic end or purpose for some groups in society. The entire educational system, for example, depends on the extended period of childhood that has come to seem "natural" in the United States.[3]

Children also provide economic benefits to the helping professions: social workers, guidance counsellors, psychotherapists, and mental health workers. Pointing out that people employed in these professions profit from the people whom they serve is often a contentious point. It may offend those who argue that people in the helping professions take on this work with the best of intentions and are often poorly recompensed relative to their education. However, intention and amount of economic return do not alter the fact that most of these jobs are linked to the existence and continuance of certain "social problems," of which many are socially constructed. I am certainly not the first to make the argument that problem solvers need problems to solve. In 1960, the British social scientist Barbara Wootton (1960, 383) made a similar point when she noted that social workers are trained to think that, as professionals, they

> understand others better than they understand themselves. It is small wonder that social workers find it hard to appreciate that the great majority of their clients require only some specific service – small wonder, in short, that caseworkers are under constant temptation to create cases.

And in a classic article on the societal benefits of poverty, sociologist Herbert Gans (1972, 277-78) writes:

> Associating poverty with positive functions seems at first glance to be unimaginable. Of course, the slumlord and the loan shark are commonly known to profit from the existence of poverty, but they are viewed as evil men, so their activities are classified among the dysfunctions of poverty. However, what is less often recognized, at least by the conventional wisdom, is that poverty also makes possible the existence or expansion of respectable professions and occupations, for example, penology, criminology, social work, and public health.

In this chapter, I discuss how children's negative social behaviour is framed in a way that creates a product – the pathologized child – that benefits and has economic value for certain groups.

The Study

My analysis is based on research that I conducted by observing an innovative state program that deals with serious cases of school truancy. In the last ten years, many states have implemented programs that are intended to deal with the truant behaviour of school children. In one New England state, a truancy-deterrent program for middle school children (sixth, seventh, and eighth graders) established special "truancy courts" within the state family court system. These courts deal solely with cases in which a child has so many unexcused absences that a truancy petition is filed with the family court by the school district's truant officer. Between September 2001 and December 2003, I conducted weekly observations in three truancy courts serving three separate school districts that together contained seven middle schools. I obtained permission from the truancy court judge and the chief judge of the family court to observe the court proceedings on an ongoing basis.[4] My argument in this chapter is based on over two years of field notes on the interactions in three court sites on approximately 300 individual truancy cases.

The school districts served by the courts that I observed are racially and ethnically diverse and include the children of recent immigrants from a variety of countries as well as White, Black, and Hispanic children whose families have lived in the United States for generations. The racial/ethnic breakdown varies between schools within the same district. In one school district, for example, a school in an upper-middle-class area of the district was 83 percent White, while another was only 43 percent White. The families served by the courts that I observed also vary in their class position and socio-economic status. Race/ethnicity and socio-economic status are highly correlated in the schools that are the most racially homogeneous. In other words, schools in which the students were predominantly White were the schools with the highest proportion of students from middle- and upper-middle-class families; schools in which students were primarily from families of colour were also the schools with the largest proportion of families in the lowest socio-economic brackets. However, the children of White working class and working poor families were all well represented in most of the schools covered by the courts in this study. The sex ratio of truancy cases across courts was 58 percent boys and 42 percent girls.

This study is not about "truancy" per se. I am not studying "correlations" between children's behaviour and family characteristics, nor am I studying "outcomes." Rather, I see the truancy court as a *setting* that provides a particular *context* in which to study a variety of questions about interactions between families and other institutions, such as schools, social service agencies, the legal system, and the state. As Clifford Geertz (2001, 22) points out, "anthropologists don't study villages (tribes, towns, neighbourhoods); they study *in* villages." In the same spirit, I am not studying truancy courts; I am studying *in* truancy courts.

The Truancy Court Setting

The truancy court is a "problem-solving court." The structure of problem-solving courts varies, but what distinguishes them from other kinds of courts is that they are intended to address issues that underlie and contribute to the actions that have resulted in charges of a legal offence. Their purpose is to change future behaviour rather than simply punish past violations. This goal usually involves a multidisciplinary team approach, in which the court collaborates with social service agencies, mental health practitioners, and other groups (Casey and Rottman 2006).[5]

Modelled on drug courts, truancy courts monitor a child's behaviour over time in an effort to get the child back on track – attending school, behaving appropriately, and achieving academically. If a child gets back on track and thereby successfully completes the court process, the case is dismissed and there is no notation of the offence on the child's permanent records. Being monitored over time and having the opportunity to emerge with a clean record are two of the main differences between staying in truancy court and having a case adjudicated in the regular family court.

In the program I observed, the truancy court hearings are physically located in the schools, so that the judge, bailiff, and court clerk convene court in a school room or school auditorium rather than at the courthouse in the city centre. The court moves from school to school, meeting once a week in each school that it covers (for example, in School A on Mondays, School B on Tuesdays, and so forth). Although located in the school, the truancy court is not a school program nor is it run by the school. It is run by the state family court, which has powers that the school does not have. The location of the "courtroom" in the school brings with it some unique features. For example, the school guidance counsellors attend regularly and present reports on the progress or lack thereof of each student who appears in court. The school principal, vice-principal, school social workers, and school psychologists often attend all or part of the proceedings, either out of some connection to a particular case or interest in a particular child. Although the setting is less formal than in most courtrooms, the power and authority of the court is no less real. Truancy court judges have temporarily removed children from their homes, placed children in psychiatric facilities for observation, ordered home investigations by the state's Department of Child Protective Services, and issued arrest warrants for truant children who fail to appear.

The number of incidents of truancy that have to occur before a truancy petition is filed varies by school district. A commonly used definition is ten unexcused absences or 10 percent of the number of school days at any point during the year. Most of the children brought before the truancy court have far more absences than the school district minimum for truancy court referral. After the formal arraignment part of the hearing, the judge asks the child why he or she has been repeatedly absent from school, which is the beginning of trying to identify and address the underlying causes. Goals are set, such as attending school every day, catching up on homework, or making up a missed test, and these goals are reviewed the following week. The child attends court weekly, and the child's parent must attend for at least the first three weeks. If, after a few weeks, the child is back on track (attending school, being on time, doing schoolwork, and behaving well), then the parent does not have to come to court with the child unless problems reoccur or new problems arise.

At each weekly review, the truancy officer reports on the child's attendance and the guidance counsellors report on behaviour and relay the teachers' reports of the child's academic work. Some time is usually spent on "problem solving," and the judge issues court orders that attempt to address what are perceived to be either the underlying or the immediate cause of the child's attendance problem. Court-ordered interventions or solutions may include family counselling, educational testing, mental health evaluations, an eye exam and eyeglasses, and so forth. Children usually remain in the truancy court for seven to twelve months from the time they are arraigned. Most of them are eventually dismissed on the basis of successful completion of the program, a few are deemed incorrigible and referred out of the truancy court to the main family court, and some children leave because they move out of the court's jurisdiction.

Framing the Problem

In this chapter, I describe typical court cases to illustrate how truant behaviour is framed by the representatives of the judicial, educational, and social service systems in a problem-solving court. I examine the way in which children's truancy and other socially negative behaviour are framed as problems of mental health and personal pathology and how medicalized labels are then used to explain the cause of the behaviour that brought the child into court. I am not suggesting that mental illness or psychological disorders do not exist, but I am arguing that an *a priori* mental health framework is being used as the first, and often the only, way to explain and treat the causes of the truant behaviour that brought the child to the attention of the court.

Miguel: Bad Behaviour or a "Sick" Child

Miguel is a fourteen-year-old Puerto Rican boy in the seventh grade. He was arraigned in the truancy court and, for a short period, was removed from his home for failing to comply with the court order to attend school. While he was in the custody of the State Department of Families and Children, a routine psychiatric evaluation was conducted. He was then returned to his home, and his behaviour and attendance improved for about a month, at which point Miguel was suspended for threatening a teacher. At the court review following this incident, both Miguel and his mother were present. The truancy officer began by telling the judge: "His [Miguel's] words were 'I'm going to stick him.' It was difficult getting mom in." The judge then said to Miguel: "What do you have to say?"

> *Miguel:* I didn't mean I was going to stick him.
> *Judge:* What did you mean? Did you mean you were going to poke him? That's threatening a teacher. You touch a teacher and you go to the state juvenile detention centre. What are you doing while you're suspended?
> *Miguel:* I'm doing my school work.
> *Judge:* I am so mad at you for threatening a teacher! You're lucky I'm not removing you [from your home] today.
> *Judge:* Why did you threaten your teacher?
> *Miguel:* He gave me an attitude. Told me, "Go to your locker and go to your room." I'm not going – and she started yelling. I don't like people ordering me around.
> *Judge:* Hey! Too bad! You're a juvenile. People can order you around.

Mother: His father is a very *very* strict person ... He tell him, you go to school in Puerto Rico and see how bad it is. He's going to end up sending him to Puerto Rico.
Court Aide: [sotto voce] He needs a beating.

The judge ordered Miguel to do community service at the police station and asked the school's police officer liaison (who was in the room) to handle this request. The police officer told Miguel that, on Sunday, he should "report to Sergeant Smith for work. Be there at 8:00 a.m. You can clean toilets and wash cars." Then he added: "I had Miguel in class. He was no problem. I'm surprised." To which the judge replied: "Yes, he's a good kid. I'm shocked." After Miguel and his mother left, the judge and the guidance counsellor each commented that both Miguel and his mother look better than they have before, and the police officer said again: "I'm surprised. He was never mean." The guidance counsellor agrees, and the judge added: "The psychiatric evaluation says nothing about anger."

Threatening a teacher is understandably labelled as problem behaviour, but what kind of problem behaviour is it? Miguel does not deny that he threatened the teacher, but he explains his behaviour as a reasonable response to being yelled at and ordered around. According to Miguel, he meant "back off" and not that he was really going "to stick him."[6] However, the judge rejected Miguel's account, reminding him that, as a juvenile, he needs to expect and accept being ordered around – and responding to a teacher with threatening statements is not a reasonable response. What accounts for Miguel's acting in an unreasonable manner? The authorities in the room are perplexed about how to explain his behaviour because up to now they have all perceived Miguel as "a good kid."

I want to stop here a moment to focus on a linguistic manoeuvre that both represents and leads toward pathologizing Miguel. The police officer and the judge both discuss the act of threatening a teacher not so much as something Miguel *did* but, rather, as something that represents who Miguel *is*. They do not use their experience of Miguel as "a good kid," "no problem," and "never mean" to question the incident but, rather, to question their assessment of Miguel. The police officer thinks of the threat as a manifestation of "meanness" – a personality trait – but not one that he or the guidance counsellor would have previously applied to Miguel. And the judge thinks of Miguel's behaviour toward the teacher as one that might indicate a psychological problem with anger by noting, with puzzlement in her voice, that Miguel's psychological evaluation did not include anything about an anger problem. The judge is therefore "shocked," and the police officer and the guidance counsellor are "surprised" because they have trouble reconciling a "good kid" with a "bad act." Miguel's mother and the court aide, on the other hand, appear to share a different interpretation of the problem. In their view, Miguel is not "sick"; he simply needs disciplining. Their respective suggestions for dealing with the problem – having his "strict" father intervene or using corporal punishment – are consistent with a view of children as people who need training in the way to do the right things and discipline to bring them back in line when they misbehave. Unlike the finesse of translating *the act* into *the person,* this latter approach does not require categorizing children into "good kids" and "bad kids," nor does it immediately cast an undesirable action as a symptom of problems in psychological adjustment or emotional well-being.[7] These are not the only two possible approaches to dealing with children's socially negative behaviour, nor am I suggesting that the approach offered by Miguel's mother and the court aide is better than that of the judge and the guidance counsellor. My point is that the pathologizing approach of the court is not the only way to frame children's behaviour. The authorities in this case struggle with their previous perception of Miguel within a perspective that sees negative behaviour as signalling psychological or emotional problems that can be labelled according to the *Diagnostic and Statistical Manual of Mental Disorders* (2000).

Trisha: A "Sick" Child or a "Toxic" Situation?

Mental health labels not only name and situate the underlying causes of children's socially negative behaviours, but they also work to turn attention away from situations and events that offer alternative explanations for the same behaviours. Trisha is a thirteen-year-old eighth grader who was habitually truant and failing all of her classes. The judge ordered a psychological assessment in response to Trisha's continued truancy and refusal to do her schoolwork. Her guidance counsellor thought Trisha "just didn't care." She was removed from her home by the court and placed in a shelter until a diagnostic assessment could be completed. During a review of her case while she was still in the shelter, the social worker assigned to her reported to the court that Trisha seemed to be doing better since going to the shelter and that Trisha's teachers and guidance counsellor said that she was smiling and talking more now. When Trisha and her mother came into the courtroom, Trisha's demeanour was indeed different than on earlier occasions, when she would avoid eye contact, stare at the floor, and say little. This time she talked more, volunteered information, looked at the judge when speaking to her, and smiled. Trisha told the judge that although she had failed all of her classes except for English, she had a plan for fixing her grades. She also explained to the judge that she liked the shelter because there were special activities, other girls who understood what she was going through, three meals a day, and a snack after school. As she said this, Trisha's mother turned her head away and said: "Guess I'm not fun."

Trisha started skipping school the year her parents were divorcing, and she moved with her mother and brother to a new school district and changed schools. During the year in which her case was reviewed at least biweekly, Trisha's family was evicted from their apartment and had to move, the family's car was impounded by the police because it was not insured, the family had to move for a third time, and Trisha's mother experienced job loss and periods of unemployment. At the same time, interaction at home was stressful and ridden with conflict; Trisha and her twelve-year-old brother were constantly bickering and often getting into physical fights; Trisha's mother was not home much and was said to spend a lot of time at the local bar;[8] Trisha and her mother were arguing a lot; and Trisha's mother remarried a man whom Trisha did not like and who, she reported, called her names. Trisha seemed to have very little contact with her father, and Trisha's adult sister, with whom she was close, was estranged from their mother. Moving from the town where her parents had lived together before their divorce meant that Trisha no longer had access to the support she had previously received from her old school friends. Given this situation, it is not surprising that the behaviours that resulted in the court order for a diagnostic assessment diminished or were replaced by more positive behaviours when Trisha was in an environment that she felt was less stressful and more predictable and supportive.

Trisha's diagnostic assessment report stated that she suffered from depression, anxiety disorder, and school phobia. Prozac, as well as family and individual counselling, were prescribed. A long waiting list for counselling through community service agencies and a lack of follow-through by Trisha's mother resulted in no counselling ever taking place. One of the judge's regular questions to Trisha became: "Are you taking your meds?" Whether or not anti-depressants were called for, and I do not claim to have the expertise to argue for or against their use in Trisha's case, there were overwhelming structural and interactional factors that were also at play.[9] The microsystems of family, school, friends, and neighbourhood were not considered by the court, the school, or the social service agencies as being directly related to Trisha's truancy or to her diagnosis of depression (Bronfenbrenner 1979).[10] Rather, these contextual factors were regarded as the (unfortunate) situation in which Trisha found herself but not as the underlying cause of her truant behaviour. The judge, guidance counsellors, and social workers were not oblivious to Trisha's situation. They were aware of, and troubled by, the oppressive, tragic, and often desperate situations of some children, but they did not see these situations as either the direct or indirect causes of truancy. Indeed, information on the court's webpage about the nature of the program's team approach clearly conveys the court's perspective on the likely causes of children's truancy:

> In each of the Truancy Courts the local community mental health organization is present. They are there to provide the families with the appropriate services and make referrals to help the child and family cope with the everyday struggles of life.

Not only is this an explicit statement of the program's focus on the child's mental health as the cause of the truancy problem, but it also frames the child's environment at both home and school as "the everyday struggles of life," as if all situations were simply ordinary "challenges" to be dealt with appropriately and never "causes" in their own right.

Implications of Pathologizing Childhood

In problem-solving courts, the problem to be dealt with is the behaviour that has resulted in the defendant's appearance in court. In truancy court, the problem is unexcused absences from school. However, rather than simply ordering the child to attend school, putting the child on probation, and following up on his or her school attendance after some months (the customary way in which truant children were handled by the family court in this state before the implementation of the truancy court), the judge, in collaboration with the school, mental health professionals, and social service agencies, attempts to find and address the underlying reason that the child is not going to school. Once a cause is discovered, the court relies on external interventions and treatments – tutoring, psychotherapy, medication, or family counselling are among the most frequent. The choice of interventions and treatments follows logically from what are identified as the causes of a child's excessive absence from school.

"Cause" can be thought about in a number of ways. Social psychologists, for example, have studied how people assign cause to behaviour. Findings suggest that, in general, people emphasize personality characteristics (internal causes) as the cause of others' behaviour but focus on environmental or situational factors (external causes) as the reason for their own actions.[11] Demographers who study fertility distinguish between immediate (proximate) determinants that directly influence fertility behaviour (that is, biological states and specific behaviours) and the social and cultural factors that influence those determinants (Bongaarts 1978). It is easier to see intermediate or direct causes than it is to see ultimate causes, and, in fairness, the truancy court is not intended to address social and cultural factors. Its aim is to get children back to school. In Trisha's case, the direct cause of her truancy was identified as her lack of motivation, which was seen as being linked to her psychological condition, of which lack of motivation is a symptom. If the reasons that children are truant or display socially negative behaviour are framed as biological or psychological factors located in the person rather than social and cultural factors located in the situation, then the interventions and treatments will be ones that are intended to directly change the individual person rather than to address the larger contextual situation.

Once an illness has been defined, cases of it can be identified. The definition includes the criteria for identification of a disorder. People can be tested or evaluated for a wide range of learning, cognitive, behavioural, and personality disorders. When there are no standard tests for a particular named condition, experts define certain patterns of behaviour as indicating the presence of the disorder. For example, the *Diagnostic and Statistical Manual of Mental Disorders* (2000, Code 313.81, note A) states that a diagnosis of oppositional defiance disorder may be applied to children who display negative, hostile, and defiant behaviour "more frequently than is typically observed in individuals of comparable age and developmental level" for at least six months. The behaviours in question include: often losing his or her temper, frequently arguing with adults, often disregarding adults' requests or rules, deliberately trying to provoke people, frequently blaming others for his or her mistakes or misbehaviour, often being easily irritated by others, often being angry and resentful, and often being spiteful. I think it likely that most parents of adolescents would recognize these behaviours, and I find it interesting that the definition of this psychological disorder is explicitly contingent on cultural and social norms by applying the diagnosis only to those children who display these behaviours more frequently than their peers.

Once cases are identified, treatments can be prescribed.[12] If the source of the truancy problem is in the makeup of individual children, it follows logically that appropriate treatments should be directed at that source. So the recommended treatments include special education, medication, counselling, individualized education programs, anger management training, and so on. Mental health professionals, social workers, educational specialists, guidance counsellors, and a plethora of others in the helping professions are the people who provide the diagnoses, treatment, and educational and therapeutic programs. Pathologizing childhood ensures the health of this industry. Relatively easy for the court to prescribe, interventions and treatments such as these not only provide a sense of efficacy for those who are charged with addressing problems such as truancy but also direct attention away from causes that are not rooted in the individual.

Personal Problems or Public Issues?

In *The Sociological Imagination*, C. Wright Mills (1959, 8) made his now classic distinction between "'the personal problems of milieu' and 'the public issues of social structure'":

> *Troubles* occur within the character of the individual and within the range of his immediate relations with others; they have to do with his self and with those limited areas of social life of which he is directly and personally aware ... *Issues* have to do with matters that transcend these local environments of the individual and the range of his inner life. They have to do with the organization of many such milieux into the institutions of an historical society as a whole, with the ways in which various milieux overlap and interpenetrate to form the larger structure of social and historical life [emphasis in original].

The view that individual pathology is the cause of truancy and children's other socially negative behaviour erases Mills's distinction.

It is possible to imagine a different approach that treats problems ascribed to children, such as truancy, as public issues. The team approach that would accompany a "public issues" perspective would look very different from the one currently used. From a public issues perspective, team approach programs would focus on the community itself. Communities and institutions would become objects of intervention rather than simply sources of intervention and service agents, and the salient question would become: "What policies and programs will create the kinds of communities that are conducive to the well-being of their inhabitants, including children?" Some examples of the questions needed to develop such policies might be: "What sorts of publicly supported community gathering places for children and adolescents might provide predictability and support in their lives?" "How should educational policies about the number of days of school each year, the starting and ending times of the school day, school vacation days, sanctions for missing school, and accommodations for student illness be designed to take account of their family-shaping and community-shaping effects?" "How might school district policies be designed to prevent the necessity of changing schools for children during times of family change and crisis (divorce, eviction, and so on)?" and "How do we construct a community that recognizes the interdependence of family members with each other and with other social institutions?"

Unlike private problems, public issues do not have the same neat connections between definition, identification, and solution. If poverty, unemployment, homelessness, or overcrowded and under-funded schools are some of the public issues creating problems of school attendance, then what is the solution and how do we get there? About these problems, there is much less agreement.

Conclusion

My use of the phrase "pathologizing childhood" in the title of this chapter is intended to suggest three things. First, that "childhood" has not only become a problem to be dealt with but also a particular kind of problem – a problem related to the health of the child, in particular, the child's mental health. Second, that what is being defined and treated within a mental health framework is not really individual children but, rather, the relationship between this stage in the life course and other social structures. Children are pathologized on the basis of their behaviour in relation to social norms about education, respect, authority, age-appropriate behaviour, and so forth. And, third, my title is intended to suggest a focus on the activity of pathologizing, not a static condition of pathology.

Although not intended as an employment program for the helping professions, this is one result of the current focus on individual pathology as the cause of social problems – and there is less motivation to look at the social causes of adolescent behaviour problems when an individual pathology approach is paying the bills. The fact that most people in the helping professions chose this sphere of employment because they want to help people and make the world a better place does not alter the point that one of the ends of childhood is to provide the raw materials by which they make their livelihood. Just as children in the United States were once part of a family economy in which they helped to produce the agricultural and trade products that could be used by the family and sold in the market, they are now part of a service economy. What they produce are the "problems" or issues that occupy people in the therapeutic industries.

Notes

1 Although I am using the singular "childhood," it is important to keep in mind that there can be more than one kind of childhood within a society since social constructions of childhood will vary by race, class, and gender.

2 A report by Grandparents.com, an online resource for grandparents, and Focalyst, a consumer research company that focuses on the baby boomer generation, states that grandparents in the United States spend $50 billion annually on their grandchildren. From before the birth to the end of the child's first year, grandparents spend an average of $1,691 on each new grandchild. "Key Findings Reveal How and Why Grandparents are Spending Billions Annually on Their Grandchildren," Press Release, 6 December 2007, PR Newswire, http://www.prnewswire.com/.

3 With the extension of childhood, and of the years of education needed to obtain workplace qualifications, young adults between the ages of eighteen and twenty-three no longer fit easily into the life-course category of "adult," and a new term, "emerging adulthood," has been coined to better capture this life stage (Arnett 2000).

4 Since it deals with juveniles, the truancy court is a "closed court." The public is not allowed to attend court proceedings, and juvenile records are confidential.

5 In drug courts, for example, defendants are usually ordered to attend Alcoholics Anonymous or Narcotics Anonymous, and the facilitators of the groups co-operate with the courts by signing attendance cards for these people.

6 A zero tolerance of threats toward teachers is understandable, and I am not suggesting that the court should have sympathized with Miguel's actions. However, zero tolerance for certain actions can blind authorities to situational contexts that may affect how underlying problems are defined and dealt with. Touching between kindergarten children and violence in creative writing are two other areas where a zero tolerance approach may misrepresent actions and result in inappropriate sanctions.

7 Based on extensive in-depth interviews with parents about the daily monitoring of their children, Margaret Nelson's book *Parenting Out of Control* (2010) describes a dichotomy in parenting between those who see their children's behaviour as a reflection of the whole child and a litmus test of the degree of trust between parent and child and those who give much less existential meaning to children's behaviour, expect children to misbehave, and consider misbehaviour to be a situation that calls for training and, often, punishment.

8   My field notes record that comments about Trisha's mother never being home and staying out drinking came from several sources: Trisha, Trisha's adult sister, and the truancy officer. On one occasion, someone in the court reported that he smelled alcohol on Trisha's mother's breath during the court hearing.

9   The *Diagnostic and Statistical Manual of Mental Disorders* (1994) identifies a number of different kinds of depression, one of which is "situational depression." In this kind of depression, symptoms of depression occur in response to specific situations or events, such as divorce, an involuntary or disruptive move, loss of a job, and so on. With situational depression, symptoms usually end within six months of the stressor's end. Although situational depression can interfere with a person's routine or usual functioning, it does not meet the criteria for major depressive disorders.

10   In a study of homeless women at two shelters, Eliot Liebow (1993, xiii) notes that "sometimes mental illness seemed to be a 'now-you-see-it, now-you-don't' phenomenon; some of the women were fine when their public assistance checks arrived, but became increasingly 'symptomatic' as the month progressed and their money (security?) diminished, coming full circle when the next check arrived" [parenthetical question in original].

11   This phenomenon is known as "the fundamental attribution error," a term coined by social psychologist Lee Ross (1977). Studies have looked at the way in which internal or external cause is attributed based on whether the action to be explained is positive or negative (a success or a failure), is performed by a man or by a woman, or is performed by someone with whom the person attributing cause shares a group identity.

12   Although there may be some debate about the appropriate treatment for a particular disorder or disability, there are usually commonly accepted approaches recommended by those who are deemed to be authorities in the field. For example, despite the fact that some people with bipolar disorder reject medication of any kind, lithium is the standard treatment and is prescribed by physicians and psychiatrists as the effective approach to this disorder.

References

Arnett, J. 2000. "Emerging Adulthood: A Theory of Development from the Late Teens through the Twenties." *American Psychologist* 55: 469-80.

Bongaarts, J. 1978. "A Framework for Analyzing the Proximate Determinants of Fertility." *Population and Development Review* 4: 105-32.

Bronfenbrenner, U. 1979. *The Ecology of Human Development.* Cambridge, MA: Harvard University Press.

Casey, P., and D. Rottman. 2006. *Problem-Solving Courts: Models and Trends.* Williamsburg, VA: National Center for State Courts.

Diagnostic and Statistical Manual of Mental Disorders. 2000. 4th edition. Washington DC: American Psychiatric Association. http://online.statref.com/.

Gans, H.J. 1972. "The Positive Functions of Poverty." *American Journal of Sociology* 78: 275-89.

Geertz, C. 2001. "Life among the Anthros." *New York Review,* 8 February, 8-22.

Liebow, E. 1993. *Tell Them Who I Am: The Lives of Homeless Women.* New York: Penguin Books.

Mills, C.W. 1959. *The Sociological Imagination.* New York: Oxford University Press.

Mintz, S. 2004. *Huck's Raft: A History of American Childhood.* Cambridge, MA: Harvard University Press.

Nelson, M. 2010. *Parenting Out of Control.* New York: New York University Press.

Pugh, A. 2009. *Longing and Belonging: Parents, Children, and Consumer Culture.* Berkeley, CA: University of California Press.

Ross, L. 1977. "The Intuitive Psychologist and His Shortcomings: Distortions in the Attribution Process." In L. Berkowitz, ed., *Advances in Experimental Social Psychology,* volume 10, 174-221. New York: Academic Press.

Schor, J. 2004. *Born to Buy: The Commercialized Child and the New Consumer Culture.* New York: Scribner.

Wootton, B. 1960. "Review: The Image of the Social Worker." *British Journal of Sociology* 11: 373-85.

Zelizer, V. 1985. *Pricing the Priceless Child.* New York: Basic.

CONCLUSION
From Children to Child: Ending in China
Jing Zhao, Nathanael Lauster, and Graham Allan

In this volume, various authors have attempted to grapple with the twin ideas of the end of children and the end of childhood. In this final chapter, we return to these ideas and their critics. As made clear in multiple chapters in this volume, while fertility has declined, children are not in imminent danger of disappearing. Similarly, while childhoods are changing, childhood as a socially constructed and carefully distinguished portion of the life course also seems in no danger of disappearing (even if it is sometimes ignored by policy makers, as discussed in Chapter 7 by Edward Kruk). We are not at the end of childhood.

So perhaps we have made the challenge for our contributors too simple, setting up straw arguments for easy demolition. In this concluding chapter, we consider a different way of defining the end of children, one with real world implications that are less easy to dismiss. In short, we could define the end of children in terms of parental expectations. Instead of expecting multiple children (a cultural norm in North America, as Rebecca Upton notes in Chapter 3), parents might come to expect a single child. In such a way, the end of children might mean the rise of the single child. There is a real world example of a country that has gone quite far in this direction, of course. In this chapter, we first return to some of the themes of this collection, then apply them to how we might think about the one-child policy and the rise of single children in China. What other ideas might have been discussed had we explored this case?

In the introduction, we laid out some of the prominent themes binding this volume together, including heterogeneity, the idea of the child, and the contrast between the child we live with and the child we live by. Heterogeneity captures the differences between groups in both childbearing experience and understandings of childhood. Grappling with heterogeneity speaks to the ways in which the positions of people matter with respect to how they live and understand their lives. Acknowledging heterogeneity means acknowledging the complexity of social life. Nathanael Lauster, Todd Martin, and James White's exploration of fertility differentials across cultural boundaries in Canada in Chapter 2 directly speaks to heterogeneity. They find that culture matters with respect to fertility and that not all Canadians are alike. However, their chapter also creates questions as to how well we can measure and understand cultural difference by placing people into the sort of narrow groupings that have become commonplace in demographic analysis. Other chapters also speak to diversity in childbearing, along the lines of cultural understandings of marriage and childbearing (Mira Whyman, Megan Lemmon, and Jay Teachman in Chapter 1), social class (Nathanael Lauster in Chapter 4), perception of mortality (Nicholas Townsend in Chapter 5), and orientation toward social norms (Upton in Chapter 3).

Heterogeneity is also present in how people understand the meaning of children. This is certainly true for the authors in this book. The meaning of a child, as discussed in this volume, might include: a material cost or benefit (Whyman, Lemmon, and Teachman in Chapter 1 and Anita Garey in Chapter 9), a means of establishing moral worth (Upton in Chapter 3 and Lauster in Chapter 4), a means of maintaining community (Lauster, Martin, and White in Chapter 2), an optional means of personal fulfillment (Whyman, Lemmon, and Teachman in Chapter 1), a necessary means of obtaining immortality (Townsend in Chapter 5), an adaptable survivor of parental circumstance (Adena Miller in Chapter 6), a policy shortcoming (Kruk in Chapter 7), or a normatively bound, morally ambiguous being, frequently disciplined and marginalized by institutional pathologization (Mona Gleason in Chapter 8 and Garey in Chapter 9). The fact that a child could mean all of these things, of course, speaks to the power of the child as an idea.

The power of the child as an idea is felt in daily life as well as in academia. Planned children all have their starts in parental ideas of a child, as discussed most poignantly in the chapters by Upton and Townsend in this volume. Yet no matter how much planning goes into a child, once children are born the idea of the child potentially conflicts with the behaviour of actual children, setting up a contrast between the child we live by and the child we live with. Actual children do not always bear out ideas, with potentially tragic consequences. Both Gleason (Chapter 8) and Garey (Chapter 9) discuss how institutions dealing with children attempt to categorize and discipline them or, alternatively, to discard them. No surprise, then, that children often seek to leave the trappings of childhood behind, as in Miller's discussion of children leaving home in Chapter 6.

The chapters in the book make clear that neither children nor childhood are in the process of ending. However, this is not to say that the authors do not express any concerns. As suggested by the first two chapters, real declines in fertility have occurred, with potentially far-reaching consequences. For countries such as Canada, where the fertility rate has fallen far below replacement level, there remain uncertainties about where the workers of the future are likely to come from. Reducing the size of the workforce could mean reducing the security of those relying on the social welfare system in their retirement. Immigration offers a possible solution to this problem, but it raises other issues of how immigrants might be made to feel at home or, alternatively, provide challenges to the cultural project of nation building.

The authors in this volume also develop a better understanding of how individual parents and prospective parents-to-be negotiate child-bearing, and, in the process, they suggest various cultural concerns. As discussed by Townsend in Chapter 5, adulthood is meaningless without children, and children are a force that provides meaning to both life and death. Townsend addresses the possibility of existential crises for those without children. Chapters 3 and 4 by Upton and Lauster respectively explore the normative pressures facing parents and those wishing to become parents. Both authors make the suggestion that parents face powerful and moral quandaries about how they should present themselves to others. Instead of going away, the specialness of childhood as a cherished and morally loaded state, or the child that parents live by, is if anything becoming stronger. At least in part as a result of new pressures to create ideal childhoods for children, the authors suggest that changes in the meaning of childhood make the path to parenthood more fraught.

As Townsend suggests, childhood is defined only in reference to adulthood and vice versa. Mismatches between the ideals of childhood and actual children are mirrored by, and inform the mismatches between, the ideals of adulthood and actual adults. As discussed in the chapters by Gleason (Chapter 8) and Garey (Chapter 9), on the one hand, adults attempt to define childhood against actual children. Power allows adults to ignore or discipline children to fit with their ideals, especially when power is encoded within institutions such as schools, hospitals, and courts. On the other hand, children also define what is meant by adulthood against actual adults. This idea is particularly well illustrated in Chapter 6 by Miller, where children experiencing parental divorce are more likely to challenge normative ideals of what adulthood means. Kruk (Chapter 7) also touches on this theme, as he measures the responsibility of policy makers by how well they look after children.

Can the ideas discussed in this book be taken further? Can they be applied outside of North America? Could they inform a different childbearing environment and a different policy context? We believe they can. To illustrate this claim, we turn to a consideration of China. As discussed earlier, the rise of the so-called "one-child policy" in China seems to have brought about an end to children, if only in the sense of ending the parental expectation of having more than one child. The contexts and meanings of childhood in this context are likely to have changed as well. What do we know about the Chinese experience and what can we say to it? Perhaps more interestingly, what other sorts of themes and insights might be developed by broadening the discussion?

China's "One-Child Policy"

Recent Chinese promotion of fertility limitation began in earnest in the early 1970s, when the government promoted birth-planning programs emphasizing *wan, xi, shao,* or later marriage, longer birth intervals, and fewer children (Greenhalgh and Winckler 2005; Liang and Lee 2006). In 1979, government engineers – surprisingly enough real engineers with backgrounds in aerospace science and control systems – took over the program and introduced what became known as the one-child policy, which attempted to directly reduce fertility, eventually limiting most couples to one child each (Greenhalgh and Winckler 2005). The one-child policy is actually a misnomer, in that there are, and always have been, many policies, and not all couples are limited to one child. Nevertheless, any reckoning of the context for childbearing in China necessarily extends discussion of the role of policy makers, something that is little discussed in the introduction to the demographic theories offered by Whyman, Lemmon, and Teachman in Chapter 1 of this volume.

Social engineering meant that the initial family planning policies pursued in the early 1970s (especially those encouraging and mandating later marriage) were weakened in favour of the more draconian single-child policy (Morgan, Zhigang, and Hayford 2009). By 1980, expectations of "one child per couple" applied to all members of the Communist Party and the Communist Youth League (Peng 1997). One-child expectations also eventually became applied to government employees and urban dwellers and residents in rural townships, although Chinese peasants were still routinely allowed two children, especially following the "open a small hole" adjustment to the one-child policy in 1984 (Greenhalgh and Winckler 2005). Since the one-child policy was carried out at the local level, a variety of different exemptions arose. Minorities whose population was under ten million, rural residents whose first born were daughters, the parents of the disabled, and those in dangerous occupations (for example, miners) were often allowed a second child (Hesketh, Lu, and Xing, 2005; Liang and Lee 2006). Similarly, those couples made up of individuals who were themselves single children were allowed a second child in some places. By 1990, most of the regulatory apparatus to carry out the one-child policy had been put in place and stabilized (Morgan, Zhigang, and Hayford 2009). The fact that this regulatory apparatus explicitly recognized and encouraged cultural difference provides a counterpoint to the discussion of Canadian multiculturalism in Chapter 2 by Lauster, Martin, and White. In the Chinese context, the state moved beyond the recognition of multiculturalism to the reinforcement of ethnic distinctions and also established a very strong distinction between rural and urban. Ethnic and urban/rural distinctions reified by the state through family planning policies (and elsewhere) became the sources of possible tension in a different way than in the Canadian context, where immigration has been so significant, opening up a new line of thinking about policy impacts.

The ways the regulatory apparatus of the one-child policy worked varied from place to place. In general, it became required to receive a childbearing permit, which in turn became linked to the birth quota allotted to various localities. Having a child inside the permit system usually meant having only a single child, but it also meant receiving access to various state benefits – for example, longer parental leave with pay. Having a child outside of the permit system was technically not allowed and was prevented in many places by the insertion of an inter-uterine device, sterilization, or forced abortion (although it should be noted that the abortion rate in China remains well below the rate in the United States) (see Hesketh, Lu, and Xing 2005). Since 1980, those people managing to have children outside the permit system faced various penalties, ranging from salary deductions to a loss of status and work (especially for state employees and urban residents) (Scharping 2003).

More recently, especially after 2002, certain aspects of the one-child policy were relaxed, making it possible to have a first birth without a permit and giving individuals more open contraceptive choices. Such changes fit with the broader shift since the turn of the millennium from mandatory regulation to incentive management, from limiting the quantity of births to raising the quality of childrearing, and from strengthening contraceptive regimes to improving health services (Greenhalgh and Winckler 2005). This shift might be fruitfully discussed with respect to the cautionary policy-related tales of the authors in this volume. In Chapter 7, Kruk pushes for policies that enable, rather than discipline, parents to spend time with their children. Broadly speaking, Garey in Chapter 9 also cautions against policies that rely on disciplining the powerless. Gleason's contribution to the volume in Chapter 8 offers a particularly powerful warning against policies that make some children disappear, which is an especially important point in the Chinese context, where so many children, especially girls, have literally disappeared. The state's efforts to avoid this outcome through relaxing restrictions on childbearing in some situations have paradoxically led to the lesser value of some children (especially girls and the disabled) becoming encoded into the policies carried out by the state.

The way the state carried out fertility regulation is interesting to consider in light of the cultural theories forwarded by Townsend, by Upton, and by Lauster in this volume. Townsend's discussion of mortality and ancestor worship in Chapter 5 accords quite well with the understandings of obligation belonging to Confucian thought in Chinese history, providing another case in which to consider how Townsend's analysis of childbearing motivation works (Tang 1995). Townsend's work might also describe the kind of forces – the kind of cultural norms – that Chinese social engineers felt they were up against (or simply overlooked) as they devised family planning policies. In Chapter 3, Upton considers how individuals draw on various cultural narratives to explain their deviations from cultural norms and navigate cultural contradictions, especially between work demands and family demands. Her work draws attention to the similar processes that are likely to be at work in the Chinese context, where, on the one hand, women not wishing to have more than one child could employ loyalty to state policies as an explanation for resisting more traditional family demands for larger families or for male heirs. On the other hand, those pleading for leniency in the face of state sanctions against parents of multiple children might justify their actions with reference to widely understood traditional expectations. The different evasive justifications that might be employed in these situations speak to the contradictory pressures faced by many, and illustrate the importance of considering cultural and economic factors in any analysis of policy change. How has the one-child policy both responded to and altered Chinese expectations about children? Has it operated in accordance with the status-related processes that Lauster suggests in Chapter 5 were at work behind American cultural change? If so, the post-Mao era in China provides exciting terrain for understanding how status and culture operate together (Hanser 2008).

Would Chinese fertility have declined without the one-child policy? At first glance, state interventions seem to have had a dramatic effect on fertility in China. The total fertility rate (TFR) in 1965 stood at approximately six children per woman. By 1979, following the "later, longer, fewer" family planning initiatives, this figure had been more than halved to approximately 2.7 children expected per woman (Liang and Lee 2006). During the 1980s, immediately after the one-child policy came into effect, the fertility rate did not greatly decline in China. However, the end of the 1980s brought a return to declines, following the stabilization of the enforcement of its one-child policies. By the mid-1990s, Chinese TFRs ranged from 1.4 to 1.5 births per woman, which was roughly in line with the calculations of the number of children technically permitted under various provincial programs (Morgan, Zhigang, and Hayford 2009). It is worth noting that China's low fertility is mirrored in the surrounding states and sub-states with similar cultural roots but without a comparable policy history, including Hong Kong, Taiwan, and Singapore as well as South Korea and Japan.

China provides a further study of how trends in childbearing and constructions of childhood might relate to one another. The children born after sharp declines in fertility were unlikely to grow up facing childhoods similar to their parents, aunts, and uncles. The grandchildren of the one-child policy are unlikely to have aunts and uncles at all. Shifts in the number of children alter the relationships between children and adults. The only children of China have been labelled "little emperors," spoiled in the attention and resources they receive from the adults around them. Yet as Vanessa Fong (2004) points out, all that attention also has a downside in that children become the "only hope" of their extended families, shouldering huge burdens of expectations. As in North America, the idea of the child that the Chinese live by and the actual child that Chinese families commonly live with are different things, with similar repercussions for definitions of adulthood. Similar to Miller's analysis of children of divorce in Chapter 6 in this volume, the children of the one-child policy may grow up redefining the responsibilities of adulthood.

Overall, even a cursory glance beyond North American borders reveals a wealth of possibilities for extending the discussion begun in this volume. The Chinese case, in particular, provides fuel for new conversations. As a result, we complete a volume dedicated to the end of children and the end of childhood most concerned with beginnings. As authors, we hope the interdisciplinary collaboration on efforts to understand changes in childbearing and childhood will continue well into the future.

References

Fong, V.L. 2004. *Only Hope: Coming of Age under China's One-Child Policy.* Palo Alto, CA: Stanford University Press.

Greenhalgh, S., and E. Winckler. 2005. *Governing China's Population: From Leninist to Neoliberal Biopolitics.* Stanford, CA: Stanford University Press.

Hanser, A. 2008. *Service Encounters: Class, Gender, and the Market for Social Distinction in Urban China.* Stanford, CA: Stanford University Press.

Hesketh, T., L. Lu, and Z.W. Xing. 2005. "The Effect of China's One-Child Family Policy after Twenty-Five Years." *New England Journal of Medicine* 353: 1171-76.

Liang, Q., and C-F. Lee. 2006. "Fertility and Population Policy: An Overview." In D. Poston Jr., C.-F. Lee, C-F. Chang, S. McKibben, and C. Walther, eds., *Fertility, Family Planning, and Population Policy in China,* 8-19. New York: Routledge.

Morgan, S., G. Zhigang, and S. Hayford. 2009. "China's Below Replacement Fertility: Recent Trends and Future Prospects." *Population and Development Review* 35: 605-29.

Peng, P. 1997. "China's Population Policy." *Population and Development Review* 23: 926.

Scharping, T. 2003. *Birth Control in China, 1949-2000: Population Policy and Demographic Development.* London: Routledge.

Tang, Z. 1995. "Confucianism, Chinese Culture, and Reproductive Behavior." *Population and Environment* 16: 269-84.

Contributors

Graham Allan is Emeritus Professor of Sociology at Keele University in the United Kingdom. Between 2005 and 2007, he was Visiting Professor in Family Studies at the University of British Columbia. His research has focused principally on the sociology of informal relationships, including friendships, family ties, and community sociology. He has published widely in these areas. Recently, he has acted as one of the advisory editors for George Ritzer's *Encyclopedia of Sociology*. He is also co-editor of the *Palgrave Studies in Family and Intimate Life* series.

Anita Ilta Garey is an Associate Professor of Human Development and Family Studies and Sociology at the University of Connecticut. Her research and teaching focus on families in relation to social institutions and within specific social and cultural contexts. Her book *Weaving Work and Motherhood* (1999) won the 2000 William J. Goode Book Award from the Family Section of the American Sociological Association. Her other works include *Who's Watching: Daily Practices of Surveillance among Contemporary Families* (co-edited with Margaret K. Nelson, 2009), which addresses how family members monitor each other, other families, and their own borders, and *At the Heart of Work and Family: Engaging the Ideas of Arlie Hochschild* (co-edited with Karen V. Hansen, 2011).

Mona Gleason is an Associate Professor in the Department of Educational Studies at the University of British Columbia. She is the author of *Normalizing the Ideal: Psychology, Schooling and Family in Postwar Canada* (1999) and co-editor of *Rethinking Canada: The Promise of Women's History,* 4th, 5th and 6th editions (2002; 2006; 2010), *Children, Teachers and Schools in the History of British Columbia,* 2nd edition (2003), and *Lost Kids: Vulnerable Children and Youth in Twentieth-Century Canada and the United States* (2010). Her current book project is entitled *Small Matters: Children in Sickness and Health in Canada, 1900 to 1940.*

Edward Kruk, MSW, Ph.D., is an Associate Professor in the School of Social Work at the University of British Columbia, specializing in child and family policy and practice. He has over thirty years of clinical and community work experience as a professional social worker. He is author of *Divorce and Disengagement* (1993), *Mediation and Conflict Resolution in Social Work and the Human Services* (1997), and *Children's Needs and Paternal Responsibilities* (2011) and has published widely in a variety of academic and professional journals. He is currently completing work on a book on child custody law reform. Edward is the father of two boys, Stephan, who is twenty-eight, and Liam, who is fifteen.

Nathanael Lauster is an Assistant Professor in the Department of Sociology at the University of British Columbia and was formerly also a member of this university's school containing Family Studies. His research focuses on the intersections between culture and how people negotiate their built environments along the way to forming families, households, and other social connections. He has published in a variety of outlets, including the *Journal of Marriage and Family, Social Problems, Health and Place, Population Research and Policy Review,* and *Housing Studies.* In addition to co-editing this volume, he recently co-edited a special issue of *Housing Studies* on housing and the family.

Megan Lemmon is a recent sociology graduate of Western Washington University. She has been working with Jay Teachman and Mira Whyman on a project funded by the National Science Foundation that is concerned with military service and health. Her future plans are to attend graduate school in sociology, specializing in family demography.

Todd F. Martin is a Ph.D. candidate in the Department of Sociology at the University of British Columbia. His main research interests are in the changing contexts of family formation throughout the life course. He has published on the topic of the religious socialization of children in the *Journal of Adolescent Research* and the labour force integration of recent Canadian immigrants in *International Migration Review.*

Adena B.K. Miller is a Ph.D. candidate at the University of Western Ontario. Her main research interests focus on the sociology of family, youth, and personal relationships. She has recently published "Young Adult Daughters' Accounts of Relationships with Non-Residential Fathers: Relational Damage, Repair and Maintenance" in the *Journal of Divorce and Remarriage,* based on her Master's thesis in family studies at the University of British Columbia. The topic of her Ph.D. is the personal relationships of young people.

Jay Teachman is a Professor in the Department of Sociology at Western Washington University. Teachman maintains a long-standing interest in the demography of families. He has published numerous articles on topics such as divorce, remarriage, child support, and cohabitation. His latest project, which is supported by a grant from the National Science Foundation, involves an in-depth analysis of the family and life-course consequences of military service for young men. The study, in which Megan Lemmon and Mira Whyman are also involved, is concerned especially with military service and later health outcomes.

Nicholas W. Townsend is an Associate Professor in the Department of Anthropology at Brown University. His research focuses on the cultural meanings and social organization relevant to social reproduction and cultural continuity, the social organization of domestic lives in a comparative perspective, and the relationships and roles of men in families. He has investigated the cultural meanings of fatherhood in three different groups: the contemporary American middle class; migrant men from Botswana, one of the labour reserves of apartheid South Africa; and a poor, rural population in South Africa. He is author of *The Package Deal: Marriage, Work, and Fatherhood in Men's Lives* (2002).

Rebecca L. Upton is an Associate Professor at DePauw University and currently holds the Edward Myers Dolan Chair in Sociology and Anthropology. She was a Fulbright Scholar at the University of Botswana for 2009-10 at the Centre for the Study of HIV/AIDS. Her research focuses on infertility and HIV/AIDS in northern Botswana, the influence of migration on family structure, women's health and fertility outcomes in this region, and the intersections of qualitative and quantitative methodologies. She has spent the past ten years researching the advent and impact of a second child in the American dual-earning middle class. She has published in the *Journal of Contemporary Ethnography, Gender and Society, Gender and Development,* the *Journal of Southern African Studies,* and the *African Journal of Reproductive Health,* among others. She is currently writing a book for Oxford University Press on the failure of public health initiatives and HIV/AIDS prevention programs in Botswana.

James White is a Professor in the Department of Sociology at the University of British Columbia. His research interests include theories of fertility; ethnic identity, enclaves and fertility; problems with levels of analysis in social theory; and disability and family. He is co-author with David Klein of *Family Theories,* 3rd edition (2008); *Families in Canada,* 3rd edition (2005); and *Advancing Family Theories* (2004). He is currently the editor of the *Journal of Comparative Family Studies.*

Mira Whyman graduated from Western Washington University with a degree in sociology. With Jay Teachman and Megan Lemmon, she has recently been studying the family and life-course consequences of military service for young men, especially with regard to their future health experiences. She is planning on attending law school, with the aim of providing legal assistance to individuals and groups who are often deprived of legal counsel.

Jing Zhao is a Ph.D. student in the Department of Sociology at the University of British Columbia. She earned an MA in 2009 from the University of British Columbia and an LL.B. in 2001 from the University of Science and Technology, Beijing. Her research interests include immigrant fertility, family formation, and population policy. Her MA thesis explores how immigrants' reproductive behaviours are structured by cultural norms and population policies in the sending country as well as by immigration and integration policies in the receiving country.

Index

privileged, 79, 80, 82, 85, 88, 89; staged and unstaged, 88; stay-at-home, 80, 81, 82, 83, 86, 88
Motiejunaite, A., 134
Mulder, Clara, 89
Multiculturalism: Canadian, 34, 35-37, 48, 51n2, 181
multidisciplinary team approach, 164
Mundie, Gordon S., 143, 148, 149, 150
Muslim, 47, 48
Mustard, J.F., 124
Myers, T., 141

Narcotics Anonymous, 174n5
National Association of Women and the Law, 135n4
National Center on Addiction and Substance Abuse, 123
National Center for Education: *National Work-Life Conflict Study* Statistics (US), 125
National Children's Alliance, 135n2, 155
National Family Child Care Association, 135n2
National Institute of Child Health and Development (NICHD), 124, 125, 123
Nazi holocaust, 144
Neidert, L., 33
Nelson, Margaret, 174n7
Neufeldt, A., 156
New Ways for Old, 152
New York Times, 14
normative markers and timetables, 108, 117, 118
norms: optimal, prescriptive, and statistical, 74-75, 76
North Vancouver High School, BC, 151

Obama, Barack, 28
Office for National Statistics, 96
Office of the Public Advocate of New York, 129
Ontario Public School Hygiene, 148

opportunity cost theory, 18
oppositional defiance disorder, 171
Orillia Asylum, ON, 144
orphanages, 141, 144
Ouellet, G., 20

Palmer, S., 130
Parada, H., 129
parental custody: outcomes, 128
parental divorce, 109, 110, 111, 117, 127; and leaving home, 116-17; outcomes for children, 109
parental leave, 134
parental role strain, 122, 125
parenthood, 93-94, 96, 97, 98, 102, 103; performance of, 70, 72-73, 74, 76, 89
parenting: shared, 127, 128-29, 131, 133, 135; state support for, 132, 133-34, 135
Parenting Out of Control, 174n7
parents: time spent with children, 122, 123
Park, Deborah, 157n8
pater, 96, 98
pathologizing, process of, 167-68, 173
patrilineal descendents, 98
Peng, P., 180
Perin, Constance, 89
personal problems of milieu, 172
philanthropic organizations, 140, 144
Pivot Legal Society, 130, 135n9
poliomyelitis, 145, 146, 150, 151, 152
Popenoe, D., 6
Population Bomb, 5
Population Reference Bureau, 4, 5, 32
Portes, A., 50
Postman, Neil, 5
poverty: impact on children, 27; societal benefits of, 162
pregnant body, 62, 63
Preston, H.S., 20, 26
privileged vs. unprivileged, 72, 73, 74-77, 79, 80, 81-82, 88
problem-solving courts, 170-71
professional class women, 77
pro-natalist policies, 32